¡Viva Elfego!

"One Man, One War"
Elfego Baca & His Mission
Memorial Sculpture for Reserve, New Mexico

James N. Muir was commissioned to create the sculpture of Elfego Baca on the cover of this book by the village of Reserve, New Mexico as a memorial. Here is how he describes his concept:

> This sculpture is a tribute to a "Courageousness" that transcends ethnic or temporal differences and pays honor to the highest and best that lies deep within all human beings. The objective is not to further the divisiveness of bigotry that Elfego Baca fought against, and which continues to this day, but rather to unite us all in the relentless struggle against tyranny.
>
> The design captures Baca's signature moment — his single-handed gunfight against overwhelming force of eighty Texas cowboys in Reserve, New Mexico. He is stepping up through a doorway in the demolished wall of the "jacal," as if rising from a grave into the light of life, with a determination born of true courage. He has looked death in the eyes and not flinched for his strength comes from a higher Power.

James N. Muir says: "I am proud to have been selected for this monumental sculpture. It has great importance and messages for humanity. I appreciate working with the town of Reserve, New Mexico in their vision and dedication to the preservation of this true hero. I see this memorial for Elfego Baca as a testimony to the power of one human being to stand up, alone if necessary, against the oppression of tyranny in order that others may live free."

¡VIVA ELFEGO!

The Case for Elfego Baca, Hispanic Hero

by
Stan Sager

SANTA FE

Sunstone books may be purchased for educational, business, or sales promotional use. For information please write: Special Markets Department, Sunstone Press, P.O. Box 2321, Santa Fe, New Mexico 87504-2321.

Library of Congress Cataloging-in-Publication Data

Sager, Stan.
 ¡Viva Elfego! : the case for Elfego Baca, Hispanic hero / by Stan Sager.
   p. cm.
 Includes bibliographical references.
 ISBN 978-0-86534-608-6 (softcover : alk. paper)
 1. Baca, Elfego, 1864-1945. 2. Frontier and pioneer life--New Mexico.
3. Hispanic Americans--New Mexico--Biography. 4. Sheriffs--New Mexico--
Biography. 5. Heroes--New Mexico--Biography. 6. Crime--New Mexico--History.
7. New Mexico--History--1848- 8. Socorro County (N.M.)--History. I. Title.

F801.B15S24 2008
978.9'052092--dc22
[B]
                                2007048935

Published in

WWW.SUNSTONEPRESS.COM

SUNSTONE PRESS / POST OFFICE BOX 2321 / SANTA FE, NM 87504-2321 /USA
(505) 988-4418 / ORDERS ONLY (800) 243-5644 / FAX (505) 988-1025

◆ FOR OUR GRANDKIDS

◈ CONTENTS

It's sometimes said that Hispanics have no heroes. Those who say it have either not heard of Elfego Baca, or they've bought into anti-Baca arguments that claim that his life story was more fabrication than fact.

But when I was doing the research for an article on Elfego Baca for an issue of the *Bar Journal*, a publication of the State Bar of New Mexico, I realized that tales of Baca's heroism were based on eyewitness accounts, including courtroom testimony under oath. That kind of proof, to a lawyer such as I am, is just as acceptable for establishing fact as any other and better than most. Yet, Elfego Baca has been relegated by history to be remembered, if at all, as simply another in a long list of ho-hum frontier gunfighters,[1] and no researcher who digs into the Chicano civil rights movement will find a trace of evidence that he ever lived.[2]

It's true that Elfego Baca first became newsworthy when he showcased his skill with a six-gun by standing off some eighty trigger-happy Texas cowboys, then by beating two murder raps arising out of the fracas. The shoot-out flared for thirty-six hours in October, 1884, at Frisco, in the Territory of New Mexico, when Baca was nineteen. It earned the young man instant notoriety in the Territory. But on the Western frontier gunfighters, including young ones, were a dime a dozen, and little would have come of the episode had there not been more to Elfego Baca than skill with a pistol.

His substance begins with the reason why the teenage store

clerk rode off to battle the Texans: he took on the cowhands in order to protect Hispanic settlers from atrocities. Baca's courage in offering his life for his people in a stand for human rights makes it demeaning to brand him as "just another gunfighter." The man has earned more than that from history, but he has been denied the honor he deserves. To be restored to his rightful place so long after his death in 1945, he needs an advocate. That's why I decided to write this book. I figured that if Elfego Baca had enough bravado to pin a fake sheriff's badge to his shirt and set out to right the wrongs being inflicted on the Mexican settlers before he hit the age of twenty, I was bold enough to name myself as his mouthpiece.

The advocacy begins by exploring the actions that resulted in his short-term standing as savior of the Hispanics, then by inquiring into why and how he lost that reputation. Looking into those issues will begin to shed light on whether he actually earned the credentials to be called "hero," and then to question whether the loss of his status was justified. The first four chapters spell out his heroic acts and the motivation behind them. I think they prove, beyond a reasonable doubt, that he earned the title.

How and why Elfego lost that hero reputation is less easy to pin down. There are two reasons for it. First, Hispanic heroes, dating back to the American Revolution and Juan de Miralles and Bernardo de Galvez, have rarely been given their due in this country, and Elfego provided no exception to the practice of prejudice. And second, Baca lived too long and too impulsively, giving him six decades to destroy the reputation he had earned in two days. During the sixty-one years that followed Frisco until his death at age eighty, Elfego attacked his own reputation by turning himself into a scoundrel, a scalawag, and a lawyer often known for sleaze, a politician suspected of dealing under the table, a failure with his wife and his finances, and a hothead who flew off the handle and pulled his six-gun at the wink of an eye. With the enigma that was Elfego, however, to find an answer to one question is to raise another. Once how Elfego lost his reputation is explained, the next question is: Why? Why did he turn himself into such a mischief-maker? For that, too, there was a cause.

The foundation for the man Elfego became was laid during his tragic childhood, when his mother and two siblings died and his father dumped him in an orphanage. It all happened when he had just turned seven. The result was a child filled with feelings of inferiority and the need to compensate, a child at risk to adverse effects from subsequent trauma. Twelve years after this multiple abandonment by his mother, siblings and father, the teen found himself lying on the cold ground locked inside a dark hut, cowering at death threats shouted by murderous cowhands, ducking thousands of bullets, dynamite blasts, and flaming logs. But he shot back; he always rose up to shoot back.

No superman could have escaped unscathed from those young adulthood events laid over such a traumatic childhood. It is not surprising that Elfego was filled with suppressed anxieties that would flare into bizarre and inappropriate reactions when stimulated.

My interviews with a thoughtful psychologist, Antonio Gonçalves, Ph.D, then with the University of New Mexico Cancer Center, put a name to Elfego's condition: He exhibited the classic symptoms of post traumatic stress disorder, or PTSD, in past years called "shell shock." The likelihood that this disorder is what triggered inappropriate reactive responses to stimuli in Elfego's life was confirmed by Dr. Bruce Huyser, a psychologist with the Veterans Affairs Medical Center, Albuquerque, who evaluates veterans to determine the presence of the disorder.[3] Over Elfego's life, the psychiatric disorder burst forth in patterns of scrapes and brawls. His violent responses to trivial stimuli stained the hero image he would have been guaranteed had he taken a bullet to the heart and died at nineteen, as happened to his ideal, Billy the Kid. But no, Elfego lived, and he was ever after open to critics and demonizers.

Though he survived the gunfire, Baca did not have the luxury of living in a time during which PTSD could be diagnosed and treated. His only recourse was to tough it out, resort to alcohol, blunder through the episodes that led him to lose his temper, brawl, fight and pull his six-gun. The effect on his reputation was inevitable. The public grew so tired of his escapades that they viewed him as a laughing-stock.

If the PTSD were not enough, there was an additional obstacle to lasting honor that Baca set up for himself. In reaction to his critics, he made himself a relentless self-promoter to the point that his horn-blowing began to sound like fiction and to be labeled as legend rather than fact. Resentment at his image-making caused Baca enemies to challenge the accuracy of his claims for himself. My research disclosed that "legends" about Baca's life are generally, though not always, supported by reports from those who were on the scene. This book records eyewitness accounts as facts.

All of this reinforces the conclusion that Elfego Baca was his own worst enemy when it came to preserving his reputation as hero. No matter what he did, his focus soon blurred, and before long he slipped out of control.

This book tells story after story from Elfego's life. Some have been told before, some have not. They are collected here so that readers can recognize for themselves the patterns of bizarre activity as they played out, while developing insights into the character of the hero. Once the stories are told, the book explains just why, no matter how hard he tried to stay perched on his pedestal, the hero always tumbled off. Sometimes, though, he was up there on the top looking down long enough to forge some real accomplishments worthy of admiration. He was a kingmaker, a force to be reckoned with in the Republican party and later in the Democratic party. He pioneered a Spanish-language newspaper; he supported the Mexican Revolution because it aimed to improve the lot of poor Mexican peasants; and he worked his way up through elective office after office until he had credible, though losing, shots at both the U. S. House of Representatives and the governorship.

Despite the burden of carrying the affliction of Post Traumatic Stress Disorder, the fact that Baca was able to accomplish as much as he did was one more measure of the man's heroism. Yet, instead of leading to acclaim for his courage in so often rising above the effects of the PTSD, the behavior contributed to by the disorder made Elfego into a figure to ridicule, and the butt of jokes and scorn. What hero could bear such a burden?

It is my hope that *¡Viva Elfego!* will lead its readers to think about and to understand the reasons why Elfego destroyed his reputation, and then to remember that for all his long adult life he was a true champion for his people. In the end, it was the revenge of the *Tejanos*, inflicted through the PTSD they unwittingly planted in his mind, that shot down his hero status. But with understanding can come forgiveness, and with forgiveness, perhaps Elfego Baca can reclaim his status as a hero who laid his life on the line in the defense of his people.

Chapters 1-4, in a modified form, appeared in *The Bar Journal*, Spring, 2001, issue, as an article entitled "One Man, One War: Elfego Baca and his Mission." The State Bar of New Mexico has kindly returned all rights to the author.

—Stan Sager

❖ ACKNOWLEDGEMENTS

Thanks to Henry Martinez, President of The Elfego Baca Project, Inc., who started me on this project and read and critiqued the manuscript, and to Howard Bryan, who for many years wrote New Mexico history articles for the *Albuquerque Tribune*, and who authored a fine book about Elfego Baca entitled *Incredible Elfego Baca, Good Man, Bad Man of the Old West*. Howard read the manuscript and pointed out errors. Any that remain are mine, not his. Antonio Gonçalves, Ph.D, offered guidance in helping me draw conclusions from Elfego Baca's early life and about how the siege at Frisco affected him, as did Bruce Huyser, Ph.D. My daughter, Gayle Sager Keenan, read the manuscript and made suggestions that improved it. Eric Jeffries, Esq., Max L. Kiehne, Bradley D. Tepper, Esq., Howard Henry and Meg Keenan also helped.

Ruby Vialpando Mayer, legal assistant to the Supreme Court Clerk, Santa Fe, dug out trial transcripts, and Marene Sweeney, NARA, Denver, the staffs of the New Mexico State Archives and Records Center and the New Mexico State Library, Santa Fe, found obscure records. Gilbert Eugene Baca loaned me his family's files of A. B. Baca and located photos belonging to Elfego Baca's granddaughter, Juanita E. Hartson of San Diego, who willingly supplied them.

I also owe a debt of gratitude to Professor Larry D. Ball, whose thoroughly researched book, *Elfego Baca in Life and Legend* (El Paso: Texas Western Press, 1992) is an essential read for anyone truly interested in the facts and legends of Elfego Baca's life.

Finally, thanks to my wife, Shirley, for patience.

1

◈ THE MESSAGE

It was an October day in 1884 in Socorro, in the Territory of New Mexico, when teenager Elfego Baca got mad. It happened just after Socorro County Deputy Sheriff Pedro Sarracino galloped up to the mercantile store owned by Juan José Baca.

Store clerk Elfego watched through the open door while the deputy dismounted and flipped the reins around one of the posts supporting the overhanging balcony. Sarracino strode inside, marched across the dirt floor and stopped in front of the counter.[4]

Though there's no record of the precise words that were spoken, the facts that the deputy told the young store clerk were remembered by Baca in his little book, Here Comes Elfego![5] There were more details in stories Elfego told to the Baca family disclosed in a Ron Hamm interview of Elfego's nephew, A. B. Baca, carried in the *New Mexico Magazine* in 1981. These sources contain the tale that the store clerk heard from the deputy.

Sarracino asked the young clerk for J. J., as the store's owner was known. J. J. was the deputy's brother-in-law. Elfego told him his boss was still in bed in the living quarters in the back of the building. But Sarracino could hold his story no longer. He told it all to Elfego, and it wasn't pretty.

Texas cowboys working at ranches around the western Socorro County village of Frisco, Sarracino's beat, had gone beyond treating the Hispanic population as inferiors to be tolerated. It had been bad enough for the locals when the cowhands rode up and down the lone street in the town firing their six-guns at chickens and other small creatures that moved, but the newcomers had turned vicious.

They'd held a man known only as *El Burro* on the counter in Milligan's Store and Whiskey Bar in Frisco while they anesthetized their consciences with liquor, whetted their knives, and then castrated him. One of the Hispanic farmers, Epitacio Martinez, had stepped up to plea that they shouldn't do it. The cowboys threw a rope around Martinez, made him watch the surgery, then took him outside, lashed him to a post, paced off twenty paces or so, and used him for target practice. The crowd that had cheered in Milligan's Store and Whiskey Bar while El Burro lost his manhood lined up to watch. One man held the stakes for bets on which shooter had the best aim. The losers bought drinks for the house. Martinez lived, but he was hit four times.

Then they'd roped a "Spanish lady" and dragged her off. Nobody could tell Deputy Sarracino what happened to her.

Elfego had heard enough. That's when he got mad. He ripped off his store-clerk apron, threw it on the packed earth floor, and shouted at the deputy, shaming him for hiding behind that big badge while he did nothing. The answer he got was that he could either do nothing or die by the shots of the cowboys, and that if Elfego wanted the job of cleaning up Frisco, he could have it.

Elfego didn't think twice. Anglo vigilantes in Socorro had taken Hispanics out of the administration of "justice" in Socorro and hanged one of the Baca boys not long before, but mutilations, human targets and a woman victim were too much. He told Sarracino that if he'd take him to Frisco, "I'll make myself a self-made deputy."

The result of Deputy Sheriff Pedro Sarracino's bulletin about the atrocities in Frisco was that when Sarracino finished his business in town, the pair headed west. Equipped with his six-guns, a deputy's badge he'd found somewhere, and his complete lack of fear, Elfego Baca was off to save the "Mexicans" from the *Tejanos*.

But Elfego did not ride off astride a rearing stallion. He left bouncing alongside Sarracino on the seat of the deputy's buckboard, behind the east end of a mule trotting west. If the *Tejanos* had known he was on the way, and why, they would surely have laughed out loud.

The store of J. J. Baca where Elfego Baca worked when he got the message from Deputy Sarracino. In 2002, when this photo was taken, the building was used as a restaurant. Photograph by the author.

2

◈   ELFEGO ARRESTS A COWBOY — TWICE

Young Baca would never have been elected to protect the human rights of an Hispanic population, or anybody else, if it had been put to a vote. Elfego claimed that he stood 5 feet 7 with his boots on, but that was stretching it. He couldn't speak Spanish, and he was afraid of Mexicans.

Though he was born in Socorro in the New Mexico Territory of Hispanic parents, his mother and father had packed up their household goods, loaded their six kids into a wagon and joined an ox train leaving for Topeka when Elfego, their youngest, was about a year old. They'd heard that the schools were better in Kansas, parents Francisco and Juanita Baca told the extended family left behind. The move proved to be a bad choice.

Elfego was fifteen or so when he returned to New Mexico. In the meantime, he grew up in the Kansas capital speaking English. Years later, he reported in a political tract that when he came back he barely spoke any Spanish at all. "As a matter of fact, I was afraid of what they called Mexicans," he wrote. But the events of the few days following his receipt of Sarracino's message would prove he feared nothing else.

One reason for his lack of fear was that Elfego, a couple of years after returning to Socorro from Topeka, had developed a skill that was wasted in the store where he clerked: he could handle a six-gun like few others. He'd picked up the talent, he claimed, from hanging out with another New Mexican, Billy the Kid. It can't be verified that Baca's teacher was the Billy the Kid who was shot by Sheriff Pat

Garret in Lincoln County in July of 1881, or whether he learned from some other frontier rowdy who used the same nickname. What is known is that by age nineteen Baca could stand up and draw against the best and shoot with an accuracy he bragged about even when he was pushing eighty.[6]

Ranch foremen James Cook and William French, and Elfego Baca biographer Kyle Crichton, as well as Elfego himself, were later to write reports of the action that took place after Sarracino and Baca arrived in Frisco. The account that follows has been put together from those sources and from the coverage of Elfego's murder trial that followed the action, as published in the *Albuquerque Evening Democrat*.[7]

When the pair reached the tiny mountain community of Frisco, named after the San Francisco River whose banks it lay along, Sarracino drove the buckboard to his home in the Frisco Lower Plaza, the furthest south of the village's three plazas. The little settlements were scattered along the valley and identified as the Upper, Middle and Lower Plazas, each separated from the next by about two miles. At Sarracino's place, they plotted how Elfego might reconnoiter the terrain and the forces that might line up against him while they rested their tired backs and bruised kidneys. When they'd recovered, on October 28, it was time for Elfego to start the action.

That day, Baca made his first visit to the cowboys' hangout in Upper Frisco, Milligan's Store and Whiskey Bar. He left his revolvers at Sarracino's place. When Elfego stepped through the door he ran into a pair of trouble-making Texans. The two had been whiling away their afternoon off work by shooting up the town. They had stopped in to quench their thirst with other cowboys who were also guzzling Milligan's whiskey. The pair had brought their six-guns with them, and they spiced their booze with shots into the ceiling. Elfego watched and listened as barkeep Milligan shouted and pounded his fists on the bar in anger at the damage.

When Baca edged up to a local justice of the peace, who was himself hoisting a few with the boys, to ask why the shooters were allowed to sit there drinking and firing off their guns, he got an earful. The J. P., Judge Lopez, told him that the cowboys worked for the Slaughter outfit, that it had about 150 cowboys on the payroll, that when they came to town their idea of fun was to shoot chickens, dogs, cats and most anything else that moved. He, for one, wasn't about to set out to break their habit for fear that he'd share the fate of the chickens.

But what His Honor had seen as a threat to his life, Elfego saw as an opportunity. While the young store clerk may not have given any thought to the symbolic significance to the Texans were he, one of the despised "Mexicans," to arrest an American cowboy and make it stick, if he did, it didn't hold him back. It didn't hold him back, either, that there was no suggestion that either of the troublemakers had been a party to the castration of *El Burro* or had fired any of the shots at target Epitacio Martinez. On that particular day, the day Elfego Baca first entered the Whiskey Bar, the pair in front of him was causing trouble for the settlers, and to end trouble was exactly the reason why Elfego had declared that he was a "self-made deputy."

So Baca walked up to the principal agitator, a young cowpoke named Charley McCarthy, and told him he was under arrest for firing his pistol in town. Without any hassle, Elfego passed up Judge Lopez and took his prisoner to the Middle Plaza for a trial by a justice of the peace he thought would be more likely to stand up against a cowboy than Judge Lopez. McCarthy promptly paid a fine to the J. P. and was turned loose. But it wasn't long until the cowboy was back in Milligan's place, tossing off a few more drinks and once again firing bullets into the ceiling. Elfego was outside, exchanging words with some of the cowboys not far from Milligan's door.

With more holes to let the sunshine through his building, saloon-keeper Milligan flew into a rage again. He ran out of his store and at the top of his voice yelled for the help of the Mexican who a few minutes before had had the guts to arrest cowboy McCarthy. By this time McCarthy's friends surrounded Baca, curious as to the tan-skinned intruder who had stood up to a Texan having a little good clean fun. McCarthy himself was probably too drunk to understand that what was brewing was close to turning into a race war.

Though caught between Milligan and the crowd outside the bar, Baca once more refused to back down. He took a step backwards, and in a voice loud enough to be heard by the tipplers inside, announced, "I will show them there is at least one Mexican in the country who is not afraid of an American cowboy."

At that point, prodded by the laughter that choked the listening cowboys, the diminutive Baca, unarmed and backed only by Milligan's cursing at the shooter who had riddled his saloon, walked up to Charlie McCarthy again. He stuck out his chest with his phony badge pinned to it, grabbed McCarthy's revolver out of its holster, and proclaimed once more that he was a self-made deputy there to keep order. McCarthy was not impressed. He wheeled, pulled the pistol of his friend, William Young Parham, from its scabbard and fired off a shot. Elfego felt the wind of a bullet whiz just over his head and watched his hat sail into the air.

Baca failed to blink. The cowboy did a double-take and dashed out of the tavern. Baca and one "very brave man" named Francisquito Naranjo took off right behind. McCarthy made it to the ranch where he worked, which was only a few hundred yards away. Elfego, once he spotted where McCarthy had holed up, delayed long enough to gallop back to Sarracino's home, dash in, and grab his revolvers. Once armed, he returned and called for back-up from among the handful of Hispanic farmers who were hanging around, though they were scared to their cores at the sight of a fellow Mexican with backbone enough to stand up against the *Tejanos*.

Baca reappeared at the ranch. Trailing at a safe distance was a handful of his reluctant admirers. Though McCarthy was surrounded by some thirty gun-toting Texans, they and McCarthy's ranch house sanctuary weren't enough to protect him. Baca arrested McCarthy once again as the cowboy stumbled out the back door of the house. By this time, it was surely clear to Elfego just how provocative his actions were in arresting a Texas cowhand for the second time. But it was too late to turn back, even if he'd been inclined to do so.

3

❖ THE COWBOYS BRACE FOR TROUBLE

Baca, with McCarthy in hand and feigning an attitude that all this was simply routine, turned his back on the cowhands and escorted his prisoner back to Milligan's Whiskey Bar. There, at first Baca decided he could let the rampaging cowboy out on bail. The self-made deputy sat at one of the tables and began to write out a bail bond that would guarantee McCarthy's appearance at trial. Young Parham agreed to act as bondsman, as did Pedro Sarracino, perhaps trying to walk a tightrope between both factions. But Milligan banged on the bar and demanded that the deputy deny bail. Baca agreed, tore up the bond, and left to escort his prisoner to a residence in Middle Frisco. There, he arranged for a guard until he could take the drunken McCarthy to Socorro for trial. It was at this point that Milligan proved to be a fickle ally.

W. R. Milligan stretched up a foot-and a half or so taller than Elfego Baca and outweighed him by well over a hundred pounds. Rancher William French was amazed when he first met the man. "His head almost touched the ceiling," French wrote, "and his hands were the largest I have ever seen on a human being. He was all length and breadth without any superfluous attachments except a fringe of hair some six or eight inches long on an otherwise bald head."[8]

Apparently realizing his bread was buttered by the whiskey-drinking cowboys whose tabs fattened his receipts, in the evening the drunken Milligan and a dozen allies appeared at the house where Elfego held McCarthy. The barkeep demanded McCarthy's release, telling Baca he had "arms to release the prisoner."

But Elfego refused to fold. He told Milligan, "You will not take McCarthy from me in any manner." When Milligan stood fast, Baca drew a pistol and shot into the ground at the tavern-owner's feet.

"You are a bad shot," Milligan said, enunciating his words clearly and swaying like a Ponderosa pine in a high wind. "You didn't hit me."

"I didn't want to shoot anybody," Elfego said. "I just want you to go away."

Milligan turned to leave, but no sooner had he reached his horse than he wheeled and lurched back, talking to Elfego "very insultingly." Again Elfego told him to go away, that he (Milligan) was making him tired. Milligan mounted his horse, only to dismount and endeavor once more to intimidate Baca with his whiskey breath and his slurred threats. "The devil may take me if I don't get Charley McCarthy out," he said.[9]

Baca had reached his limit. He faced the Milligan-led gang and laid down an ultimatum: either they would leave, or he would count to three and start shooting.

In what might have been the quickest three-count in the history of gun-fighting, Elfego finished the count, drew his Colt, shot one cowboy, Tabe Allen, in the knee and shot the horse of another. It fell on its rider, Young Parham, inflicting injuries from which he would soon die. Milligan and the remaining cowhands, realizing they'd lost the quick-draw contest literally hands-down, lost interest in freeing the prisoner.

As they rode off, the cowboys suddenly realized that lawmen were available to address issues of shootings and other infractions of the law. It was a possibility that hadn't occurred to them when they were the shooters and mutilators and the local residents were the victims. Snubbing the local deputy, Sarracino, who had picked his side by lending his Frisco home as a temporary jail for prisoner McCarthy and by standing by Elfego, the cowhands sent a rider off to Alma, a village some thirty miles south of Frisco. The messenger was to sound the alarm along the way and fetch Dan Bechtol, the only Anglo deputy in riding distance. His assignment would be to arrest Baca for killing the cowboy who'd been crushed by his horse.

Hours later, at the WS spread near Alma, ranch foreman James H. Cook listened and acted on the announcement carried by the rider who galloped up from Frisco. Cook's account of the rider's report said:

> One evening in the fall of 1884, a rider came at a furious gait up to my ranch house door and hurriedly informed me that the Mexicans had gone on the warpath at a little settlement up the San Francisco River, about thirty miles away. He stated that they had killed one of Mr. Slaughter's cowboys and were going to wipe out all the Americans living near their settlement. . . . [The messenger] had been sent to warn Americans along the San Francisco River of their danger and to get as many men as possible to go immediately and help guard the homes of the Americans living near the Mexican settlement.[10]

Cook, and as many of his men as he could spare from their duties at the ranch, rode off to another ranch nearer to Frisco. There, Cook found a horde of recruits from the vicinity. The place had been made into a staging area for the battle that was in the making.

Others rode to the SU ranch to sound the alarm. Expecting to find the place in flames, apparently believing that it must have taken a small army of "Mexicans" to arrest a single Texan and that the army was marching with flaming torches, the riders found everyone at the SU in bed asleep.

After themselves snatching a few hours rest after the hard night's riding, the cowboys were awakened by the return of the messenger they'd sent to Alma. With him was Deputy Dan Bechtol and more cowboys from Alma. The gunmen dallied while Dan snoozed for a few hours. Some of the bunch themselves dozed, then they all saddled up and rode out to find a pliable justice of the peace to assure that Charlie McCarthy got their version of a fair trial. Armed with the hand-picked judge and Deputy Dan, they cantered into Frisco Plaza to wait for Baca to appear with his prisoner.

The next morning at about eight o'clock two cowboys showed up to heckle Elfego at the Sarracino residence in Middle Frisco. But word about Baca's handiness with a pistol had gotten around, and the pair stayed a respectful two hundred yards away. Elfego identified them as Clemente Hightower and Gyrone Martin.[11] The pair shouted to Elfego that he should take his prisoner to Upper Frisco for trial.

Elfego waved his pistols as the men drew nearer. They pulled back. Then one of the cowboys told him that there were about a hundred men waiting for him in a canyon he'd have to pass on the way to the Upper Plaza.

Young Elfego balanced the odds: a hundred Texans to one teen-aged Mexican seemed about right. He told the hecklers he'd take his prisoner there in a while, then waved the two away.

When the men left, Elfego again demonstrated his concern for the Hispanics of the village. He passed the word to the Middle Frisco community that the women and children had better get out of the line of fire. The plea drew about a hundred-twenty-five people. Elfego shepherded them to the small village church, where they huddled inside behind its thick adobe walls to avoid the *Tejano* bullets.

Baca then rode with his prisoner the two miles or so to Upper Frisco without further trouble. The "hundred men" waiting in a canyon didn't materialize until shortly after Elfego arrived, though there were about a dozen cowhands standing around in the Upper Frisco plaza. According to the account by Kyle Crichton, Elfego's biographer, the horde from the Slaughter outfit swung up from an arroyo to the justice of the peace's office and swept down on Baca as he stood by the building.[12]

Meanwhile, word had reached the cowboys in surrounding ranches that there was a bunch of Mexicans threatening their buddies in Upper Frisco, and the revolution needed to be dealt with. The report said that a cowboy from the Spur ranch had been killed, and another, Charlie McCarthy, was being held hostage. While Baca was guarding Charlie McCarthy, more cowboys from surrounding ranches galloped up in a cloud of dust with their justice of the peace in tow. Added to the Texans already present, the tally of the forces lined up against Baca stood at about eighty.

Baca recognized two of the Texans and walked over to the pair. His reputation had been made the night before; they pulled out their pistols and threw them to the ground.

Another of the bunch, a Mr. Wilson, also known to Baca, sidled up to the man with the badge and cussed him out. But Wilson was careful to hold his hands away from his revolvers. A man behind Wilson took a pot-shot in Baca's direction from the middle of the crowd of gunmen milling around outside Milligan's Whiskey Bar. Apparently the shooter intentionally fired in the air. If he'd taken a direct shot and missed, he would have gunned down one of the angry cowhands circled around Baca.

Despite these provocations, somehow the pot didn't quite come to a boil until after McCarthy had been escorted by Deputy Bechtol to a near-by house for his second trial. By the time the party disappeared through the door, Milligan had remembered that his survival depended on alliance with the hard-drinking Texans who spent their pay at his bar, and that the holes through his ceiling and roof were worth it. Every remaining trace of support for the trouble-making Baca evaporated. Even so, the Milligan hospitality may have played a role in quieting things down temporarily. Many of the cowboys spent the next hour or so sampling the Whiskey Bar's refreshments, leaving the trial and the proceedings outside the justice of the peace's house to play out whatever course they took. A handful of the Texans wanted to be close enough to the trial to see what happened when it was over. They squatted in the dirt outside the bar and played a game of "mumble-de-peg" with an open-bladed knife.

It was not until over three decades later that shenanigans in the back room of Milligan's place while McCarthy was being dealt with would come to light.

In a house down the road from Milligan's place, the justice of the peace convened his court for McCarthy's second trial. In half an hour, Elfego dashed out the door, his hat pulled low over his eyes, and disappeared into a nearby *jacal*, a small residence made of wooden pickets driven into the ground and smeared with mud inside and out. Baca asked the owner of the *jacal*, Geronimo Armijo, to leave with his family, including his eight year old son, Molo, and another boy, who were husking corn on the mud roof. The boys jumped down and ran off, leaving the structure to Baca. As she left, Mrs. Armijo locked the hut's only door behind her with a padlock. Baca was inside with no way to get out.[13]

A few minutes later, McCarthy walked out of the J. P.'s residence a free man. He'd been found guilty of shooting up the town and had paid a five dollar fine. But the amount of the fine in no way reflected the significance of events that began when a Mexican arrested a Texas cowboy. And the punishment meted out by the justice of the peace did not end the affair, but was more of a beginning.

4

◆ THE GUN-BATTLE

After the cowboys had offered their congratulations and lifted a few toasts to McCarthy's freedom at Milligan's, some of the bunch stopped to reflect. It didn't take long for them to decide that the fellow who'd fired a shot that killed a cowboy on the count of three the night before ought to pay for the offense. A few of the cowboys claimed they'd been given the okay to arrest Baca by their justice of the peace. They would execute a warrantless arrest, or just maybe the trouble-maker might be shot resisting arrest. If he survived, they'd charge him with murder.

After they'd had time to fortify themselves further with Milligan's nectar, and after Milligan had whipped them into a killing mood with his shouts, fist-waving and banging on the bar, a stream of cowboys poured out of the Whiskey Bar. They jumped on their horses and raced the hundred yards or so down the street to the *jacal*. As they reined in, some of the more exuberant Texans fired a few shots through the door.

Among the leaders was a Texan named William B. "Burt" Hearne, from the Spur outfit. Hearne pulled up outside the *jacal* and leaped off his horse, saying, "I'll get that little Mexican out of there." He swaggered up to the door. Close behind was William French, later to become foreman of the WS outfit and still later to write an account of the affair. McCarthy was also in the forefront, hoping to recover the revolver that Baca had seized from him.

Jerome Wadsworth, one of the Texans, had somehow gotten the key to the house and fumbled to get it into the padlock. Others present were convinced it wasn't locked, and shoved up to the front to push it open. Hearne banged on the door and commanded that anyone inside surrender. Elfego kept quiet, tiptoeing around the inside of the place while he scouted out how to defend himself.

Baca heard voices in the crowd saying, "Let's kill him." As the Texans lost patience, one yelled, "Let's fire," and they did.[14]

Elfego answered by spraying a few shots of his own from the window high in the wall at one end of the structure, then the crowd pushed on the door again. When there was no answer to his demand to be let in, Hearne took a step back and kicked the door as hard as he could. Two shots were fired through it by "someone in the house," as Wadsworth testified to the incident. Baca had discharged each of his two 45s.

"Boys, I'm killed," Hearne cried. He clutched his abdomen. As he fell to the ground, his friends picked him up and carried him to Milligan's back room, where they made him comfortable until he died.

Some of the cooler heads among the Texans suggested that it was time for action from the deputy on duty. They chased down Dan Bechtol. They found him snoring in a corner of the storeroom at the back of Milligan's, catching more rest after his exertions of the day before. The cowboys roused him. But Dan turned down the invitation to keep the peace in favor of returning to his backroom snooze. The cowboys were on their own again, and the siege began.

William French, the literate Irishman who worked for the WS ranch and later became its foreman, wrote of the action that followed from the Texans' perspective. He and his friend, "Old Charley" Moore, who had just ridden up only to have his hat shot off by Baca, decided to "fog up" the trapped self-made deputy, as French put it in his book, by proving to him that he was not the only one with ammunition. The two hid behind the adobe buttresses of the Upper Frisco village church across the street, peeking out from time to time to throw shots into the *jacal*. At each gunshot, Baca retaliated, his bullets causing chunks of adobe to fly.

The shots were heard by a troop of cowboys who had ridden out of Upper Frisco to head home following the celebration of the freedom of Charlie McCarthy. Not wanting to miss the action, they turned back, led by Jim Cook, the WS foreman who later also wrote an eyewitness account. The headcount of the Texans was back up to eighty. Cook described the assembly to his brother and a number of English friends who were with him at the Plaza. He said, "I considered the Americans gathered at the Plaza as nothing more or less than a mob." But it took Cook only a few minutes to decide to throw in with the mob and to elect himself its de facto leader, at least when it came to later parleys to end the shooting.

When they met at the scene, Cook and French conferred out of the reach of Baca's gunfire. The result was an effort to negotiate with the trapped Baca through shouted offers. But the cowboys chose the wrong medium for communication. They yelled their proposals in Spanish. The hitch in the plan was that Baca didn't speak Spanish. He answered by firing more shots.

The slugs fired at them from Baca's guns settled it for the cowboys; they riddled the *jacal* with bullet holes for twenty minutes, top to bottom, right to left, before they paused to check the result. During the barrage, Baca's revolvers were silent.

It must have occurred to the cowboys that there was a reason why Elfego didn't fire back every time they loosed a salvo. The "Mexican" was trapped with a limited amount of ammunition, so he needed to expend it carefully. When Elfego had dashed inside after the McCarthy trial, he would have carried no more than the six rounds in each Colt less the two he had fired the night before, and an ammunition belt, or maybe two, around his waist. He may have had a few more shots in McCarthy's pistol, although it's probable that McCarthy had emptied it firing into the ceiling at Milligan's. Baca probably could have fired some sixty shots before his supply ran out. There is no report that the Armijo residence included any store of ammunition.

At the end of the concentrated fusillade the Texans figured Baca was a sieve. One of the boys, Ed Erway, showed himself in order to reconnoiter. In a moment, Baca peppered a couple of shots in his direction, driving him back. The cowboys' salvos started once again, riddling "every nook and cranny where a bullet could possibly penetrate." The assault quieted Baca for a time, giving the siege forces the opportunity to plan their strategy for the night, since the sun was about to set.

Testimony later estimated 4,000 rounds were fired into the house during the entire siege, 367 were said to have penetrated the door. What is not disputed was the attackers' awe that Elfego, through it all, returned the fire. Unknown to the cowboys, Baca had an ally in whoever had built the *jacal*. The floor was a foot to eighteen inches lower than the grade level at the entry door. The excavation may have been the source of the mud smeared on the hut's walls. It was this feature of the building that Baca used to save himself, rising up only to punch his pistols through the mud, fire his shots between the pickets, then duck back while the Texas bullets whined through one wall and out the opposite one.

As the sun began its slide behind the mountains to the west, Cook and French set sentries to watch for an attempted night-time escape. French himself took a post, creeping around from time to time to check the other guards to be sure they were keeping their eyes open. He found few as dedicated to staying awake as he was. The slumbering lookouts would have been unlikely to have detected Elfego if he had tiptoed away, if only he could have escaped from the hut.

Or maybe Elfego knew it was no use to try to sneak off. The door was padlocked on the outside; to force open the hut's window would have made enough noise to rouse the Texans.

But did Elfego sleep? In the peace of the moonlight after the day's blizzard of bullets, was his stomach so twisted, his bowels so knotted, that he spent the night vomiting in a corner of the hut behind the fireplace? It's not something he ever admitted. Maybe it never happened. Maybe he found some of the Armijo family bedclothes, cocooned himself in them against the October mountain cold, stretched out on the floor and slept the sleep of the innocent for a full eight hours.

Following the quiet night, the leaders of the cowboys figured that Baca had either slipped away or was dead. To test the theory, French made an oblique run across the street. Baca's shots proved he was still hale and hearty.

There was more evidence confirming the conclusion. Wisps of smoke rose from the chimney of the *jacal*, and the cowboys caught whiffs of breakfast cooking. In the face of the enemy's gunfire Elfego had found beef and flour left behind by Mrs. Armijo, fired up the embers in the fireplace, made beef stew, tortillas and coffee. Either Elfego was thumbing his nose in the face of the cowboys, or he had emptied his stomach and intestines so many times that he couldn't go on without nourishment. Or both.

Down the street at Milligan's multi-purpose establishment the cowboys also had breakfast, though the eyewitnesses did not record what was on their menu. With stomachs filled on both sides, the participants picked up where they'd left off the day before, and the day's target practice began.

During the morning the cowboys received a report that a horde of Mexicans was approaching. When reconnoitering showed the Texans that there were a number of local farmers and ranchers riding over the hills on both sides of the village, they fired a few shots in their direction. The groups dispersed. It was later discovered that the locals had no hostile intentions but were on their way to Socorro to seek help from the authorities.

After this diversion, some of the more restrained Texans decided it was time for another parley. The records don't show the language used to offer to Baca that he would suffer no personal harm if he were to give himself up, though it was probably Spanish since the response was the same as it had been before: more shots. This led the cowboys to greater ingenuity.

They sent a party a few miles to the Cooney mining camp for dynamite. While waiting for it, they tossed burning logs on the *jacal* roof. The mud wouldn't ignite. When the blasting party returned, they blew out a wall with the miner's dynamite. It crumbled, but left a fortress of rubble that shielded Elfego. They strung up blankets between the buildings across the street from the *jacal* so they could run between the structures without exposure to Elfego's 45s. Baca fired at their shadows. Later, he claimed four dead, eight wounded for his stay in Frisco, though the cowboys admitted to only two dead.

One Texan scuttled across the street toward the *jacal* crouched behind an iron stove-front held up as a shield. Elfego's first shot creased his scalp as his head periscoped above the barrier. The fellow turned tail and ran around in circles, clutching his head, yelling, "He killed me. He killed me." It was the only laugh the Texans had had since Elfego Baca pulled his six-guns.

But the second day of the battle was waning, and the Texans were getting bored at the prospect that the only chance for victory was to starve out the pesky Mexican. At this point an unexpected diversion, in the form of a "tall American" named Frank Ross, drove up in a buckboard from the direction of Socorro. One of the farmers had reached him with a report of the activities at Upper Frisco and was alongside him in the buckboard. Ross had two indicia of his claim to be a deputy: a badge and an air of authority.

Ross took charge, though Deputy Dan suddenly appeared

when the firing stopped, strutting around the scene to the annoyance of French. Dan's posturing ended when it was suggested he return to Milligan's, where French's report says he "found consolation."

Then Ross devised another parley. He drafted as a peace intermediary the man who had gone to Socorro to bring him back to Upper Frisco. But Baca didn't understand the Spanish the fellow spoke any better than he'd understood the cowboys' language the day before. Ross himself then switched to English. This time Baca understood and listened.

In a few minutes a truce was negotiated, and surrender terms for escorting Baca back to Socorro for trial for Hearne's killing were struck.

With all but the leaders of the cowboys out of sight, Baca appeared, not through the front door as those who had stayed at the scene had expected, apparently forgetting about the padlock on the outside of the door, but through the small window in the gable at one end of the house. French described the effect the attacks had had on Elfego: "He was like a wild animal, stripped to his shirt, with a revolver in each hand, looking suspiciously on every side of him, as if fearing treachery." Outside Baca's flimsy refuge in the presence of Ross no treachery surfaced.

Ross, however, also feared the possibility of shots into his prisoner's back. To reduce the odds, he convinced a handful of the cowboys to stay in Frisco for a time rather than hitting the road back to their ranches with the news of Elfego's transportation to Socorro. His worry was that some of the army of Texans who had left early to pay their respects at the burial of the dead cowboy, Hearne, might return and take Baca when they got the news that Elfego was still alive and on his way to jail in the county seat. The remaining Texans agreed, and a curious event followed.

Ross turned custody of his prisoner, still in possession of his 45s, over to the cowboys with no objections from Elfego. They escorted him to Milligan's to wash up and join in sampling some of the hospitality of the now genial proprietor. There is no report of who paid the tab, but there is no doubt that Baca was the toast of the town.

During the break, the cowhands quizzed Baca about the events of the past couple of days with particular interest in how he happened to be alive. Elfego explained that he had managed to dodge their bullets by flattening himself on the sunken floor. The Texans who crossed the street to check out the *jacal* while the others were drinking with Baca reported back that everything in the place was "reduced to splinters." A broom handle was pocked with eight bullet holes, but a six-hundred year old statue of *La Señora Santa Ana*, said to be sacred, was unmarked. It was never explained how the icon happened to be in the humble residence.

After the bi-partisan celebration of Baca's heroism, apparently the next morning, Elfego rode off toward Socorro as agreed during his negotiations with Ross, riding on the back seat of a buckboard pulled by a mule, his hands resting on his twin Colts. Ross and his driver sat on the front seat. Six Texans on horseback led the way, in position so that Elfego could keep an eye on them while they stayed alert for an ambush. He was taken to Socorro, where he was held in shackles in the new jail while awaiting trial.

As they rode off, some of the Texans remembered Elfego Baca's words spoken before the fracas began: "I will show them that there is at least one Mexican in the country who is not afraid of an American cowboy."

Peace returned to the communities of Upper, Middle and Lower Frisco.

There are no further reports of atrocities against Hispanics in western Socorro County.

As French wrote, "the honours [sic] were with Baca. . . ."[15]

Baca had quieted the Texans by earning their respect. But while his mission was accomplished, and for the first time Mexican-

Americans in Socorro County could walk up to a pistol-toting Texas cowboy and look him in the eye, Elfego himself was heading into more danger from the cattlemen. And though he may have thought he had left the siege at Frisco behind forever, he would live with the effects it planted in his mind for the rest of his life.

5

◈ THE AFTERMATH

Not all the Texans were willing to join William French in award-ing "honours" to the uppity Mexican. There were a few whose rage had built up to such a point that they hatched a plan to hang Elfego from a tree limb if he should escape the shoot-out. But they continued to underestimate the teenager. Elfego was a step ahead, for he had an idea of what they were up to.

Elfego understood that for the cowboys, the deal to transport him to Socorro for trial was part of a game that had no rules, a game in which the young Mexican sand-burr under their saddle-blankets was the pawn. For the Texans, it was a matter of pride and dominance. The kid had bested them by arresting a Texan, then by escaping all the bullets and the rest of the messengers of death they could throw at him. And their nemesis was one of a racial group expected to cow-tow and look at the ground when Texans approached. If one of these second-rate citizens showed backbone, others might be inspired to do the same unless the troublemaker was dealt with. For Elfego, it was a matter of life and death, and only half his problem was to survive the few minutes following his exit from the *jacal*. Once he was out in the open, he had to continue to live until he reached Socorro and the relative safety of the county jail.

Elfego had done his best to protect himself as he yelled his three non-negotiable demands to Ross through the walls of the *jacal*. First, Ross must guarantee that he (Ross) and his driver would ride in the front of the buckboard; Elfego himself would sit on the rear seat.

Hispanics. Tell you what I think. I think Elfego Baca taught a lot of Anglos that Hispanics are Americans, and just like them. And it stuck. I don't know how else to explain it. I can tell you this, it's not that way other places."

Henry Martinez agrees. "Hispanics and Anglos [in Reserve] were never afraid of each other. Everybody was just like everybody else. Then when I went away, I found it wasn't like that in other places. Hispanics were afraid of Anglos, Anglos were afraid of Hispanics. I couldn't believe it. I'd never known that."[23]

The integration in Reserve has another dimension. Take the treasurer of the Elfego Baca Project, Max L. Kiene, for example. Kiene is a Harvard-educated real estate developer who returns to his native Reserve at least every weekend from his base of operations in Los Lunas, on the south edge of Albuquerque. Kiehne believes in Reserve and makes his principal home there.

Kiehne is a descendant of Emil Kiehne, who came to the area in 1882 as a sixteen year old boy, two years before the gunfight. Young Emil rode in with his uncle, August Kiehne, driving a herd all the way from Fredericksburg, Texas, to feast on the grass in the San Augustine Plains. He and his cattle stayed. Kiehne ranch hands didn't participate in the siege at Frisco, nor did they contribute to the hell-raising a few of the cowboys thought was fun but which one hundred percent of the Hispanic population recognized as oppression. Their cattle operation was proof that not all the Texans were trouble-makers and can lead to the conclusion that the cowboys who gave Elfego such a hard time were probably a minority.

The Kiehne family is one that has fully integrated. Its relationships reflect how shadows of the old Frisco are stitched into the pattern of the present Reserve.

The young Emil Kiehne married a local girl, Eufalia Chavez. Eufalia's father, Bernavel Chavez, was one of the Frisco Nine who stood by Elfego Baca when he was first accosted by the mob of angry

Texans because he had arrested cowboy Charley McCarthy. Their son, Max C. Kiehne, married Teresita Lopez, who was a granddaughter of deputy sheriff Pedro Sarracino, with whom Elfego rode into Frisco. While Spanish-speaking Hispanic families in the area were discouraging their children from speaking the Spanish language with the hope that fluency only in English would lead to more full social acceptance, the Kiehne-Chavez-Lopez family brought up their children to be bilingual.[24] They still are. And so it goes in Reserve today.

But even in the years following the commencement of a new millennium, citizens of Reserve can now and then be heard to wonder aloud what life would be like if Elfego Baca and his six-guns were to return for a while. "Maybe," they say, "just maybe, he could run the scumbags that sell drugs to the school-kids out of town. That, I'd like to see."

6

◆ THE FIRST MURDER TRIAL

Once Deputy Ross, Elfego Baca and the six Texans riding in the vanguard cleared the "Point of Timber," passed over the San Augustine Plain, through Magdalena, and Baca was in the custody of the sheriff in Socorro, the danger had just begun. But the threat was no longer from the six-guns of the Texans. It was from the rope of the hangman.

Less than sixty days after the cell door slammed on Elfego, on January 1, 1885, Sheriff Pedro Simpson left office. He was replaced by the candidate of the cattlemen, Charles T. Russell. The new sheriff was another resident of Socorro County who had turned his back on Texas to find his fortune in the New Mexico Territory. With the Texans in charge, the cattlemen and the young hotheads they employed were suppressing their anger, and the Hispanics, for a while, were slow to take any lip from them. Racial relationships were upside down, at least on the surface. At the center of the tilted universe of Socorro County was Elfego Baca. The prior tenuous state of balance between the Americans and the Mexicans, as both factions called themselves, would never be the same.

Baca was held in the newly built Socorro County jail to wait trial for the murder of William B. Hearne. The complaint was sworn to by Frank Ross. The sheriff had only to walk a few paces to serve on Elfego a warrant to "arrest [sic] the person of A. Baca eney [sic] where you may find him in Socorro County." The document was not filed until three weeks after Baca and Ross had ridden into Socorro on Ross's buckboard, on November 25, 1884. The warrant had been issued by

Anglo Justice of the Peace, William A. Wilson. At some point, Baca was apparently released on bond, since an appearance bond signed by Baca, with Lorenzo Rivera, Abdenago Baca (Elfego's brother) and Pedro Martin as sureties, was filed in the court records.

Not until March 31, 1885, did the Socorro County grand jury issue its true bill of indictment stating the facts of the crime as the D.A. saw them. The defendant was arraigned and pleaded not guilty on the same day.

The handwritten collection of redundancies issued over the grand jury name was signed by Charles C. McComas, district attorney for the Second District of New Mexico. It was filled with the repetitions required by the law's attention to detail so as to nail down at least twice every step needed to convict, and it bubbled over with anger at the foolhardy Mexican who had upset the system by keeping the peace. The grand jurors charged that

> Elfigo [sic] Baca, late of the County of Socorro, Territory of New Mexico, on the thirtieth day of October, in the year of our Lord One Thousand Eight Hundred and Eighty four at and in the County of Socorro aforesaid: with force and arms in and upon one William B. Hearne in the peace of the said Territory . . . of his malice aforethought and from a pre-meditated design to effect the death of him, the said William B. Hearne, did make an assault: and that the Said Elfigo Baca a certain pistol then and there loaded and charged with gunpowder and leaden bullets, which said pistol he the said Elfigo Baca in his hands then and there had and held, to, against, and upon the Said William B. Hearne then and there unlawfully . . . and from a premeditated design to effect the death of him the said William B. Hearne, did Shoot and discharge; and that the Said Elfigo Baca with the leaden bullets aforesaid, out of the pistol aforesaid then and there by force of the gun powder shot and

sent forth as aforesaid the Said William B. Hearne, in and upon the body of him the Said William B. Hearne . . . did strike, penetrate, and wound, given [sic] to the Said William B. Hearne then and there with the leaden bullets aforesaid . . . one mortal wound of the depth of ten inches, of which Said mortal wound the Said William B. Hearne there and then instantly died; and so the grand Jurors . . . do say, that the Said Elfigo Baca . . . from a premeditated design to effect the death of him the said William B. Hearne did kill and murder contrary to the form of the statute in such case made and provided, and against the peace and dignity of the Territory of New Mexico.[25]

In Socorro, Elfego Baca was represented by John M. Shaw, a respected trial lawyer who later served on the Territorial Supreme Court. The quality of the representation may have accounted for the fact that for charges arising from the Hearne killing, the Socorro County trial judge granted a defense motion for a change of venue. The matter was moved to Bernalillo County, where Albuquerque was the county seat, as it is today.

Changes of venue, or changes in the location of a trial, can be granted if the court concludes that the defendant probably cannot receive a fair trial in the community in which the charges were filed. Though the only portions of the Hearne murder file that remain are in the files of N. C. Laughlin in the New Mexico State Records Center and Archives, Santa Fe, since they do not include the motion John Shaw filed for Elfego, it is speculation to guess whether it charged the Cattle Growers Association with financing the prosecution and stirring up anti-Baca feelings. Based on the language of the motion for a change of venue made in the murder case filed later against Elfego arising out of the death of Young Parham, one can conclude that accusations of that kind were probably made. The Parham murder trial is addressed in another chapter.

Whatever the specific grounds for the motion, it was granted, and Elfego was transported from Socorro to Albuquerque. The Hero of Frisco had arrived in the largest city in the territory to stand trial for the murder of William B. Hearne.

The best account of the trial that remains is one written at the time by an anonymous reporter for the *Albuquerque Evening Democrat*, although only the last two days of the three day trial were reported.

The trial began in Albuquerque on May 7, 1885. The prosecutors were Charles McComas, Socorro County District Attorney, who had signed the grand jury presentment, and his assistant, Neil B. Field. Baca was represented by Bernard Rodey of Albuquerque, one of the leading lawyers in the Territory, as well as H. B. Hamilton and John Shaw of Socorro. The role of N.C. Laughlin, in whose files the surviving trial records came to rest, is not identified.

There is no indication of how Baca, the twenty dollar per month store clerk, might have paid his battery of high-priced lawyers. Perhaps counsel did it anticipating that their names would be plastered all over the newspapers as a result of appearing alongside the notorious and handsome defendant in the high-profile murder case. Or maybe Elfego's brother, Abdenago Baca, who signed his bond and is reported to have owned substantial assets, footed the bill. At any rate, the legal talent that lined up on Elfego Baca's side of the table was a "dream team" of territorial legal talent.

Elfego's lawyers grabbed a huge advantage when they exercised their peremptory challenges to send home jurors they didn't want. They were able to seat a one-hundred percent Hispanic jury. Those who were left to hear the evidence were Demetrio Garcia, Ramon Martin, Elisio Guiterrez [sic], Soto Armijo, Cecilio Garcia, Jesus Perea, Thomas Garcie y Montoya, Juan Guiterrez, Andres Lucero, Felipe Garcia, Juan C. Greigor and Juan Garcia y Rael.

Copies of subpoenas issued to require the attendance of witnesses have survived in court records, though the witnesses called on the first day of the trial were not listed by the newspaper. The proceedings on that day were "too late to be reported for *The Democrat*," according to a brief note appearing in the paper's edition of that day. What is known is that the prosecution filed a cost bill showing that twelve oaths were administered on the first day to witnesses called by the D. A. Deputy Sheriff Frank Rose and Charley McCarthy appeared, the latter paid for traveling 280 miles to the trial, though McCarthy was short-changed since the round trip was longer than that. Milligan was one of those sworn to tell the truth, as was Tabe Allen.

Day two got underway, probably before a packed house, at 10 a.m. on May 8, when the prosecution called cowhand Jerome Wadsworth.

An account of Wadsworth's testimony was carried in *The Evening Democrat*. At least some of his testimony was reported as verbatim, though it did not include the questions asked by the attorneys nor rulings of the court on what apparently were constant objections.[26]

The testimony developed that when Elfego had McCarthy under arrest in Frisco, Wadsworth saw it all. He walked up to Baca and his prisoner, and Elfego demanded he explain whether he was friend or foe. Assuming the question was whether he was a friend or a foe of McCarthy, Wadsworth told Elfego he was a friend, that he'd heard McCarthy was sick, and that "they," presumably referring to the horde of cowboys in town, wanted to see him.

Wadsworth's testimony is the only indication that McCarthy was ill while he was in the custody of Elfego Baca. It sounds plausible. The cowboy was probably carrying a mammoth hangover from the shot after shot of Milligan's cheap whiskey he had tossed down the day before.

Baca then told Wadsworth that he would produce McCarthy for trial, but he tacked on a condition. The group must sign an agreement saying they would not harm him (Baca). The cowhand did not testify whether the agreement was signed. Apparently it was, by somebody, because the document is referred to later in Wadsworth's testimony.

At this point, Wadsworth gave the defense an opening to attack his memory and his credibility during cross-examination. At first, he said that Baca and McCarthy were together when he rode up, but later in his testimony, he reported that it was he (Wadsworth) and Baca who went to the Upper Plaza together, and it was only then that Elfego brought McCarthy out of the temporary jail to turn over to Wadsworth and his friends. It was while McCarthy was still standing outside the house used as the lock-up that the horde from the Slaughter outfit rode up to the justice's office and McCarthy said, "Look at the crowd of men coming here."

Then Wadsworth explained the nature of the charges that Baca had filed against McCarthy. They weren't just for shooting off a firearm in town. According to the reporter's account, "Baca had filed a complaint against McCarthy for attempting murder on him. . . ." The charge probably referred to the incident in which McCarthy shot off his hat and missed shattering his skull by a fraction of an inch.

When the Slaughter men drew near, Elfego paused long enough to consider that none of them could know about the agreement that he was not to be harmed. He then disappeared out of the back door of the justice's office and wasn't seen again. In an hour or so, some of the men went out to look for him. Somehow, they discovered he was locked inside the Armijo place. Wadsworth hunted down a key. When he'd found it, this is what he said happened:

> [I] tried to unlock the door; one of the men said the door was not locked, and Burt Hurn [sic] tried to open it; as he pushed on the door two shots were fired by someone in the
> house, and Burt staggered back and said: "Boys, I'm killed."

Hurn staggered off about twenty feet and fell; he got over the fence and fell again; when he fell the last time two of the men ran to where he was and picked him up and carried him into Mulligan's [sic] store, where he died in about an hour.

While Wadsworth told the facts of the beginning of the encounter, it was Crichton who gave insight into Baca's mood and the reaction of the cowboys as the eighty rode up to the justice of the peace's office. Crichton quoted Cook, leader of the cowboys, as describing the meeting going this way: "'Good morning, Mr. Wilson,' said Baca affably. 'Good morning, you dirty Mexican blankety blank,' replied Wilson in turn, following it up by words of like purport. It was then also that a shot was fired by one of the Slaughter crowd."[27] During his testimony, Wadsworth would not admit that any of the cowboys had fired the first shot nor that it had been provoked by a jovial greeting.

Wadsworth was not asked about the shots fired into the *jacal* by the angry cowhands nor the shouted threats reported later by Elfego Baca when it was his turn to testify, but it is not clear whether all of the Wadsworth testimony is reported by the newspaper.

It surely must have boosted the defense strategy of attacking the credibility of the witness when Wadsworth claimed he "did not know of any shots fired on the outside [of the *jacal*]. . . ." It is not likely that there was any man on the all-Hispanic jury who had not, at one time or another, huddled with his family behind a locked door while his town was "shot up" by a bunch of trigger-happy Texas cowboys out to have a good time. And the horde chasing Baca felt they had been provoked by the brash kid with the quick gun who'd arrested one of their own, making it less likely that they kept their pistols in their holsters.

After telling the story that no cowboy fired his gun, Wadsworth testified that the men were all around, but "they did not furnish McCarthy with any arms." Of course, by then it was obvious that McCarthy was the only one of the bunch who was not carrying at least one pistol that he was ready and willing to use. Overall, defense counsel's handling of Wadsworth's cross-examination probably left positives for Elfego's case in the jurors' memories.

Wadsworth was followed on the stand by O. B. Bishop. His opening testimony made a gift to the defense by undercutting the count of eight or nine men that Wadsworth had just testified to as present when the fifty rode up out of the arroyo. Not only did he call the waiting men a "gang," but he put their numbers at "between forty-five and fifty." They were in town, he said, to see McCarthy because a man had come to the ranch to say that McCarthy was to have a trial that afternoon, and that he would not be freed on bail. At first, Bishop said nothing suggesting that the crier who galloped up also reported that the Mexicans were on the warpath.

The prosecution at this point seemed to have understood the vulnerability of Bishop's testimony, for it tried to squeeze additional information from its witness. Bishop gave "an additional answer to the questions put by the prosecution: — The men came because of information that one or two cowboys had been killed." The admission was late in coming, probably because the prosecution had wanted to steer clear of any suggestion that the cowhands riding up were out to avenge the killings by doing a little killing of their own.

When Bishop had once again taken his seat in the audience, the reporter wrote, the testimony of "several other witnesses [unidentified by the paper] was taken, but all told nearly the same story as is given above."

Another bit of testimony not reported by the newspaper, probably for the reason that it was said on the first day of the trial, is told in Crichton's book. Crichton wrote that one of the cowboys, whom he does not identify, testified that if a Colt 45 were fired into the center of Elfego's chest from a foot away, there would have been no effect, and the reason had more to do with the devil than with God.[28]

In a move that seems from the newspaper account to have followed a tepid prosecution case, District Attorney McComas rested. In fairness, it should be remembered that since the first day of the trial was not reported, it cannot be known with certainty all the witnesses who testified or what they said. It would have been predictable, however, had District Attorney McComas started with a few strong witnesses, filled in with his weakest, and saved the most damning testimony for last.

In any event, it was time for the motions of defense counsel asking the court to terminate the prosecution and to send Elfego Baca home as a free man. If such motions were made, and they surely were, they were not reported. The next account the *Democrat* carried was the opening statement of the defense when it was time to present Elfego Baca's case.

The opening by Baca's lawyer was reported tersely, but it impressed the reporter. After hearing it, he felt the case was in the bag for the defense. The statement in its entirety, as summarized by the Albuquerque press, is:

> [Baca's lawyer] Judge Shaw made the opening statement, and it went to show that Defendant, Baca, was sheriff at San Francisco; that he had arrested McCarthy for discharging his pistol in the city limits; that as soon as his cowboy friends heard that McCarthy was under arrest, they immediately went to the town in full force and threatened to kill the sheriff and wipe out the town; that the defendant, in order to keep from being killed, went to another house, and that if he did shoot the man, it was perfectly justifiable. Taken all in all, the judge [lawyer Shaw] made a very clear and concise statement, and the opinion is that Baca will be released.

Lawyer Rodey and his team had succeeded with the newspaper — Baca was pictured as "sheriff" twice in a single paragraph, McCarthy had been portrayed as under arrest, and justification was the centerpiece on the table. The reporter did not record whether the jury appeared to respond as favorably to the defense lawyer's statement as he had.

Defense counsel Shaw and Rodey kept mum about Baca's self-appointed deputy status in their opening statement. The report of the Defendant's case that followed does not mention ex-sheriff Pedro Simpson's affidavit appointing Elfego Baca a deputy. Simpson did not testify, as far as can be determined. He was not listed among those subpoenaed by the prosecution, and the paper's coverage picked up the entire defense case without mentioning Simpson.

Time and again since the trial the question has come up as to whether Elfego Baca was in Frisco as a real deputy sheriff, sent there to campaign for the reelection of Sheriff Pedro Simpson, or whether he was a self-made deputy, as Elfego claimed. The mystery of whether Simpson back-dated an affidavit reflecting Elfego as a deputy, marked as a trial exhibit, must remain a mystery. The affidavit was not mentioned, either by the prosecution or by the defense, in any of the reported testimony.

There was probably a reason why the defense lawyers did not raise the issue. Elfego Baca acting as a real-life deputy sheriff was more defensible than a kid playing lawman with a borrowed badge pinned to his chest and two dead men laid out in Milligan's storeroom. Why the prosecution kept quiet is less easy to understand, unless the answer is that the issue was addressed during the part of the trial not reported by the paper. Perhaps Elfego had been so convincing in his role as deputy that no one suspected he was self-made, especially once Sheriff Simpson had signed an affidavit that ratified acts that had been so successful. Or maybe Elfego was "self-made" in the sense that he went to Simpson before he and Sarracino set out for Frisco and persuaded the sheriff to issue him a deputy's commission for the trip.

At the opening of court on May 9, the third day of the trial, Elfego Baca took the stand as the first and only witness to be called in his defense. For Baca, there was no sitting back while claiming the right to remain silent. Not when his very life was at stake.

He testified that on the morning of October 28 he had arrested a man for firing a revolver in Milligan's "house," presumably referring to the Whiskey Bar in that way since Milligan and his family lived in the back. The arrest was made in the upper precinct, "but as there was no justice of the peace there I took him to the middle precinct, or plaza."

As they set out for the plaza, Baca did not take his prisoner's revolver. It was a failure that surely demonstrated what a rookie the self-made deputy was in the precautions to be taken by arresting officers. The pair, Elfego and his prisoner, walked to Milligan's saloon, Baca said. His testimony continued,

> McCarthy, my prisoner, commenced firing off his revolver, at everything and everybody; Milligan went out yelling; he knew I was a deputy sheriff, and asked me to help him; when I asked McCarthy to stop he had fired five shots and instead of stopping he fired the last of the five shots at me; then I went home [to Sarracino's place] and got some men to help me arrest him, because I had no arms at the time; I got eight or nine men and went back to Milligan's house and did not find McCarthy there; I went to a ranch two or three hundred yards away, and again did not find him; but when coming back I met him on the road; he started to run and I asked one of my

deputies who it was that was running, and he said it was McCarthy; then I had the guards arrest him; all the way up to jail he abused us in a very insulting manner, stopping every minute or so, and crying he did not need to be taken and wouldn't have to go if he didn't want to; he was very drunk; at the upper plaza a large number of cowboys had assembled and as there was no justice [of the peace] there I took him down to the middle plaza; he drew Perham's [sic—referring to Young Parham, later to be killed by his falling horse] pistol and shot it at me; I then refused to let him off or have any bail; Sorcino [sic] and Perham were willing to be his bondsmen.

After Elfego had written the opening few words of the bond, Milligan blew up again, and Baca changed his mind about letting McCarthy out on bail. The previously reported episode with the changeable Milligan took place when the saloon keeper threatened Baca, as Elfego testified to in some detail. When he ended the tale of his adventure with Milligan, Baca moved on to tell about what happened the next day.

The self-made deputy did not take his prisoner to the justice's office at nine o'clock that following morning as he'd intended, he told the jury. At around ten, McCarthy escaped. Baca pursued, overtook him near Milligan's place and again put him under arrest. It was only then that a "large number of cowboys came to town from their ranches; they asked me why I didn't give him an examination; I told them I didn't know what to do with him; that I knew that there were men waiting for me in the upper precinct."

Finally, Baca testified, he made it to the upper plaza, where he sat down to pencil out a list of the witnesses required for McCarthy's trial. When an individual identified as J. Parpzia, perhaps the justice of the peace's bailiff or process server, left to seek the witnesses, "we saw a lot of men coming; they were all armed; carried their arms in their hands. . . . " Of course, there was already a "large number" present.

After the episode with the man named Wilson who insulted Elfego, Baca dashed for the house of "Jeronomo" (Geronimo Armijo). There, he went inside, and the door was padlocked by Mrs. Armijo as she left. There was no way out except through the single window in one end of the hut. Baca's own report of the commencement of the shooting followed in the newspaper's account:

> I heard several men around the house; I heard their talk, and they wanted to kill me; one of them said in English that it was just a padlock that fastened the door, and they had better go and get a key; they went away and returned in a few minutes, and pushed the door, they again went around the house; one of them said, this door is not locked; he shoved the door at one of the middle rooms; the others were trying to unlock the door; I remained where I was; they pushed on the door but did not open it; when they did not open the door; they all said, let us fire; they commenced firing through all the doors, and I fired a few shots through the windows, then they pushed the door again, and I fired two shots through the door; this is all I know.

With that, the court recessed for the day.

The next morning Elfego Baca was back on the stand. He testified only long enough to contradict Wadsworth's claim that the cowboys present, except for Hearne, were on their horses with their guns in their scabbards. Baca's version was that he could see them through the window, some had rifles but all had pistols. "They had their weapons in their hands; they came to the house with pistols and said they would get me out."

At that point, Elfego's attorney sat down, and it was the prosecution's turn to grill Elfego.

The cross-examination as reported is brief and not helpful to the prosecution. It established, probably to District Attorney Mc-Comas' dismay, that the cowboys rode around the house and fired through the door when one of the cowboys said they would get Baca out. Surely in those frontier times when Texas cowboys liked to shoot up Mexican communities, the testimony conjured up in the minds of the Hispanic jurors and the audience an image of a band of drunks galloping, circling, firing at the hut and anything and everything that moved, yipping at the tops of their voices, just as Charley McCarthy had done the day Elfego arrested him.

Baca's cross examination ended with another word picture — the overtaking of the wagon with the coffin on the way to Socorro with Deputy Ross, and Baca's observation that he feared he might soon be in one himself.

It was probably a tactical mistake for the prosecution to stop its questioning at that point. Baca's comment, made almost as an aside, may have been discussed in advance between defense counsel and their young client. It helped dispel the notion that Elfego was a killer who was out to shoot as many Texas cowboys as he could line up in his sights, and it came while the prosecution was asking the questions. The restraint by the dream team in electing not to conduct any redirect examination was lawyering of the style expected from the Territory's best attorneys. The result was that at the end of Baca's testimony the jury was left with an understanding of the fear that Baca had faced and overcome in standing up to his cowboy persecu-tors. The young man had portrayed himself as anything but a preda-tor whose aim was to kill.

The defense rested.

The Territory paraded four witnesses before the jury in its re-buttal. Wadsworth took the stand again to testify that he "was with the gang all the time."

The signed agreement resurfaced, continuing to have importance to the Territory's case. The agreement boiled down to a promise that the Texans would not harm Elfego, though its precise terms were argued about since the document did not survive. Wadsworth said it was written in Spanish.

McComas' case was largely based on this signed document. The district attorney had to establish that the cowboys were no threat to Baca, and that the feisty upstart was not justified in shooting Hearne. But there was a flaw in the McComas theory, and it was big enough so that defense lawyers Shaw and Rodey could drive their buggies through it. The twelve Hispanics on the jury and the defense team sitting at the their table knew, if Mr. McComas did not, that the safe conduct memo had been signed by a handful of cowboys before the main force rode up, and no one had testified that the newcomers had bought into it or even knew about it. Of course, during the trial, the plot to ambush Elfego on his way to the Socorro jail with Deputy Ross, in breach of the safe conduct deal, was not yet out in the open so as to confirm that some of the Texans were scheming to stretch Elfego's neck alongside the road to Socorro.

McComas was left to try to draw clarification from his witness about the number of cowboys present. The response seemed to muddy the water. Wadsworth said once more that there were only "eight or nine of the boys with me where the killing occurred. . . " leaving everyone who was paying attention to wonder what had happened to the bunch from the Slaughter outfit that had ridden up. The implication left was that they must have been outside the house where Elfego holed up, and that the total was about eighty.

McComas tried to highlight the agreement that had grown so important to the prosecution, though defense lawyers were probably chuckling up their sleeves while McComas chased the issue. Wadsworth testified that the document did not require Baca to be disarmed; that it said that "no one of the party would molest him." On cross examination he maintained again that he did not violate the contract, though he said nothing about the Texans who had not signed.

The prosecution next called A. M. Loftis and O. B. Bishop, neither of whom provided significant additional facts.

Finally, Charley McCarthy was sworn in to talk about the contract, which by that time seemed like a red herring the prosecution had drawn across its own case. He was there when it was signed, McCarthy said, though he was not questioned about whether he was sober or whether he was hung over. McCarthy did not say he signed it, or whether he or Elfego Baca could read the Spanish it was written in, or whether anyone except Wadsworth had signed for the cowboys. He was also there, McCarthy said, when Hearne was killed; he heard all the conversation but heard no threats against Elfego Baca, though he would have if any had been uttered.

There was no cross-examination, and McCarthy sat back down. It was late on Saturday afternoon and the prosecution had no one else to call. The case was ready for the jury.

The newspaper account does not report the charges given the jury, but some of them have survived in the N. C. Laughlin file.

After defining the terms "feloniously," "unlawfully," "willfully," "premeditated design to effect death," and "malice," the trial judge instructed the jury that if they believed "from the evidence that the defendant Elfigo [sic] Baca did on the 30th day of October 1884, or at any other time within ten years next before the filing of the indictment . . . without authority of law willfully shoot and kill William B. Hearne . . . from a premeditated design to effect the death of said William B. Hearne . . . you will find him guilty of murder in the first degree and simply so state in your verdict."[29]

When those words had been delivered to the jury, the court went on to read from its sheaf of heavy, legal-sized paper the handwritten instructions for second degree murder, or murder without premeditation. The judge then concluded there was no evidence warranting giving instructions for third or fourth degree murder, but gave an instruction on murder in the fifth degree, or death inflicted by unjustified or inexcusable "culpable neglect." The penalty for that offense was one to ten years in the Territorial prison.

Over the written objections of both defense counsel J. M. Shaw and Bernard Rodey, the prosecution persuaded the court to give an instruction on the issue of provocation: "Mere words however insulting will not justify an assault and the Court instructs the jury that if they believe from the evidence that the defendant fired the fatal shot, if he did fire it, in resentment or revenge for any insult or supposed insult which he had received by words He [sic] cannot avail himself of the plea of self defense therefor.[30]

At last, to the relief of the listening Elfego Baca, the court came to the justifiable killing instruction. It provided a peg on which the jurors could hang their verdict if they decided to acquit. In defining justifiable killing for the jury, the judge said that it is "one committed . . . in resisting any attempt to murder the person doing the killing or to commit any felony upon him or . . . when committed in the lawful defense of his person when there shall be reasonable ground to apprehend a design upon the part of the person killed to commit a felony upon the person doing the killing or to do him some great personal injury and there shall be imminent danger of such design being accomplished."[31]

No account tells how long the jury deliberated, but presumably the court stayed in session well into Saturday night, long after *The Evening Democrat* had cleared the presses.

The *Democrat* seems to have lost interest in the case quickly, since its edition of Monday, May 11, did not carry the outcome, nor did it make any other reference to the trial after its Saturday issue.

But the word soon spread out from the courthouse: Elfego Baca had been acquitted. Round two was over, and Baca had won again.

In some respects, the trial had been a replay of the shootout. A parade of angry Texans had lined up to take potshots, this time verbal, at the Mexican kid who had upset the balance of Texan supremacy; the outcome had been the same as it had been in Frisco, and the cowmen were just as upset as they had been before. As before, they were not satisfied to let it rest.

7

❖   THE SECOND MURDER TRIAL – THE FRISCO NINE

The second murder trial that sprung from the events at Frisco was for the death-by-falling-horse of William Young Parham. It quickly turned into warfare between the cattlemen and the Hispanics, and Elfego was still at the center, still the champion, still taking the fire. The fact that there were no bullets flying and that the war was fought on paper made it no less bitter and no less critical to Elfego's survival nor to the preservation of the sputtering flame of pride that he had kindled in his Mexican-American contemporaries.

Following Elfego Baca's May 10, 1885, acquittal for the murder of Hearne, it took the cattlemen nearly seven months to organize their next attack in the campaign to stamp out the rebellion of the Mexicans by locking up their teen-aged leader for good or making him dance at the end of a rope. This time, the Texans cast their net in an arc wide enough to catch a handful of the Frisco farmers who had stood by Baca during the confrontation with saloonkeeper Milligan at the time Baca shot Young Parham's horse. Nine persons were charged with Parham's murder. Surely that would be enough to suppress the insurrection.

On December 5, 1885, the Socorro County grand jury returned a true bill of indictment directed against "Elfego Baca, José Andres, Bernavél Chavez, Juan Luna, Pedro Sarracino, Ché Narranjo, Francisquito Narranjo, Patrosinio Romero, Quico Narranjo, and diverse others whose names are to the Grand Jurors unknown." They will collectively be called here the "Frisco Nine."

Elfego Baca at about age 20, after he was tried for murder the second time.
Apparently Elfego was wearing a borrowed coat.
Photograph by Edwin A. Bass, courtesy of Museum of New Mexico, Negative No. 75265.

The crime charged, in three sheets of cramped handwritten allegations, was murder in the death of William Young Parham. In view of the size of the crowd of defendants named and that the cattlemen seemed to have been behind it all, the real offense must have been that the Frisco Nine had had the guts to stand beside Elfego as he challenged cattleman power over the people of Frisco.

After listing all the men charged, and asserting that the alleged offenses occurred on October 28, 1884, in Socorro County, the bill alleged that the Frisco Nine:

> in and upon one William Young Parham, the said William Young Parham then and there being mounted and riding upon the back of a certain horse, feloniously, willfully, of their malice aforethought and from a premeditated design to effect the death of him . . . did make an assault; and that the said [Frisco Nine] certain pistols and rifles then and there loaded with gunpowder and leaden balls [they] then and there had and held to, upon and against the said William Young Parham, being so mounted and riding upon the back of a certain horse as aforesaid . . . and that the said [Frisco Nine] with the leaden balls aforesaid out of the pistols and rifles aforesaid so shot and discharged . . . did strike wound and instantly kill: and that the said horse . . . ridden by the said William Young Parham, being so shot, struck, wounded and instantly killed as aforesaid by the said [Frisco Nine], in consequence . . . did . . . fall against and upon him the said William Young Parham, giving to him . . . in and upon the breast of him . . . one mortal wound; of which . . . William Young Parham . . . then and there instantly died, [and the Frisco Nine in this way] the said William Young Parham did kill and murder.[32]

The indictment was signed by the new district attorney, Democrat Harvey B. Fergusson. In 1911, Fergusson was to edge out Republican candidate Elfego Baca in a race for New Mexico's second seat in Congress.[33]

Though the Socorro county court file remaining has preserved only a few documents, they are revealing as to the temper of the times in Socorro county following the Frisco incident. The paperwork, and the courthouse fireworks, started with a motion filed by Elfego's lawyers.

This time around, Elfego Baca was represented by local Socorro legal talent with no Albuquerque reinforcements. On Baca's behalf, without referring to the other eight defendants, H. L. Warren, of the law firm of Fox & Sniffen, drafted and filed a motion for change of venue on March 24, 1886. Warren asked the court to change the location for Elfego Baca's trial from Socorro County "to some County free from exception for the reason that the said Defendant can not have justice done him at the trial of his cause in the County of Socorro." At some point not disclosed by the surviving records, the other eight defendants jumped on the change of venue bandwagon.

The defendants claimed the court and the jury panel were prejudiced. The prosecution denied it, and the arguments flew back and forth. Support for the charges of prejudice began with an affidavit filed to support the defense lawyers' motion to change the venue. All nine of the defendants signed. In the three page handwritten document, the Frisco Nine peeled the cover off years of resentment against the power of the ranchers and their cowhands and against Texan arrogance toward the Mexicans. In laying out information that might cause the judge to send the case away for trial at any place but Socorro, the attorneys who drafted the affidavit alleged a conspiracy between the cattlemen and the prosecution. They claimed the cattlemen had hammered together a plan to convict the Nine, that it involved spending a lot of money to support the prosecution, and that it would rob the defendants of a fair trial.

According to the affidavit, the Central New Mexican Cattle Association was "an organized body of men . . . composed of a large number of men residing and carrying on the business of raising and dealing in live stock and cattle in various parts of [Socorro County] and possessed of great wealth power and influance [sic] in said County and having in their employ and service a very large number of men throughout said county." It asserted that both men killed at the Frisco shootout, Hearn and Parham, "were respectively at the time of there [sic] death members or employees of the said Association. . . ."

Then the affidavit got down to brass tacks. It charged that "all the members and employees of the same have combined and confederated together to posecute [sic] and procure the conviction of the said Defendants and each of them of the said crime alleged in the indictment in this case and have subscribed and expended and are expending large sums of money for that purpose . . . [and] several of the members of the present panel of the Pettie [sic] Jurors of the Court are members or employees of the said Association and violently prejudiced against these Defendants [who] are innocent of the said alleged murder. . . ."

The net result of all this influence and money spent, according to the affidavit, was to influence and control "the minds of the persons upon said present panel of Jurors and other persons subject to jury duty . . . [so] that it will be impossible for said defendants or either of them to have a fair and impartial trial. . . ."[34]

On March 26, two days after the motion was filed, another affidavit supporting the motion for change of venue was placed in the court file. It is a curious document in that it identifies itself as the sworn statement of one "John W. Virginia," who the affidavit says is "a member of the Central New Mexico Cattle Growers Association," but nowhere in the affidavit can the signature of Virginia be found, though it bears the signatures of six other persons. Virginia's name appears to have been inserted in the body of the document in a different hand and with a finer nib pen than the one in which the rest of the affidavit was written. Page one of the document, below Virginia's name, reads as though it were the statement of a single person, but the second page shifts to the plural.

The document raises several questions: Did cattleman John W. Virginia agree to provide an affidavit on behalf of the defendants, then change his mind? If so, did he reverse his position when he felt the heat from fellow cattlemen who had learned that he was about to go on record as a turn-coat, and did he then turn tail and run, to duck out of town instead of showing up at the lawyer's office to sign? Was he threatened by the cattlemen?

Perhaps the reason John W. Virginia did not sign what started out to be his affidavit is no more sinister than that he changed his mind, or was suddenly called back to his ranch while the Frisco Nine's lawyer was drafting the paperwork. After all, even back in 1885 lawyers must have had a reputation for dragging their feet in drafting important pleadings and documents. And if that is what happened, maybe because of the labor-intensive task involved in writing long legal documents by hand with a pen dipped in an inkwell, when Virginia excused himself the law office decided to make do with page one, which had already been drafted, and simply to rewrite the second page where the signatures appear.

The document recites that "John W. Virginia, being duly sworn says that he is a member of The Central New Mexico Cattle Growers Association . . ." The Association, it said, had a large number of members and employees in Socorro County, two of whom had been W. B. Hearn and William Young Parham, "for the murder of whome [sic] the defendants stand indicted in this Court . . ." Following the killings, according to John W. Virginia or whomever was to have spoken the words in the affidavit, "the facts and circumstances attending said pretended murder have been discussed and talked about to such an extend [sic] among the members of said Association and the inhabitants of said County that this affiant believes that said Defendants can not have a fair and impartial trial in the County of Socorro on the account of the bias and prejudice of the inhabitance [sic] of said County." That concluded page one.

Page two recited that the "affiants [shifting to the plural] respectively believe that for the reasons stated in said affidavit the said Defendants can not nor can either of them have a fair and impartial trial of said cause in said county of Socorro."[35] The paper was signed by Socorro County residents Disimirio Jaramillo, Buck Adams, Sam Edgington, Monto Butler and Jose Baca. Juan Baca also signed—by an "X" mark, apparently being unable to read or to write his name.

The group signed and swore to the document before former sheriff Pedro A. Simpson, now a Notary Public. Simpson had apparently been enlisted to do his part against the cattlemen who had organized to defeat him in his bid for reelection. It can be concluded from the appearance of the document that the pen used by Simpson in signing was the one used to insert the name of John W. Virginia in the body of the affidavit, though that is speculation.

But the affidavit-signing individuals were soon challenged. It took only a couple of days for the cattlemen to fire back through two affidavits filed on March 29.

One was signed by Charles T. Russell, the county sheriff himself, who had beaten out Pedro Simpson and who was not about to let Elfego Baca and friends slip through his fingers. Russell wrote that he was the sheriff, that he knew the citizens of Socorro County and people who were likely to be called for jury duty in the case. He'd done some figuring, apparently, and had concluded that the number of men who were in the cattle business in the county was small compared to the total population. He'd also measured "public sentiment" and had come to a conclusion, which he stated for the benefit of the court: "[I]n the opinion of affiant there is no such prejudice in the minds of the qualified jurors of said County against any of the defendants as would prevent them or any of them from having a fair and impartial trial. . . . Indeed affiant believes that a very large majority of the qualified jurors . . . have never heard of the said defendants and know nothing of the facts of the alleged killing. . . ."[36]

Then the cattlemen dealt what was probably the death blow to the effort of the Nine to move the trial out of Socorro. They produced a second affidavit, this one signed by George L. Brooks. Brooks called himself the former "Secretary of the Central New Mexico Cattle Growers Association during its entire existence . . ." This document claimed that the Association had "disbanded on the 16th day of March, 1886 [and] on said day there were but thirty one members of the said association who reside in the County of Socorro and that the said association has never contributed any sum of money whatever to the prosecution of the defendants in the above entitled cause or to any person or persons for that purpose and further affiant saith not."[37]

The affidavit did not deny that the individual members of the then-defunct association might have made private contributions to the prosecution, though there is no evidence that they did, except for inferences that might be drawn from the affidavit of the Frisco Nine. It also shied away from any mention of how many cowhands those thirty one members had on their payrolls and over how many thousands of acres their ranches were spread.

The paper warfare seems to have ended at this point, at least as far as documents preserved for history are concerned. The defendants lost, and the trial was called for Socorro in the new county courthouse. The next round was the jury selection.

Though the venue arguments had not gone well for them, the Frisco Nine carried the day in picking the jury. The twelve jurors seated were largely Hispanics, though a reliable list of all those who served has not survived. Though two Anglos, H. Zoller and Joseph Wickham, remained on the panel, it appears that all the rest were Hispanic.

The witnesses called by the prosecution, according to a subpoena in the court file, were W. R. Milligan, M. B. Allen alias Tobe Allen, Charles McCarthy and W. W. Wilson. Tobe Allen was the person identified by William Cook in his account as "one of the Americans, Allen by name," who was shot in the knee by Elfego during the confrontation with the Milligan forces when Parham was crushed by his horse.[38]

Defendants subpoenaed Bernardo Chavez, Bartolo Hernñandez, Andres Benevides, Esperidion Armijo and Guadalupe Sarracino, the wife of Deputy Pedro Sarracino. No record of the trial proceedings remains.

The verdict was for acquittal. Elfego had won round three, and he was once again a free man.

But though the two jury trials had milked the witnesses for all the facts of the events at Frisco for Elfego's short stay in the village, the testimony and the arguments of the lawyers did not explore the reasons why the racial tensions in and around the little community had come within a hair's-breadth of flaring into a bloody race war. And one can scarcely endeavor to evaluate Elfego Baca's actions without delving into the racial setting in which he found himself.

8

◈   SETTING THE SCENE FOR THE SIEGE AT FRISCO

William French described Frisco as a "peaceful Mexican community" at the time that Elfego Baca rode into town. If his description had been apt, when the word arrived at the ranch where French worked, reporting that a revolution was brewing, the cowboys and their bosses would surely have chuckled, shrugged off the news as too improbable to be believed, and gone back to branding their cattle. But they loaded their firearms, saddled up and rode out to quell what they thought was a budding rebellion. So what was going on? Why did ranch foreman William H. Cook, and French himself, believe the cry of the messenger who carried the word that "the Mexicans are on the warpath?"

The reason was that the peacefulness was a veneer that covered layers of resentment and ill feeling that virtually everyone knew existed.

One historian, Ralph Emerson Twitchell, concluded that antagonisms between the Anglos and the Hispanics within the Territory dated all the way back to the first intrusion of Lt. Zebulon Pike's expedition in 1806. Following Pike's adventure, Americans began to move into Texas. Later they spread from Texas into New Mexico, where they shoved aside those who were already there, settlers from Mexico who had arrived while the Spanish were ruling. The result was bitterness on the part of the Mexican farmers, though their culture did not promote overt demonstrations of anger.

The hostility was nurtured for years. As late as 1912, the *Albuquerque Morning Journal* ran a lengthy article on the relationship, based substantially on Twitchell's work. It was titled, "The Texas-Santa Fe Expedition." The story recalled that when the Texas Republic's President Lamar sent a force of three hundred men to Santa Fe in 1841 to exercise the Republic's muscle by persuading the New Mexicans to become Texans, the "New Mexicans were not ready to hail the Texans as deliverers. . . ." To the contrary, the writer reported, New Mexico Governor Manuel Armijo characterized the Texans as, "being a choice assortment of reckless and desperate men from whom nothing other than pillage, murder, and outrage could be expected."[39]

But the issue that lifted the New Mexico-Texas quarrels to top billing on the national political scene was a claim that Texas made to lands of New Mexico extending all the way westward to the banks of the Rio Grande in mid-New Mexico. The claim to a chunk of New Mexico was raised shortly after the end of the Mexican War, when another delegation from Texas rode into Santa Fe in 1848. This contingent came to supervise the addition to Texas of a newly created county they wanted to be carved out of New Mexico.

According to historian Warren A. Beck, the Santa Fe newspaper reported the reactions to the invasion in that ancient city: "There is not a citizen, either American or Mexican, that will ever acknowledge themselves as citizens of Texas. . . . New Mexico does not belong, nor has Texas ever had a right to claim her as a part of Texas. . . . Texas should show some little sense, and drop this question."[40]

The fact was that New Mexicans supported statehood for themselves as preferable to bowing down to the rule of the Texas government in Austin. They set out to get it. When they called a New Mexico constitutional convention in 1850, Texans were outraged; they concluded that their only recourse for bringing the intransigent New Mexicans to heel was by threatening the use of military power.

The disagreements see-sawed back and forth during the presidencies of Zachary Taylor and Millard Fillmore until Fillmore took a firm stand in support of the position of the New Mexicans, and also in favor of his United States military forces that occupied the Territory. The Texans reacted with threats of secession. The pressure got the attention of Washington.

The result was a compromise cobbled together in the halls of Congress in 1850. In return for agreement to the establishment of the boundaries of New Mexico, Texas was paid ten million dollars. But in the boundary survey that followed, New Mexico lost approximately a half million acres. Though the boundary dispute was settled, for New Mexicans the wounds were not allowed to heal.

Another series of events promoting tension between the Texas cattlemen and New Mexico Hispanic farmers and small ranchers grew out of what was called the "Great New Mexico Cattle Raid." The incursion shook eastern New Mexico in the 1870's, but it reflected the Texan's view of Hispanic settlers as untrustworthy, and worse. Charles L. Kenner wrote of these episodes in Texas-New Mexico relationships in *The New Mexico Historical Review.* Kenner found that leading up to the invasion of the New Mexico Territory by Texas ranchers was a series of Indian raids on West Texas ranches for the purpose of cattle theft.

A Texas stockman, John Hittson, told a Denver reporter for the *Rocky Mountain News* how the losses had come about. He blamed three classes of New Mexicans for his disappearing cattle: They were the merchants, who were prosperous businessmen, the *Comancheros,* or "Greasers," employed by the merchants to act as middle-men, and finally, there were the Indians.[41]

Hittson pictured a three-way conspiracy. The New Mexico merchants supplied trinkets and ultimately took possession of the stolen cattle, the "Greasers" dealt the trinkets and other items supplied to them by the merchants to the Indians. The Indians stole the cattle and turned them over to the Greasers in exchange for the trinkets.

Hittson had had enough. He resolved to get his herds back from the New Mexico ranchers on whose lands he believed they had wound up, and he had a plan for doing it. The plan worked, but part of the fall-out was to make Texas-New Mexico relations even worse.

Hittson recruited nearly a hundred ruffians in Denver, outfitted them with arms, and led them in an invasion of the New Mexico Territory. Hittson's men were ruthlessly efficient in carrying out their cattle-recovery from the Mexican-Americans.

Eventually, at the request of townsmen in Las Vegas, Don Miguel Otero, a former delegate to the United States Congress from the New Mexico Territory, was persuaded to visit the Texans' camp to urge them to have greater respect for the property of New Mexico's citizens. Otero's son, who was to be a territorial governor, quoted the answer his father was given when he asked for the return of cattle that did not belong to the Texans: "Don't attempt to interfere with what we are doing unless you are looking for trouble."[42]

The future governor concluded his report of the incident by writing that his father did not push further, knowing it was useless. But the young Otero never forgot. Thereafter, he wrote, "Tejanos" was a hated word in New Mexico. "It is said that mothers were in the habit of censuring their children with the dire threat: 'If you are not good, I'll give you to the *Tejanos*, who are coming back.'"[43]

Author Carey McWilliams, in his book, *North from Mexico*, addressed many of the same issues growing out of the movement of Hispanics from Mexico across the Rio Grande. He named a chapter "Not Counting Mexicans."

According to McWilliams, King Fisher, a notorious Texas gunman, when asked how many notches he had cut on his revolver, replied: "Thirty-seven—not counting Mexicans." The comment symbolized relationships between the two factions: Mexicans were allowed to exist, but if they got out of line, a Texan gunman could terminate their lives without a second thought.

McWilliams, in what might have described the legacy of the Great New Mexico Cattle Raid, also told of the view of Mexicans held by Anglo-American settlers in Socorro County, New Mexico Territory in the 1880s: "To them, all Mexicans were 'greasers' and unfit associates for the white man. A few brave words were all that was needed to work these men into a Mexican-killing mood."[44]

The attitude of the Texans toward the Mexican-Americans was not helped by the esteem in which the cowboys were held by some authors who glamorized them for the consumption of fans of the Old West. Writer J. Frank Dobie called the Texas cowboy a "proud rider, skilled, observant, alert, resourceful, unyielding, daring, punctilious in a code peculiar to his occupations, and faithful to his trust." The vulgar and ignorant ones did not fit in, he claimed.[45]

Writer Dobie did not comment on the mindset of the proud riders toward Mexicans, and no Hispanic author found an outlet for a voice extolling the virtues of the simple life of the farmers who had come from south of the border.

Historians Gann and Dunnigan summarized the common Texan view of the Mexican-American: "A pattern of violence, discrimination, and contempt [directed against Hispanics] made Texas probably the worst state in the Union for the Mexican American."[46] Another writer, David J. Weber, termed the Texan view of the Mexican-American as "Hispanophobia," with a particularly virulent strain infecting some who used it as a rationale to keep Mexicans "in their place."[47] A cover for the hate some of the Texans displayed was their claim that they didn't like the Hispanics of the Territory because of their "thieving" ways.

While Texas stockmen didn't make it into western Socorro County until the early 1880s, when they came, they rode in with the biases they had learned back home. They found that western Socorro County had been populated by Hispanic farmers and ranchers who had been there since shortly after the Civil War. That the settlers had been first in time was of no consequence. Ranchman James Cook, participant in the Frisco shoot-out, wrote that when Texans moved in with their herds, and "occasionally their neighbors' herds," along with their cowhands, their quest was to find free public land. As the Texans drove their cattle across the terrain, Cook said, the stockmen added more by roping and branding any "mavericks" that happened to be caught in the flow. Whose land they were trespassing over didn't matter any more than did the ownership of cattle they ran across.[48]

Some of the cattlemen came into Socorro County because they'd worn out their welcome with Texas lawmen, Cook said. There were also those who rode in carrying anger about the events at the Alamo, where 155 men lost their lives in 1836 in a siege by 2,000 Mexican troops under General Santa Ana. The rage remained buried only as long as they were sober. After a few drinks, these men turned into Texas patriots out to avenge the dead by harassing any of the locals whose skin tone matched that of the Mexican troops under Santa Ana.

But what effect did all this history have on young Elfego Baca? The impressionable kid from Kansas surely learned these lessons soon after he moved back to Socorro from Topeka. But there was more schooling about "American" vs "Mexican" relationships conducted in Elfego's own new backyard, and the lessons he learned there must have left the most lasting impressions of all.

Elfego's personalized education started not long after he took up residence in Socorro. The instruction began with events in the Socorro Methodist church on Christmas Eve, 1880, when Elfego was fifteen and just beginning to learn the ways of the New Mexico Territory.

On that night, three members of the Baca clan, Antonio, Abran and Onofre, visited the church. When the Baca boys began to harass the young women who sat in front of them, usher A. M. Conklin, editor of the *Socorro Sun*, asked them to leave. The trio walked out the door, but they waited outside for Conklin. In gunfire exchanged when the last Christmas carol had been sung, Conklin was killed by the second bullet fired by Onofre Baca.[49]

The story of the organizing done to catch the wrongdoers was told by Chester D. Potter, an eyewitness to many of the events, in a series of four articles that ran in the *Pittsburgh Gazette* beginning on May 13, 1913.[50] Potter wrote that the "Socorro Committee of Safety," a name that cloaked with respectability what was a band of vigilantes, came into being as a result of the killing of Conklin. Potter described the Christmas Eve events as a "bomb of racial hatred" that exploded, creating a breach between "greaser" and "gringo" that took years to heal, though he provided no evidence of the healing.

The three Baca boys were all nephews of Juan José Baca, according to Potter, the same Juan José Baca for whom Elfego Baca was working on that day in October of 1884 when Pedro Sarracino rode up to describe what was going on in Frisco. Recently, however, the Baca family has unearthed information to show that the relationship between Onofre Baca, the Conklin killer, and Elfego Baca was closer than as cousins. They were brothers.[51]

According to a 1995 article in *Herencia* magazine, family investigations show that birth records confirm that both Onofre and Elfego were the sons of "Francisco Baca y Juana Baca." Onofre would have been two-and-a-half years older than Elfego. Evidently, if the conclusion that the two were brothers is correct, Onofre was left behind when his parents went to Topeka. The reason for the failure of Elfego to mention the relationship over his lifetime is unexplained. Onofre grew up in the home of his uncle, Gregorio Baca and wife Maria Demetria Torres, in Socorro. It was a common practice at the time for birth parents to place young children with relatives who would care for them when it was difficult for the parents to do it themselves, and perhaps that explains why Onofre was left behind when the rest of the family headed off to Topeka.[52]

Whether the two were brothers or cousins, when the brew cooked up by the Committee of Safety began to bubble, there was no one in town who could have escaped alignment with one side or the other. Elfego's head would have been filled with versions from newspaper accounts and word on the street, all reporting that Onofre had shot a prominent local citizen, that the Anglos were fighting mad about it and the Hispanics had better take cover. It was all kept alive for weeks as the Committee rode out to chase one Mexican after another, and it was just the kind of stuff that would have grabbed the attention of a fifteen-year-old, even if the leading actor had not been a member of the extended family. The indoctrination Elfego received as training for the anger he felt at the message he was to receive from Frisco four years later was anything but theoretical. And even if the claim that Onofre was not actually his brother is accepted, Juan José Baca would have fed the coals smoldering inside his store clerk with his own rage at what had happened to his nephews.

With Conklin dead, Potter's Pittsburgh article reported, Col. Ethan W. Eaton, a citizen of the county, sent for newly-elected Sheriff Juan Maria Garcia. When the sheriff refused to jump at the beckoning of the colonel, it took only a few hours for Colonel Eaton to organize a chase to bring in the killer and his accomplices. After Eaton's bunch had arrested the sheriff and eight other "Mexicans" for dereliction of their duty to hunt and capture the Baca boys, the vigilantes set out in earnest to track down the offenders.

By December 28, Eaton and his men captured and jailed Antonio Baca. Onophre and Abran disappeared.

Ultimately, Antonio was shot and killed while trying to escape custody. Abran was captured and tried for murder, and Onofre was taken when he fled to Mexico. Onofre was returned to Socorro, where the vigilantes took him from the train despite a plea from the family to the governor begging for protection. The Committee hanged him from a gate post.[53]

The Committee of Safety (vigilantes), Socorro, with captives Martinez and Silva (the only two Hispanics in the group). Photograph by Lohn, courtesy Museum of New Mexico, Negative No. 158291.

While Onofre's swinging body doubtless attracted the attention of the teenage boys of Socorro, there is no record that Elfego paid his last respects to his brother/cousin before he was cut down, or that he attended his funeral or burial. Nor is it known whether he sat in the courtroom while Abran Baca was tried for his complicity in Conklin's death, sweating it out with the defendant, his cousin, until the all-Hispanic jury returned a verdict of acquittal. Despite the verdict, Abran escaped the vigilantes only by leaping out of a courthouse window and galloping off on a waiting horse when the verdict was read.[54]

According to Potter's story, "Three years were required to rid the city of its criminal element, to restore the legal machinery of the law [to Anglo control], and to impress this fact upon the mind of the native Mexican."[55] Potter makes no comment about what the vigilante justice impressed upon the mind of young Elfego Baca, who by then had celebrated his eighteenth birthday.

For all these reasons, resentment of the arrogant Texan invaders was alive and well among the native population of Socorro County in 1884, though the Texans lacked the sensitivity to recognize it or the motivation to mellow if they had. The effect of their insensitivity was reflected when the Slaughter outfit rode into Frisco to free their man from the insignificant Mexican who'd arrested him for doing what young Texans in New Mexico did.

All this was to come to focus within the young man living out his teens in Socorro, caught between the Anglo influences of his childhood in Topeka and the Hispanic bonds his family was forging around him. The youthful Elfego, filled with the need to compensate for the feelings of inadequacy and inferiority left by a tragic childhood, was about to be energized to take control over the instability of that early life. He was to recover that lost control by standing up to the Texas terrorists who had so long threatened the Mexican-Americans of the Territory.

It was into all this interracial pressure that the untested Elfego Baca rode on Sarracino's buckboard on that October day. He would be fighting attitudes as real as the gunshots, but in the smoke and the noise his people would find a savior. All the tensions were real enough to make James H. Cook believe the rider who galloped up to his ranch house door at a furious gait to shout that the Mexicans had gone on the warpath.

It was these stresses into which Elfego thrust himself when he jumped up onto the seat of Sarracino's buckboard and headed for Frisco. How he would respond to them was shaped by the life he had led up until that day in October.

9

◈ LIFE BEFORE FRISCO

Elfego Baca was the son and youngest child of Francisco Baca and Juanita Baca. The couple had six children, though including Onofre in the count, they had seven. Elfego was born in Socorro, in the Territory of New Mexico, in February of 1865, though the exact date is disputed. Baca himself claimed he'd appeared on the planet on the 27th of that month. Baptismal records show he was born on February 15. Elfego had a tale about his birth.

His mom, while nine months pregnant, was outside one afternoon playing ball in the February Socorro sunshine. The game was called *Las Iglesias,* and he described it as similar to the game that became known as softball. Juanita, described by her son as "short and stubby," was watching for a hit in her direction. When one came, Juanita reached to spear it, and "here comes Elfego." Elfego was so taken with the phrase used to describe his appearance that years later he named his undated twenty-two page autobiography *Here Comes Elfego! The Autobiography of Elfego Baca.*

Juanita and her son caused a halt in the game while they were taken into the Baca house to receive birthing help.[56]

But the circumstance of his birth, though unique, was just the start of his early years' adventures. Compared to episode two, it was a tame one indeed. For just before his first birthday, Elfego was captured by a band of Indians.

Pondering their children's future, Francisco and Juanita had decided to leave the Socorro area, where Francisco was "one of heavy landowners and cattle raisers," according to Elfego's autobiography. They packed up and joined an ox train heading for Topeka. Though the reason they gave for the move was so that their young son and other children could have the benefit of the better schooling the parents believed they would find in the Kansas capital, it has been speculated that they were motivated by adverse financial conditions, possibly caused by fall-out from the Civil War.[57]

The infant Elfego's trip to Topeka had progressed only as far from Socorro as the present village of Estancia, surely not more than a couple of days' journey, even by oxcart, when the travelers ran into a band of Navajo Indians on the warpath. The raiders rode off with baby Elfego, presumably squalling and yelling, tucked under the arm of one of the warriors. His kidnapping lasted only four days until the band galloped back to the encampment and tossed the brat back to his mother. They did not stop to explain why they no longer wanted the baby.[58]

The move to Topeka turned out to have been a disastrous one for the Baca family. During a period in February and March, 1872, around the time of Elfego's seventh birthday, his mother, a sister and a brother died. There is no record of the cause. Francisco, who in Topeka was a "minor contractor," apparently found it difficult to cope with the tragedy or to care for the rest of his family after his wife died. His depression deepened the pall over what was left of the family. Father Baca left Topeka to find work in Colorado, leaving Elfego behind in an orphanage. Crichton extracted from the subject of his biography an admission that life in Topeka was a "desultory existence."[59]

The Topeka years shaped the man into whom Elfego was to grow. The losses of Elfego's mother and his two siblings, followed closely by his abandonment by his father, created in the boy a persona marred by feelings of inferiority and anxiety. The seeds planted sprouted into a personality with varied needs. One aspect was the need to compensate for the feelings of inferiority. In Elfego, the need doubtless contributed to the "savior complex" that drove him to ride off to Frisco to save the settlers.

There was a second aspect to his personality. His tragic childhood probably left Elfego with an impaired ability to cope with the stress of trauma.[60] The "vulnerability" or "resilience" factors shaping an individual's response to later trauma are molded during infancy until about age seven. Such episodes as Elfego's kidnapping by the Indians and the experience of the multiple abandonment by his core family members had a lasting effect.[61] These "vulnerability" or "resistance" factors bear on an individual's reaction to trauma as the child grows into adulthood.[62]

To face the trauma Elfego would experience in the flying bullets, the exploding dynamite and the burning logs, he would need every ounce of courage and resiliency he could summon. While he found the courage, the trauma levied its toll. The vulnerable boy, grown into a vulnerable man bearing the after-effects of the stresses of the gunfight, would need even more courage just to cope with the dangers and the tensions he would experience as a lawman, a lawyer and a politician. The "shell shock," or post traumatic stress disorder, to which his childhood left him open, was the final legacy of the gunbattle. It was a recurring challenge that would tighten its grip on the Hero of Frisco every time he faced a perceived threat, an imagined insult or an apparent slur.

Baca's courage would be enough.

Elfego left Topeka in 1880, when he was about fifteen. He returned to Socorro in the company of his brother, A. B. Baca, who was later to become Socorro County assessor. Elfego lived with his grandparents in Socorro for a time after his return, he was to record in his autobiography, though Crichton reported that he lived with an uncle.[63] The two accounts can be reconciled if it is concluded that the extended family of three generations lived in the same household, at least for a while.

Elfego took back to New Mexico only a few other recollections of his stay in Kansas. One was his friendship with another schoolboy, a Kaw Indian named Charles Curtis, who was to become vice-president of the United States. The other was the fact that the only other Spanish-speaking people in Topeka had been the Sanchez family, and that Elfego spoke English in school. That accounts for the fact that when he returned to Socorro, he couldn't speak any significant Spanish.[64]

Elfego's fluency in the English language turned out to be a mixed blessing. When he returned to Socorro he was "an alien in his home town." His Spanish was "diffused through the rough hewn English of a Kansas community," as Crichton said.[65] It was probably shaped by a Kansas twang that left the Spanish-speakers of Socorro scratching their heads and grinning at the comic efforts of this Midwestern interloper to communicate with them in the Spanish that should have rolled off his tongue like a native. The fellow looked like a Mexican, dressed like a Mexican, had the name of a Mexican, but he talked like a clodhopper from the Sunflower State.

Within a year or so after Elfego's return to Socorro, Elfego's father also came back to town. The homecoming seems to have begun well for Francisco, since the elder Baca soon hired on to be town marshal of the community of Belen, some thirty miles north of Socorro. But it didn't take long for things to turn sour for Francisco. The job as lawman apparently encouraged a latent violence, because before long he found himself in the middle of a fistfight over the good points of a quarterhorse he owned that out-sped one possessed by a prominent area family. The scanty report of the event does not identify who was the aggressor, but whoever was, Francisco apparently didn't back down.

A brawl over a horserace, though, was the least of Francisco's worries. No sooner was the incident behind him than the lawman found a reason to shoot two "drunken Mexicans," as the Santa Fe newspaper called his victims. The pair had gotten into a brawl at the F. Scholle & Co. store in downtown Belen, and Francisco had felt perfectly justified in pulling his pistol and using it to keep the peace. When Eutimio Baca died in a pool of his own blood on the floor of the store, and his brother, Termino, lay stretched out beside him with serious wounds, the law disagreed with Francisco: he'd not been justified in shooting; he'd committed a crime. He was arrested and charged.[66]

Francisco was promptly tried in Los Lunas, the county seat of Valencia county, in which Belen was located. He was found guilty and sentenced to a term in the penitentiary. None of the county court records of the trial or the charges leading up to it have survived, so the name of the prosecutor and the ethnicity of the jurors are not known, nor is anything about the victims except their names. They were apparently not related to their slayer. The Baca lawman was convinced that the "powerful family" who owned the second best horse in the county was still out to get him, had been behind his prosecution, and that his trial had been a set-up. He didn't keep his suspicions to himself.

While the law was working out just how it was going to carry him to the state pen in Santa Fe, Elfego's father was held in the county lock-up in the building in which he had been tried. Elfego, then about sixteen, was upset by the jailing of the head of the family when the news reached him in Belen, especially with the part that his father had been wronged by the powerful family whose horse Francisco's had outrun.

Working up a strategy worthy of someone older and wiser, young Baca made his way to Los Lunas after the sentencing and before his father could be shackled and transported to a permanent home in the penitentiary. Tagging along with young Baca on the jaunt was a friend named Chavez. Elfego planned his trip for the feast day of Saint Teresa, when all Catholics worthy of the name, including the jailer, would be offering their devotion and their prayers and presence to the saint. The odds were that long after leaving the services at the church, and through the small hours of the night, the guards would be drinking the celebratory wine.

Neither of the boys enjoyed the luxury of the use of a horse, mule or other form of transportation, so they hoofed it the fifteen miles from Belen to Los Lunas. Nosing around, they soon located the jail on the first floor of a building that also housed the second floor county courtroom. Francisco's cell, they found as they checked out the courthouse, was right below the jury room. Due to the religious propensities of the jailer that led to his absence, the boys had plenty of time to work out the tactics of a jailbreak.

The pair found a ladder at the rear of the building and somehow came up with a saw. Climbing to the second floor, they slid open a window and climbed through into the jury room, where they set to work sawing a hole in the floor. Below them, Francisco and his cellmates whispered encouragement and closed their eyes against the falling sawdust as first one of the boys then the other took a turn at the saw. Since the church and the site of the toasting of the saint were not in the neighborhood of the courthouse, the boys didn't worry about the noise of the saw teeth ripping through the wood or the cheers from below as the hole grew larger.

Uninterrupted in the peace of the religious holiday and the dark of the night, and thankful to the saint for inspiring such dedication in the jailer that he was compelled to spend the night hoisting glass after glass to her blessed memory, their labors were successful. They soon had an access hole large enough to accommodate a man. Two other prisoners sharing the same cell offered Francisco their shoulders, and when he had exited through the escape hatch and hugged his son, he reached down and helped the pair ascend also.

Perhaps due to lingering memories of his mother's training, Elfego returned the ladder to its place behind the jail. He then scouted for provisions to sustain the little party while they hid out from the posse that would surely soon be after them. Elfego's labors to provide nourishment were met by the jailer himself, who had hung jerked venison to dry on the jailhouse clothesline. Elfego and the escapees helped themselves to this open-air larder, and they walked off with baskets of chiles and ears of corn that had been stored outside the jail.

By this point, it would seem that Francisco had probably assumed leadership of the little brigade, though out of awe at his son's ingenuity he may have deferred to young Baca. In any event, rather than running off for Belen or Socorro as a sheriff's posse might have expected from a trio eager to celebrate freedom, the three escapees and their saviors toted their food across the road. There, they stretched out in a large clump of grass a hundred yards or so from the jail and well within listening and watching distance. Elfego's account does not disclose whether the former prisoners and the pair who had made their escape possible slept any that night, but if they did, the sun rising over the courthouse across the street and the crowing of roosters in the rural neighborhood surely provided an early reveille.

Once the village began to stir, it didn't take long for the jailer to discover that his prisoners were long gone. Maybe it happened when the breakfast call was made and nobody answered. The alarm was sounded. The sheriff and his deputies promptly organized a posse with much cursing and shouting and blame-laying, all to the entertainment of the audience who parted the grasses to watch the fun. As the lawmen galloped off to beat the surrounding countryside, arms at the ready, the five reclining in the grass enjoyed a leisurely morning in the sunshine, munching on the jerky, nibbling on the chiles and corn, and for fluids eating watermelon they had found behind the grass patch. All in all, it was a good time for father and son to get reacquainted, though they had to be careful not to raise their heads too high.

Elfego Baca was to say later, after he repented of those days as a law breaker and became an enforcer of the laws, that the jail break and escape taught him a valuable lesson. What he learned was that the average criminal is likely to stay close to the scene of the crime. Generally, he concluded, that works to the offender's advantage unless the sheriff has the experience or the insight to recognize the pattern of the criminal mind and checks out the neighborhood of the spot where the crime took place.

By the end of the day the escapees noted that the activity around the courthouse had fallen off. They assumed that the fervor of the search party had burned itself out, and that most of the posse had gone home due to lack of interest. The five split up, leaving behind the grass patch, watermelons and their stash of food. The two prisoners who had been Francisco's cell mates set out for Albuquerque; Francisco and his two rescuers headed south on foot. The immediate destination of the two Bacas and young Chavez was the village of Escondida, just north of Socorro, a twenty-five mile walk from Los Lunas. There, father and son left Chavez behind and set out with a guide and three horses south toward Mexico. Though Elfego did not remain there with his father, once the pair reached Ysleta, near El Paso, Francisco found work with a brother who was a storekeeper in that village. He was to stay there for seven years.[67]

The behavior of the organizers of this little adventure can certainly be questioned, as it has been. The facts speak for themselves. The tale does shed light on the upbringing of Elfego after the death of his mother. The conclusions drawn, even trying to apply the parenting standards of a century and a quarter ago, do not reflect favorably upon the influence provided in his father's home. Elfego had little parental supervision, and what he had must have been applied by his grandparents well after he had passed his formative younger years. During the time that his personality was shaped, often felt to be around age seven, he had been left high and dry by four persons who provided the nexus of his family support—his mother and the two siblings who died, followed with abandonment by his father and his deposit in an orphanage. At the time of the jail break Elfego apparently was living with Francisco in Belen rather than with his grandparents in Socorro. After the jailing of Francisco, he seems to have been left to fend for himself. It was not an upbringing designed to provide a secure base.

Baca supporters can squeeze some solace from the story of a lonely boy who set out to rescue his father. Despite the trauma of his childhood, Elfego did what he could to pull the family together, and the family he had to work with was dear old Dad, a dad who had been separated from him by the bars of the Valencia county jail and the hot temper that got him there by leading him to shoot and kill two men. The fact that Elfego demonstrated his allegiance to his father by breaking the law doesn't blot out his motivation of family loyalty.

And there's this, too. Francisco is not reported to have gotten into any more trouble during his seven years in Ysleta, or afterwards.

But for Elfego, the importance of the jailbreak adventure was that he had cemented his position in the family and in the Hispanic community. He could no longer be viewed as the Anglo kid from Topeka masquerading as a Mexican-American. He had reinvented himself, and now he was one hundred percent acceptable to Hispanic Socorro. There was only one thing the teen had to learn in order to round out the abilities he would need to rein in the unruly young Texas cowhands he would find in Frisco. His Kansas upbringing had not exposed him to the use of the revolver. He would soon remedy that deficiency.

Elfego Baca at about age 15, shortly after he returned to Socorro from Topeka.
Photograph courtesy of Museum of New Mexico, Negative No. 48462.

10

❖ LEARNING TO USE A SIX-GUN

Elfego was proud of his brief association with Billy the Kid during the period that followed his hatching of the jail break. He often bragged that he had learned how to handle a six-gun from association with the famous outlaw. Questions have been raised, however, as to whether the young man that the fifteen-year-old Elfego Baca connected with for a time was the Billy the Kid of legend or whether it was some other young frontier hoodlum using the same moniker. Apparently the name had a ring to it that appealed to many young men named William throughout the Old West after William Bonney made the name famous.

The Billy the Kid of Lincoln County fame, the one with the full name of William Bonney, was killed by Sheriff Pat Garrett in July of 1881. At the time of Billy's death, Elfego Baca would have been sixteen. Yet, Elfego wrote that he met Billy the Kid when he (Elfego) was that age and Billy was also about sixteen.[68] If the dates are calculated, Elfego's guess about the Kid's age was three years off. Billy the Kid would have been nineteen when Elfego was sixteen, with death just over the horizon. The Kid didn't live to reach twenty.

Certainly, every day of William Bonney's time in the year before he was shot is not accounted for, though little of his activities is left open to guesswork if accounts of his Lincoln County War participation are accurate. Also well-known is the fact that Billy the Kid had a baby face that made him appear younger than his years. Still, there is doubt as to the true identity of the trouble-maker that tried his best to teach Elfego bad habits in a saloon in Albuquerque sometime in

1881. Kyle Crichton told the story at some length.

Whoever his companion was, one day Elfego and the youth known as Billy the Kid caught a ride from Socorro to Isleta, an Indian pueblo a few miles south of Albuquerque. From there they walked into town, limping the last few miles in boots that had not been made for walking.

At the time, Crichton explained, Billy the Kid was just another carefree young man who had not yet earned a reputation as a killer or as anything else except a teen-aged prankster. It is with this description of the Kid that his true identity must come into serious question. Crichton did not explain how the Kid's reputation was still unformed when in 1878, three years earlier, William Bonney had ambushed and killed his first victims on the streets of Lincoln, New Mexico. The dead men were the county sheriff and his deputy. For the next two years Billy was on the run. In 1878, Elfego Baca would have been a thirteen-year-old boy sitting behind a school desk in Topeka, and Billy the Kid would have been a sixteen-year-old cop-killer.

In any event, after their hike the pair rested up in Albuquerque's Railroad Town section by leaning against a telegraph pole on First Street. There, Crichton related, as they were taking their ease they witnessed an episode of police brutality. As they watched, a local cop drew his sidearm and shot a pedestrian who had just walked past the policeman, who was talking to another man. No sooner had the shots rung out than the accomplice the officer had been talking to fired a handgun into the air, then hurriedly placed it in the hand of the pedestrian who was bleeding to death on the sidewalk. Elfego and Billy turned their backs and sauntered off toward Old Town, wise enough to keep their mouths shut about the whole event.[69]

Elfego himself had told the same story earlier, giving it a slightly different ending. After shooting the pedestrian, the cop walked into a nearby saloon, where he bought a round of drinks for the house. While the celebration was going on, Sheriff Perfecto Armijo came up and asked who had killed the dead man on the sidewalk outside. When the policeman admitted the shooting, he was arrested and later tried and hanged.[70]

However it happened, the pair of boys walked on down to Old Town Albuquerque, where they ambled into the Martinez Bar. Their age was no barrier to their orders for drinks as they mingled among the other late afternoon patrons. They spent the rest of the afternoon and early evening strolling into and out of other Old Town bars and dance halls until they ate a late supper before returning to the Martinez watering hole.

It was then that Billy decided to have a little fun at the expense of the bouncer. Knowing what would happen, Billy pulled a tiny but noisy pistol he had been carrying, concealed it in his hand, and while everyone was watching the entertainment, fired it into the ceiling of the bar. The crowd, including bartenders, hit the floor. The music stopped. The patrons scanned the crowd, and seeing nothing threatening, eased back to their feet while the bartenders peeked from behind their mahogany fortress until it appeared to be safe to stand up.

After enough time for everyone to have forgotten the incident, once again Billy pulled his little pistol, and when no one was looking, fired once more into the ceiling. Once again, everybody dropped. This time the bouncer smelled a rat, suspecting that the grinning half of the Socorro pair was the cause of all the commotion since he was the only one standing. Confronting Billy, the bouncer and half the crowd conducted a head-to-toe search, but found no trace of a firearm anywhere on the Kid, who by this time was laughing out loud.

It happened the third time. This time a pro, Deputy Sheriff Cornelio Murphy, stepped up to make the body search. He had no better luck than the bouncer and the crowd had had, though he probed every area of Billy's clothes and anatomy that were known to man.[71]

At this point, Billy and Elfego figured they had worn out their welcome. They walked out before they could be asked to spend the night in the hoosegow, even though the only evidence against them was circumstantial. Outside, Elfego studied his companion from head to foot, looking for the noisy six shooter. Nothing. Still grinning, Billy pulled off his sombrero, reached inside the crown, and pulled out the pistol.

Neither Elfego nor his biographer, Crichton, reports any lessons learned by the young Baca by his time spent with Billy the Kid, or the subsequent death of the famous outlaw at the hands of the law, except Elfego credited his time with the Kid as sharpening his skill with a six-gun. Perhaps they practiced quick-draw moves as they walked from Los Lunas to Albuquerque. If they did, the lessons must have been unique in the history of firearms since the only weapon carried by Billy the Kid seems to have been the tiny pistol he hid in his hat.

For Elfego, the experiences with Billy the Kid were more than a teenager's night on the town. In the six-gun and in the skills in using it that young Baca learned from Billy, or whomever he was, the unconnected youth had found the equalizer, the source of power, the creator of purpose in his life, the tool for righting wrongs. From then on, Elfego was rarely without a revolver. A weapon represented power and control to the young man who had grown up with neither.[72] The fact that he chose to use that power and control to save his people, and later as a lawman, is to his credit. As an outlaw, Elfego allied with Billy the Kid would have produced a far different history. As it was, Elfego as law-abiding citizen generated more than enough turmoil. Some of that turmoil would surface shortly after the murder trials were behind him.

11

❖   BATTLES AND BRAWLS

A fter the waves of publicity that followed the two murder trial acquittals had calmed, Elfego was forced to live with two related burdens. First was the fact that he carried a reputation as the fellow who had stood up to the Texas cowboys. Second was his elevated status as a gunman. Both led to provocative episodes in which the risks were not always imaginary, though often not as dangerous as imagined by Elfego. Some of the threats he faced were real enough to require him to defend himself against living, breathing enemies. Others, however, were not real threats but were imagined dangers in the form of apparitions of ghostly Texans firing at him through the flimsy walls of the *jacal*, given momentary life by some exaggerated perception of peril.

Elfego had celebrated his acquittal for the killing of Young Parham for only six months when he was back in the bad graces of law enforcement officers in Bernalillo County. In what was to be the first of a series of scrapes with the law after the legal fallout from Frisco was behind him, Elfego pulled his pistol once more.

It was on August 14, 1886, that he was accused of drawing a weapon on a woman. It happened in Albuquerque. The court records do not show the reason he threatened Mrs. Josefa Weiner; it's likely that Elfego lost his temper and drew reflexively at a taunt that conjured up images from the past, causing him to perceive danger when none existed. In any event, for his response to what was most likely an imagined threat, he was sentenced to sixty days in jail, put under a peace bond for a year, and ordered to pay a twenty-five dollar fine plus costs. It was his first conviction. The *Albuquerque Journal* carried a brief story about the escapade. The issue of Sunday, August 15, 1886, reported, "Elfego Baca, an old town Mexican, was arraigned before Judge Heacock yesterday on a charge of displaying a deadly weapon in a threatening manner."

Elfego appealed. In October of 1886 the appeal was dismissed and the bond released for failure to prosecute. Elfego had out-waited his prosecutor.[73]

It took less than a year after the Josepha Weiner episode and some fourteen months after the acquittal of the Frisco Nine for Elfego to embroil himself in more hot water. This time, he was indicted by the Bernalillo County grand jury for unlawfully and feloniously drawing a pistol on one Charles Springer, whom he was apparently trying to arrest. It was not reported just what offense Springer was suspected of, or whether his alleged offense was simply that he had tried to make Baca mad by swearing at him. The indictment was handed down in June of 1887. Once again, Baca was represented by Albuquerque lawyer Bernard Rodey. Once again, as he had done in the Hearne murder case, Rodey played the trump card that identified his client as a deputy sheriff. This time, Rodey produced for the jury Elfego's oath of office, witnessed by Bernalillo County Sheriff Jose L. Perea.

Though the "wild animal" who had come through the window of the *jacal* at Frisco had pulled a revolver once again, it's to Elfego's credit that he didn't fire a shot. Instead, he was able to control the shoot-first reflex to a perceived threat that Frisco had pounded into him. Both parties to the confrontation walked away without injury except for Springer's hurt pride resulting from the insult of looking down the barrel of a Colt 45 waved by a man known to have used it to kill at least two others.

The instructions the judge read to the jury gave them a way to let the deputy off the legal hook. They recited that if Baca were trying to take Springer into custody after the man tried to assault him, and that Springer had used loud and indecent language and was otherwise obstreperous, then Baca would have been justified in using force to make the arrest.

The judgment or verdict of the jury is preserved in the court file. It's handwritten in Spanish and states that the jury is of the unanimous opinion that *"acusado no tiene culpa Elfigo Baca."* It is signed by "Jose Gonzales y Aragon, presidente."[74]

With the instruction given to the jury and a not guilty verdict, Elfego was probably not left with yet one more lawyer's fee to shoulder. Rodey was most likely paid by the county.

More trouble followed Elfego. In 1888, when he was twenty three and a married man with a growing family, along came Juan Baca. Juan was apparently not a relative. He worked as a policeman and deputy sheriff in the west side of Albuquerque, and there was a long-standing enmity between the pair who bore the same family name.

The newspaper that reported the quarrel the two had one night in September didn't probe into the reasons why Juan went at Elfego with a knife. Surely such a weapon was not the one of choice for bringing in a suspect in some criminal activity if lawman Juan's objective had been to arrest Elfego for some offense or other. Whatever prompted Juan's assault, Elfego ended up with a wound under the ribs in his right side. The newspaper reported it as "dangerous."

It took Juan Baca only a moment after he'd sunk his blade into Elfego to regret his folly. He dashed to the nearby office of Justice of the Peace Lucero and confessed his guilt to a charge of assault and battery. His prompt acknowledgment of guilt lends to the conclusion that probably this time Elfego was not the aggressor, and that Juan may have tried to build his own reputation by proving that while Elfego had earned a standing as a gun-slinger, his pistol was no defense to in-fighting against a stiletto.

But Elfego was young, and he was soon as good as new. It's not reported whether Juan's confession mended the breach between Elfego and himself even half as quickly as Elfego's side healed, or whether Juan might have decided it would be better for him if he moved out of town.[75]

There's no report that Elfego sought to retaliate against Juan. Perhaps Elfego's restraint came from an increasing maturity, since he had the responsibilities of a wife and children. If he were to succeed as a family man, he would need stability in his life, as well as a regular income. He figured maybe he could find both as a peace officer in Albuquerque. And his wife, Francisquita, liked the town where her father lived.

12

◆ THE OFFICE-HOLDER

Elfego's tiny autobiography lists with pride the public offices he held, both in Socorro and Bernalillo counties. At the time he wrote, in 1924, he was a candidate for district court judge in Bernalillo County, the most populous county in New Mexico. He was then fifty nine and ready to take another in a long list of turns at serving the public. He didn't make it.

Elfego's list didn't describe each and every public job he'd filled. He skipped any mention of his tour of duty as a deputy sheriff of Bernalillo County following acquittal of the Parham murder charge. Maybe he wasn't proud of the fact that to assume the deputy's duties he'd had to turn his back on Socorro. He may have felt that there was at least an implication to be drawn from his stay in Albuquerque that he'd run away from the cattlemen who were so strong in Socorro County.

What seems to have happened is that following his acquittal in 1885 for the alleged murder of William Hearne in the trial held in Albuquerque, Elfego returned to Socorro only long enough to defend himself against the charges that he'd murdered Young Parham. When the jury turned him loose with its verdict, he came back to the brighter lights of the largest city in the state. In Albuquerque, he served as deputy sheriff during the term of Santiago Baca, who was in office from 1885 through 1886, and that of Santiago's successor. Apparently Santiago and Elfego were not related.

But it's possible that Elfego hadn't run from Socorro at all. It could have been his marriage to Francisquita Pohmer in Albuquerque in 1885 and his bride's wish to be close to her father that kept him away from his old home town. Francisquita was sixteen when they were married, there is never any indication of a living mother, and there seems to have been a strong pull between father and daughter.

Whatever his motivation for staying in Albuquerque, it seems obvious that over his lifetime Elfego never enjoyed life so much as when he was enforcing the law. He was good at it. Elfego didn't stay long in Albuquerque in the early years of his marriage. By July of 1891, he was a United States Deputy Marshal arresting felons in Socorro, and two years later he was an assistant district attorney for the Socorro judicial district.[76] In October, 1893, he was appointed as county clerk of Socorro County.[77]

The county clerk job must have been a dull one indeed for the man of action. He was too young and too vital to have been pleased with a tour of duty behind a desk. It isn't difficult to imagine what sitting in a chair behind a desk did to Elfego. He surely watched his waistline grow from inactivity; he must have champed at the bit in eagerness to get outside, onto a horse and once again hunt down suspects who were terrorizing neighborhoods or towns as the Texas cowboys had done in Frisco. Maybe it was because the job was a crashing bore that caused Elfego, on an evening in spring, 1896, to drop in and sample the wares of Blavaschi's saloon, there to run into William E. Martin. The aftermath of the action that followed kept Elfego busy for several months, surely drawing his attention away from his county clerk routines.

As the pair lifted a few drinks together at Blavaschi's place, Baca began abusing Martin. Martin took it for a while, then let go with a swing. Elfego stepped back, pulled a pistol and fired three shots. Either the alcohol Elfego was drinking or the intervention of one Librado C. de Baca caused the bullets to go wild. Elfego and Martin were both arrested and put under bonds.

Francisco Padilla filed a criminal complaint with Socorro

justice of the peace H. R. Harris, charging that Elfego Baca had fired "leaden bullets" out of his pistol, "commonly called a revolver," at "the body of" William E. Martin. Baca's intent, according to Francisco, had been "to kill and murder Martin."[78] The case soon reached the grand jury. That body of citizens returned an indictment charging Elfego Baca with assault with a dangerous weapon with premeditated intent to kill.

Elfego hired A. A. Freeman as his lawyer. Freeman went to work for his client and soon had an affidavit all written up using his new office equipment, a type-writer. Elfego signed the paper. The words Freeman put into Elfego's mouth claimed that the grand jury indictment was faulty because one of the grand jurors was too old. The man was over sixty, and under the Territorial law no one who had passed three score was qualified to sit in judgment, if Freeman's take on the law was right. Not only that, but the foreman of the grand jury was the postmaster at Polvadera, in Socorro County. The implication was that any fool, especially one sitting on the judge's bench, should have known that a federal post office employee cannot sit on a grand jury, let alone act as the head man.

Just in case, Freeman typed up a second affidavit he filed at the same time he handed the first one to the court clerk. Elfego trotted over to Freeman's office and signed that one, too, this time with a pen that blobbed ink so badly his signature looked like a Rorschach test. Maybe the language of the affidavit and the memories of earlier trials it brought up made Elfego's hand shake until the ink spilled out.

Affidavit number two said that Elfego had just run for mayor, and that the story of the fracas with Martin had been front page news while Baca was campaigning. It claimed that the alleged assault had been the talk of the town, and that to keep all the negative gabbing about Elfego on street corners alive, the indictment had been filed on the very day of the election, May 5, 1896, presumably as a political move to do in candidate Baca. The final insult had come when the sheriff met Elfego at the polls with an arrest warrant and carried him off the election grounds. The talk before that had been loud enough, but now it was non-stop laughing and giggling at the would-be mayor whose political career had just met a major set-back.

As a result of all these dirty tricks, the affidavit claimed, there was so much public excitement and prejudice against Elfego Baca that there was no way an impartial jury could be found in all of Socorro County. The Freeman-prepared affidavit all sounded so reasonable, and how proud both Elfego and Freeman must have felt that the hero had limited his response to the insults by expressing his anger only in papers filed in the courthouse.

But the judge didn't like Freeman's shenanigans a bit. His honor called Elfego's lawyer in, and the two sat down for a heart to heart. Elfego's counsel backpedaled. He went back to his office, typed up an apology and filed it. He didn't ask Elfego to sign. There was no time for that with a judge who was breathing fire.

The document said that Freeman's client had not meant to be disrespectful, and it agreed that Elfego's affidavit could be stricken from the record. Freeman's act of contrition didn't identify which of the two affidavits he had prepared had been found so offensive by the judge. His honor was probably steamed by both. The bad part for Elfego was that he had signed a document that claimed he couldn't get a fair trial in his court, and that had made the judge who was the key to the Baca fate downright mad.

While all this was going on, the *Rio Grande Republican*, published in Las Cruces, reported that the controversy at Blavashi's watering hole up the river in Socorro had been stirred up by a guy named Elfego Baca, who happened to be the Socorro County clerk. W. E. Martin, the paper said, was Socorro County's representative to the last legislature. Unreported was that Martin was also the interpreter for the Socorro County district court. Though Martin later acted as clerk of the district court, it is not clear whether he held that office at the time of his altercation with Baca. If so, it would have put him in charge of shepherding the grand jury indictment and the arrest warrant through the processes of the court.

When Elfego and Martin went back to work at their desks at the courthouse, it surely must have been a tense time, but apparently there was a truce strong enough to permit both to do their jobs. But the case was not yet closed.

A few days after Freeman's apology to the judge, J. A. Archuleta, Esq., jumped into the fray to associate with Freeman as a second counsel for defendant Baca. A trial setting was promptly vacated. The case sat inactive, waiting for the next term of court to come up. When it arrived, Baca withdrew his plea and entered a guilty plea in a plea bargaining deal engineered by attorney Archuleta. On the last day of December, 1896, Elfego paid a one hundred dollar fine plus costs. He left the courthouse to go out and see the new year in, probably watching over his shoulder lest Mr. Martin should come up from behind.[79]

As far as Elfego was concerned, the case was finally over and best forgotten. But it was to come back to haunt him once again years later. It happened when lawyer Elfego made another prosecutor mad. The fellow dug up a rule that said that nobody could practice law if he'd been convicted of a felony. Then he claimed that when Elfego had pled guilty in the Martin assault it had been to a felony. Martin had had his revenge, and it was sweet indeed, though Baca slipped out of that one, too.

In 1893, when Elfego was appointed county clerk, an important part of the job was to assure that the records of real estate transactions, including mining claims, were properly kept. Equally as dull for a man who wanted the bad guys of the Territory to shake in their boots when they heard his footsteps was keeping records for certain personal property transactions, like bills of sale and chattel mortgages.

The county clerks drew no salary; they earned their keep from the fees paid to them for filing and recording documents. Apparently, the clerk had the discretion to set the amount of those fees, since in his campaign brochure Elfego told how much he charged.

He also boasted that in order to help poor people he waived the filing fees during the months of December and January. That compassion for the poor helped win his election following his initial appointed term, so that he held the office through 1896.[80]

The county clerk's position apparently wasn't enough to keep Elfego busy. While he was in the office he studied law for a short time. It was long enough to get him admitted to the bar.

Elfego served the public in two other sedentary positions in Socorro County, though there is evidence that during at least a part of his time at the indoor jobs he was also out chasing the criminal element.

Following his stint as county clerk and law clerk in Judge Hamilton's offices, Elfego moved from the clerk's office to another county job. For a time he was school superintendent for Socorro County. His greatest accomplishment in that office, the campaign brochure that grew into his short autobiography boasted, was to encourage school children to practice good study habits. He gave $5.00 dolls to every girl with perfect attendance, and a medal to each boy who showed up every day. Not much action there for a man to whom a six-gun was no stranger.

Baca was then elected mayor of Socorro. He filled the job for three years, from 1896 through 1898. By the time his mayoral tenure began, Socorro had lost much of its reputation as a strong factor in New Mexico's economy due to lack of water and the virtual cessation of the mining activity that had brought prosperity.[81]

Elfego, with the pride of a native son, termed the city he presided over "one of the best cities of the state." He backed up his boast by staying around after he left the mayor's office.

Three years after assuming the mayoral post, Elfego got the job of district attorney for Socorro and Sierra Counties. He stepped into the office when Governor Miguel Otero appointed him, with the backing of Socorro County Republican heavyweight Holm Bursum. Now Elfego was in his element. He served two years as D. A., during 1900 and 1901. He was back in the same job again in 1905 and 1906. His second term didn't have a happy ending, for reasons that are explained later in this book.

It was in 1913 that Elfego got a special call from Bernalillo County Sheriff Perfecto Armijo. It's not clear from the telling of the tale by William A. Keleher in his *Memoirs*, whether Baca was a deputy sheriff at the time, or whether Sheriff Armijo simply needed a special talent and knew that Elfego had it. He tapped Elfego to preside at the hanging of Demecio Delgadillo, a convicted murderer and resident of Chihuahua, Mexico.

Newspaperman, later lawyer, Keleher was on top of the story from the beginning. He'd covered the trial of the twenty-eight year old Delgadillo for the *Albuquerque Journal*, and he followed up by attending the hanging. It was in the Bernalillo County jail yard while the gallows were going up that he and Elfego first met.

The duties for organizing the hanging called for a man of many talents, and Elfego filled the bill. He oversaw construction of the scaffolding, ran tests when everything was set up, and dropped sand bags of appropriate weight to be sure that nothing collapsed during the main event. He acted as master of ceremonies in front of the assembled crowd gathered to watch poor Delgadillo breathe his last. When the trap with Delgadillo standing on it was finally sprung, Elfego got up close to the attending physician to listen to the last beats of the prisoner's heart. When the doctor was satisfied that it had pulsed its last, Elfego made the official announcement: "'Gentlemen, the official time is three minutes and sixteen seconds.'" He went on: "'Gentlemen, this is one of the nicest hangings I have ever seen. Everything went off beautifully.'" But he spoke through clenched teeth.

After Keleher had phoned his story to his paper, he witnessed one more incident. Father Tommasini, who had walked up the steps to the noose with Delgadillo after praying with him, approached Elfego. He asked the master of ceremonies how long it had been since he had taken the sacraments. Elfego cut and ran.[82]

13

❖ SHERIFF ONCE MORE

In 1919 Elfego was elected sheriff of Socorro County once again. During this and his earlier turn at the sheriff's office he distinguished himself by his innovative crime scene investigation techniques, ingenious cost-cutting initiatives, and inventive methods of bringing in persons charged with crimes without leaving the courthouse. But there was another accomplishment he also bragged about.

Sheriff Elfego set his prisoners to work building a garage for the county. Fortuitously, or more likely by design, his prisoner population included men with a variety of building skills. He melded them into a construction team and put them to work. The result was a garage with the estimated value of $8,000 that had cost the county only a few hundred dollars. A second benefit was that the new building saved the county rent of $100 per month it had been paying on a lease for a similar structure.[83]

Elfego later boasted that while he was sheriff there was only one prisoner who escaped. The fellow was a Texan held pending transportation to the state pen for cattle-stealing. Sheriff Baca enlisted another prisoner, also a Texan, who tracked down the man and brought him back. The episode was a minor one in a life filled with action. The fact that Elfego included it in his little autobiography may have resulted from his glee in using one Texan to bring in another.[84]

It was during his last term as sheriff of Socorro County that Elfego demonstrated another method of raising funds for the sheriff's office while demonstrating in-your-face belligerence. This time there was no gunplay involved.

Four thieves described by the *Albuquerque Evening Citizen* as dressed in "soldier suits," as the paper called their U.S. Army uniforms, drove an automobile belonging to J. M. Boyd from its parking spot in front of a drug store on Central Avenue, Albuquerque. Boyd and Deputy Sheriff Charlie Banghart gave chase. They caught up with the quartet in Socorro, where the four had been nabbed by Sheriff Elfego Baca. Naively, the pursuers expected that the sheriff would hand the keys to Boyd, as the owner of the car, and he would drive the car back home. Elfego had another idea.

After all, he was the one who had made the arrest. That had earned him, he figured, an "arrest fee" for bringing in the crooks. He handed the Bernalillo County deputy and Boyd a bill for twenty-five dollars. The Albuquerqueans screamed foul. "Too much," they cried. "It's another robbery piled on top of the first one."

Elfego wouldn't budge. He'd done his job and he expected to be paid for it, and never mind that the county handed him a salary check every month. To Boyd and Deputy Banghart, he said, in effect, "My way or the highway." Boyd and Deputy Banghart hit the road for home, side by side in the same vehicle. The four car thieves stayed behind as Elfego's guests behind locked doors for another thirty days. The car remained in Socorro in the sheriff's yard, but the length of its sentence hadn't been determined by the time the report was carried in the *Albuquerque Evening Citizen.* Once again, Elfego had won.[85]

Elfego's method of enticing criminals to turn themselves in was a cost-cutting technique that added only a few cents to the annual budget of the sheriff's office. Yet the plan saved hundreds of dollars worth of deputy's or sheriff's time. He wrote a form letter "to all the men who were wanted for arrest." The letter told the wanted man that if he didn't come in to the jail and turn himself in, he, Elfego Baca, Sheriff, would come after him. "They knew what that meant. You bet they didn't want me to come after them," Elfego explained. The ploy rarely failed. Baca's reputation was too well known, and it made no allowance for shilly-shallying. Baca boasted that the technique had worked even with a notorious cattle thief known as Henry Coleman, though to hear some accounts Coleman may have known he had little to fear from Sheriff Baca.[86]

The Coleman adventure did not cover Elfego with glory, and it resulted in making a pair of formidable enemies in the persons of A. T. Hannett and George Curry, powerful political figures.

Coleman was a well-known rancher in western Socorro County who was rumored to have a habit of treating his neighbors' cattle as his own. When his wife was brutally murdered he was a prime suspect. But it was for cattle rustling that Elfego seems to have first been called on to bring in Coleman, who went to great lengths to maintain the façade of being a reputable cattleman.

A young lawyer from Gallup, Arthur T. Hannett, who was later to become governor of New Mexico, had obtained a writ of attachment from a court directing any sheriff of the state to take possession of certain cattle belonging to his clients that were held by Coleman. With Coleman's reputation as "one of the very last of the bad men of New Mexico," as Elfego Baca characterized him, Hannett found no lawman willing to pass the time of day once he mentioned that he needed someone with a badge to serve a writ on Henry Coleman.[87] Elfego was not as shy as his colleagues. His demand letter worked, and he served the writ.

Baca also brought in Coleman on a charge of murdering his wife, or "woman companion," there being some doubt as to whether the pair ever married. The circumstances of Coleman's jailing after his arrest were curious, at best. George Curry, who had been Baca's bitter opponent in a competition for the Republican nomination for Congress in which Elfego came in second, wrote the story.

Coleman was indicted for the woman's murder. The trial court denied bail and remanded him to jail. "Sheriff Baca was friendly to Coleman," believing Coleman wasn't guilty of the killing, Curry charged. Instead of locking his prisoner in the county jail, Elfego took him to Curry's Socorro hotel, provided him with a room, and asked Curry to take charge of the prisoner until the trial was called. Baca let his prisoner keep his gun. Curry didn't seem to have been any more afraid that Coleman might shoot his way out of the hotel than Baca had been. When Elfego went back to his office, Curry lifted the firearm from Coleman's hand and stuck it in an unlocked desk drawer.

Not long before the trial was to start, Coleman went on a drinking spree. He rummaged through the hotel until he found his pistol, pulled it out of the drawer and staggered his way around the hotel lobby waving it in the air, threatening to shoot District Attorney Harry Owens. Curry disarmed Coleman, locked him in his room and called Baca.

Coleman was later shot and killed by a posse trying to serve a warrant on him. Curry, and others, criticized Baca for not having served the warrant himself. Curry asserted that while no one doubted Baca's personal courage, "He let his friendship for Coleman lead him into a clear evasion of official duty. Baca became my personal and political enemy."[88]

14

❖ THE MAN-HUNTER

When it came to campaigning for office, Elfego was not too modest to boast of any feat that might have saved the tax-payers a nickel. But it was a different matter when it came to interviews for the purpose of preserving the color he had added to the history of the Southwest as a champion of the downtrodden.

In an October, 1936, interview with Janet Smith, employee of a WPA project called "Folklore Collection," Elfego was a reluctant subject, though Ms. Smith had talked to him in his office once before, in July of that year. But she kept prodding him until finally she got him to open up about his capture of a bunch of desperadoes called "the Manzano Gang." His tale revealed Baca's talents at crime scene analysis and his endurance when in hot pursuit of a suspect.

When Smith tried to draw out the ex-lawman, she found that "he does not talk readily about himself." Ms. Smith wrote: "He brought out books and articles that had been written about him [by others], but he did not seem inclined to reminiscing and answered my questions briefly." At a loss as to where to take the interview, she finally asked him about the famous Manzano Gang she had read about. That sparked her subject's interest. He began his story, as quoted by Smith.

"There were ten of them, and I got nine." He came up one short, Baca explained, only because the fellow was shot by someone else before Elfego got to him. He went on to describe a murder that motivated him to stay in the chase. "They used to go to a place near Belen and empty the freight cars of grain and one thing and another.

Finally they killed a man at La Jolla. Contreros was his name. A very rich man with lots of money in his house, all gold. I got them for that. They were all convicted and sent to the Pen."

As far as Baca was concerned, the story was finished. But the persistent Janet Smith figured there was more. She bored in, demanding the whole story. Elfego capitulated, perhaps from appreciation for her aggressive style of cross-examination, perhaps because he was unaccustomed to being questioned by a pretty young woman.

As sheriff, Baca told his interviewer, he'd learned about the shooting of Contreros by a telephone call to his office in Socorro. When told that the victim was dying, Elfego promised he'd have the murderers locked up within forty-eight hours. It was a self-imposed rule: close the case in forty-eight hours; get on to solving the next case.

By process of elimination, he settled on the notorious Manzano Gang as the likely perpetrators, and he thought he knew where the gang holed up. He saddled up, and with two deputies alongside, cantered off to the east before sunrise to find the Gang's hideout.

As the sun rose over the Manzano Mountains, Elfego's three-man party of lawmen reached the ranch of Lazaro Cordova. There they found Cordova's son-in-law, Prancasio Saiz, brushing down his horse. The saddle-blanket was steaming, and the saddle was wet. Suspicious at what had led the man to a hard ride in the dark of the night, Elfego enlisted Saiz to join the small band of lawmen, over the suspect's objections.

Not far from the stable was a graveyard where the sheriff had heard the Gang sometimes camped out. The next events brought into play Elfego's ability to draw conclusions from a scene, long before the word "forensics" had been introduced into the popular vocabulary by television crime shows. As Baca explained to Smith,

"I rode over to it and found where they had lunched the day before. There were cans and cracker boxes and one thing and another. Then I found where one of them had had a call to nature. I told one of my men to put it in a can. Saiz didn't know about this, and in a little while he went over behind some mesquite bushes and had a call to nature. After he came back I sent my man over, and by God it was the same stuff—the same beans and red chili seeds! So I put Saiz under arrest and sent him back to the jail at Socorro with one of my deputies, although he kept saying he couldn't see what I was arresting him for."

While one of Elfego's deputies escorted Saiz back to Socorro, the sheriff and his lone remaining companion traveled on east and over the mountains to the village of Manzano.

There the pair found two of the Gang and arrested them. Elfego sent them back to Socorro with his remaining deputy. After checking for more Gang members but finding none, Elfego also set out back across the mountains for Socorro. On the way back, Elfego stopped again at the Cordova ranch. By then, it was about two a.m. He roused "the old man," put him under arrest, and took him to Socorro. Elfego had been up and on his horse for over twenty-four hours.

Elfego then told his interviewer how he, as a peace officer, used patience to obtain confessions around the turn of the twentieth century.

"I told him he was under arrest, and on the way to Socorro I told him that unless he and his son-in-law came across with a complete statement about the whole gang, I would hang both of them, for I had the goods on them and knew all right that they were both in on the killing of Contreros. I put him in the same cell with his son-in-law, and told him it was up to him to bring Saiz around. They came through with the statement. I kept on catching the rest of the gang, until I had them all.

All but the one who got himself shot before I caught up with him."

The Smith interview didn't end until Baca had told Janet another tale of frontier harassment of local Hispanic populations by cowboys. This time, the site was close to Socorro.

A long time before he became Sheriff, though while he was a "self-made deputy" sporting a mail-order badge, a couple of Texas cowboys were shooting up the town of Escondida, where Elfego had gone to visit his uncle. He told Smith:

> "They hadn't hurt anybody that time. Only frightened some girls. That's the way they did in those days—ride through town shooting at dogs and cats and if somebody happened to get in the way—powie!—too bad for him. The Sheriff came to Escondida after them. By that time they were making a couple of Mexicans dance, shooting up the ground around their feet. The Sheriff said to me 'Baca, if you want to help, come along, but there's going to be shooting.'
>
> "We rode after them and I shot one of them about three hundred yards away. The other got away—too many cottonwoods in the way.
>
> "Somebody asked me what that cowboy's name was. I said I didn't know. He wasn't able to tell me by the time I caught up with him."

Elfego told Janet Smith the sheriff's records in Socorro would show the incident, and that the place where the cowboy was buried was a little way off the main road.[89]

Another case in which Elfego's detective skills were applied with verve and imagination, this time while he was a deputy sheriff in Socorro County, was the capture of two-time murderer José Garcia.

Garcia had killed a man in Belen and was generally believed to have acted at the instigation of the dead man's wife. The killer and the widow disappeared. Some time later, the lady reappeared, but as a corpse that had been quartered and hung from a tree like a deer after the hunt. That was enough to give new motivation to the lawmen who had given up tracking down Garcia while he was believed to be holed up with his paramour in some romantic hideaway. Elfego had had enough of Garcia, too. He set out to find José and bring him in.

For three months deputy Baca searched until he finally concluded that the man was hiding in Sandoval County, a few miles north of Albuquerque, with a sheep herding outfit not known for its respect for the law. Baca, this time wearing the badge of a legitimate Socorro County under-sheriff and not a mail-order catalogue duplicate, rode to the small town of Bernalillo, county seat of Sandoval County. There he enlisted as a guide sixteen-year-old Alfredo Montoya, whose curiosity had led him to ride his horse over every square foot of Sandoval County.

Young Alfredo got his first hint of what was up when Elfego called a halt to his man-and-a-boy party a dozen or so miles out of Bernalillo. Baca dismounted, pulled out a small mirror, a piece of cork and a box of matches, and set about blackening his face, neck, hands and every other inch of his body that might show, with burnt cork. Young Montoya watched, pointing out spots he'd missed.

After half a day spent with the make-up kit, the pair moved on, watching in every direction. The sheep-herders had eyes throughout the county, and if word of the approach of a suspicious pair of riders had reached the men, Elfego knew an ambush set in some arroyo or behind some rock outcropping would spray them with shots.

Just after sundown on the sixth day out of Bernalillo, the man-hunters smelled smoke. They soon spotted the flames of a campfire.

Young Montoya, his black manservant trailing a horse-length behind, rode slowly up to four men circling a flickering cook fire. All of them were mounted, armed, and each one placed his hands on his pistols and turned to face the intruders. The sheepmen's hostility turned to welcome when they recognized Alfredo, a kid who seemed to be the friend of every person in the county. "My groom," Alfredo said, grinning, pointing to Elfego. The groom dismounted, shuffled his feet, tugged at his hat brim and helped Alfredo off his horse.

Black men were not common in the Territory, and it's doubtful if Elfego would have passed the scrutiny test of the curious sheepmen had he not stayed away from the light of the fire. As it was, he studied the men from under his lowered hat until he picked out the fugitive, who had dismounted and stood toying with his horse's saddle away from the fire, his hand inches from his six-gun. When Garcia's attention went back to his horse, Elfego pulled out his twin Colts and got the drop on him. "Elfego," Garcia breathed.

After Elfego directed Alfredo to collect the guns from the sheepmen, the two-man posse tied Garcia's hands behind his back. When Elfego had warned the remaining three men about the futility of following, and threatened them with the vengeance of Alfredo's father if the kid were to be shot from behind, the three set off on horseback. When they reached the village of Thornton on the Santa Fe tracks, they stopped to check out the train schedules. Their appearance created quite a stir, and the prisoner was soon recognized as the assassin who had killed and butchered the woman. It didn't take long for a crowd to gather nor for them to metamorphose into a mob that was in a lynching mood. It took every bit of Elfego's reputation as a gunfighter to stand them off, but once he'd told them who was hiding behind the black face, no one stepped up to demand that Garcia be turned over to them for cottonwood-tree justice.

Elfego delivered his prisoner back to Socorro, disappointed that there had been no real action. Alfredo Montoya was so taken with his role in bringing in the killer and his training by Elfego Baca in blackface that when he grew up he was elected sheriff of Sandoval County.[90]

But as for Elfego, though his first love would always be working out his aggressions by catching the bad guys, he never forgot the poor and downtrodden.

15

◈ DEFENDER OF THE POOR

There are two incidents found in accounts of Elfego's life that demonstrate Elfego's compassion for the poor. The poor were nearly uniformly Mexican-Americans. Both episodes can be interpreted to shed light on how completely Baca had worked himself into the Hispanic community when he was a young man, newly arrived in Socorro and speaking no Spanish. The stories were told by Crichton. The first involved Baca's cousin, Conrado Baca, and Conrado's business partner, Frank Shaw.

The pair of businessmen called on Elfego to put down an excess of exuberance in the little community of Kelly, just outside of Magdalena, which lies some twenty-six miles west of Socorro. The activities could be said to have been a repeat of the Texas cowboy arrogance at Frisco, this time by miners celebrating Saturday night.

Cousin Conrado and Shaw ran a store in the village. When the work week ended, the miners came to town. Nothing delighted them more than shooting up the Baca/Shaw store, making the place ring with shots ricocheting from pots, pans and other kitchen implements hanging from the rafters. When they tired of those targets, they tested their skills by shooting the buttons off the coats of the proprietors. The owners were stoic about it all until the night cousin Conrado lost two buttons, his hat, his belt buckle and his dignity. There was only one place to go from there, he figured, and that was to his burial plot in the cemetery. Who to turn to but cousin Elfego? Shaw and Baca rode out to seek help.

Elfego was temporarily unoccupied, so he responded to their

pleas. Within a few hours after he'd cantered to the rescue, he wrestled possession of the store away from the miners. But the two owners were nowhere to be seen. Elfego, though, had served his time behind a store counter at the Juan José Baca store in Socorro. He hadn't liked clerking then and he didn't like it any better in the Baca/Shaw store in Kelly. A day passed, and the owners still hadn't shown up. Elfego figured that if cousin Conrado and his partner didn't care enough about their business to come along and help save it, why should he labor on as a shop-keeper when he'd rather be doing about anything else? Elfego sent out word to the poor Mexicans of the area.

The next day was Christmas in Kelly, though the season of the year was all wrong. Elfego gave away the entire stock of the store. For a few days the native population ate as they had rarely eaten before.

There's no record of the reaction of Conrado Baca and Frank Shaw when they got back to their store and found it empty. They'd lost their stock, worth an estimated $3,500, but they'd gained in experience. To Elfego, his satisfaction in getting the miners out of the store was worth every nickel of the partners' investment, his thanks the full bellies of the poor people of Kelly.[91]

The second incident showed that Elfego's concern for the poor Mexican-Americans of his county was genuine. During his tenure as Socorro County sheriff, he took an initiative that led eventually to the overturning of an oppressive statue. The law had been passed at the behest of sheepmen, and it resulted in the jailing of persons who owed a debt to a sheep owner and did not either pay off the amount owed or work it off. The sentence could be up to sixty days in jail. The justification for the law originated in the seasonal nature of the business of raising sheep. To keep workers from moving away during the off-season, the sheep ranchers had to make loans to them so they could survive. Their pay, once the work began again, often wasn't enough to allow repayment, especially if the worker had a family to support. Sheepmen eager to collect their debts had gotten the attention of the state legislature to get a law passed. The statute had been the result.

Sheriff Baca returned one day from an out-of-town trip to find his jail had been turned into a virtual debtor's prison. Eleven prisoners filled its cells, all of them just starting out to serve sixty-day sentences. One of the men, Elfego found, had a wife and four children. The man hadn't been able to scrape up enough to pay the eleven dollars he owed to his sheep-man employer.

Elfego called the eleven into his office. "Get out," he told them, according to Crichton's biography. "Go on back home and go to work. Pay off your debts. You'll only eat us poor here."

The district attorney didn't like it. Other sheriffs around New Mexico whose budgets paid for the keep of their prisoners thought Elfego's way was little short of a god-send. District judges decided not to enforce the law. Soon, the legislature repented, and repealed the law before it could be acted on by the state supreme court.[92] Once more, Elfego was the hero of poor Mexican-Americans. Once more he had thumbed his nose at authority and turned his actions into the heroic.

16

◈ THE INTERPRETER

During Federal Works Progress Administration historical interviewer Janet Smith's first visit to lawyer Baca's office, in July,
1936, she was impressed that the courtly Elfego saw to it that she had
the coolest seat in the room. During her visit, she wheedled out of
him the story of his trip to Roswell with Judge Leland. It appears to
have happened between the time that Elfego was Socorro's mayor
and when he became county school superintendent.

During that period Baca was hired by Judge Charles A. Leland, district judge for Socorro, Eddie, Chavez and Lincoln counties,
not as the judge's lawyer, but as his interpreter. By that time, Elfego
was fluent in Spanish as well as in English.

Judge Leland had arrived in the territory from the civilized
community of Toledo, Ohio, only long enough before to learn that
when a New Mexico judge ruled against a party accused of murder
or assault, the man's brother or cousin just might take a potshot at his
honor from behind a tree. The judge decided he needed a bodyguard
to cover his back when he had to make his first annual trek to open a
term of court in Roswell, on the east end of his sprawling judicial area.
It was July of 1898, and Judge Leland had been sworn in only a week
earlier.

The judge found money in his budget for an interpreter. In
what he'd learned about Elfego Baca, he identified the skills of one
who could act both to interpret and to guard his body. While Elfego
wasn't particularly interested in the ten dollars a day the job would
pay, he decided it would be wise to get on the good side of a judge

that he would probably appear in front of as a lawyer before his legal career got much older. The two set out for Roswell, the judge armed with his court dockets, Elfego carrying his revolvers.

The cases that were called and tried are long since forgotten, and there is no record that Elfego had a reason to pull his pistol to defend his honor's back, but one tale remains. That is the story of the bondsmen that Elfego told to Janet Smith.

In Roswell, Elfego tore himself away from his courtroom duties long enough to visit a local bar. There he was approached by two Anglos whom he had seen hanging out around the courtroom in the Chavez County courthouse. One prompted the other to ask for Baca's help. As they told their story to the judge's all-purpose assistant over drinks, it developed that the pair had signed a bond to guarantee the court appearance of one of their sheep-herders. The object of their trust was an old man from Mexico who had been involved in shooting another Mexican. Their sheepherder was supposed to appear at the current term of court, but they couldn't find him. They had $2,000 in bond money on the line, and Elfego knew, as they did, that it would be forfeited if the old man didn't show.

The sheepmen concluded they would at least come out with $1,500 in their pockets if they could hire Elfego for $500 to settle the case. Elfego figured he knew how it could be done. They shook hands on the deal, and Baca set out to put his plan into effect. Approaching Judge Leland, Elfego told him the whole story, or most of it.

Judge Leland listened carefully as Elfego laid out a plan that could give the judge a day off by side-stepping a trial for the sheep-herder. After all, Baca explained, the man's fate didn't matter to the locals anyway, since both the shooter and the victim were from Mexico. Then Elfego reeled his honor in: if the D. A. would agree to take the sheepherder's plea to carrying a deadly weapon in return for a fifty dollar fine, the trial could be vacated. The judge would be a hero for collecting the fifty dollars, because the law would send it to the nearly-broke county school fund, and he could head home early. His honor snapped it up, if only the D. A. would buy in. Somehow in the conversation, the fact that the Mexican was missing never came up. Elfego left to search for the district attorney.

But before putting the plan to the D. A., Elfego found an elderly Mexican chopping wood not far from the courthouse. He soon found that the man's English was all but non-existent. After considerable dickering in Spanish, the two struck a bargain. If the Mexican would follow the script, when the play was over Elfego would pay him $25. Agreed. That done, Elfego sold the plea-bargaining plan to the district attorney.

Later in the afternoon of the day that Elfego had appeared at the woodpile, the Mexican showed up at the courthouse, just as planned.

The courtroom dialogue has been retold many times, but in the telling the color and personalities somehow get lost, and it has never been told better than in the original version written by Janet Smith in recording her July 27, 1936, interview with a contemplative Elfego Baca.

When the sheepherder's case was called, the woodcutter stand-in stepped up before the judge and was asked for his plea.

"Guilty," he smilingly replied to the Judge's question.
"Gracias," he answered when the judge pronounced a $50 fine.

The judge was annoyed at this debonair reception of his sentence. "I am going to make you Mexicans obey the law in this country," he said sternly, "and the next time I find you in my court I am going to send you to the Penitentiary. Do you understand?"

Mr. Baca translated: "The Judge says that any time you Mexicans are not treated properly by the people in Roswell, you have only to let him know."

The Mexican smiled. "Gracias," he said again.

"Tell that Mexican," roared the Judge. "Tell him that he has nothing to thank me for. Tell him that I don't like his looks. He looks to me like an outlaw and an imposter. I should presume from his appearance that he had committed some crime. Tell him that he would do well to stay out of my court hereafter."

Mr. Baca interpreted: "The Judge says that he is very much impressed with your appearance. He also likes your courtroom manner. He sends his compliments to your mother."

"Gracias," replied the irrepressible Mexican.

Impatiently the Judge dismissed court. The Mexican paid his fine to the clerk [with $50 Elfego had given him in advance]. Elfego Baca walked erectly down the aisle, the Mexican following close behind, his mind on the $25 he was to be paid.

Outside the courthouse the two Anglos from Texas, having collected their bond money, called to Baca, pulled him aside, told him he'd made a mistake. He'd brought in the wrong man. Janet Smith recorded the finale.

"'What the Hell?' said Elfego. 'What the hell do you care? The matter is settled, isn't it?' He turned to the smiling Mexican and paid him his $25."[93]

17

❖ THE LAWYER

It's guesswork as to why Elfego Baca set out to be a lawyer. Some have speculated that he began reading for the law before he left for the Frisco clean-up. Others have guessed that just maybe it was the gun-battle itself, or his admiration of the lawyers that defended him, that drove Baca to seek out the offices of Socorro lawyer Humphrey B. Hamilton to study law. It was in Judge Hamilton's office that Elfego read law while presumably providing some of the routine services of a law clerk, runner and process server, as was the custom at that time.

Judge Hamilton (the title "judge" was commonly given to respected lawyers whether or not they had ever sat on the bench) was apparently not an exacting taskmaster, since the demands he put on his charge were not burdensome. To prepare his pupil for a career in the legal profession, Judge Hamilton led Baca to read "Smith's *Elementary Law* and a few chapters of Blackstone's *Commentaries*, assuredly a scant preparation for the bar," as Albuquerque lawyer and writer William A. Keleher described the new lawyer's preparation for admission.[94]

Elfego was admitted to the practice of law by Territorial District Judge A. A. Freeman, "in the atmosphere of a friendly court," in December, 1894. He raised his hand to take the oath in Lincoln County, where Billy the Kid had won his reputation, though the reason why the ceremony took place so far away from Socorro has not been explained. At the time, Baca was Socorro county clerk, though Keleher's *Memoirs* say, "He was admitted to practice law while serving as a Socorro County Deputy Sheriff."[95] Perhaps the energetic Baca was holding down three jobs at the same time—deputy sheriff, county clerk, and law clerk to Judge Hamilton. He had a growing family, he was on the way up in the politics of the Territory, and he always had lawyers to pay to extricate himself from his scrapes, so it would not be a surprise if he had been burning his work-day candle at both ends to keep income flowing.

It wasn't long after his name was added to the lawyer rolls until Elfego hooked up with a law partner. It was a lucky break for the rookie lawyer. The senior partner of the two-man firm was Andreius A. Freeman, who had been a Territorial supreme court justice and the judge on the bench when Elfego was admitted to practice. It was an association that surely made Elfego's status as a fledgling lawyer much more credible than if he'd hung out a shingle and gone at it solo.

Justice Freeman's reputation for a well developed sense of humor survived until Kyle Crichton wrote Elfego's biography, according to the book. Crichton tells of the case of *Hargrave vs Smith,* with the opinion of the court written by the fun-loving Freeman, reporting that it was indexed in the New Mexico decisions under "humor." Maybe the *Hargrave* case was a product of Crichton's own sense of humor, since it doesn't today appear anywhere in the index of New Mexico cases, going back to the inception of the Territorial Supreme Court. Or maybe Crichton got the name of the case wrong.

It might have been that sense of humor, too, that led Freeman to team up with a man with a reputation as a gunslinger who had used a pair of revolvers to enforce justice when no one else cared. But the new partner surely knew his way around the courtroom, not because he'd completed a rigorous course of study, but because he'd survived two murder trials as the star of the show. Those experiences with his life at stake were surely more than equivalent to reading a few dozen law books and sitting through a hundred lectures on the rules of evidence, trial procedure, jury selection and the preparation of jury instructions delivered by a law professor long on talk but short on courtroom experience. Or maybe Judge Freeman simply recognized raw talent when he saw it.

Elfego's sometime counselor, Will Keleher, wrote that one of Elfego Baca's qualifications for the bar was that he "spoke excellent English, without any trace of a Spanish accent."[97] Crichton, on the other hand, after reporting that Baca was something less than a well-rounded lawyer, excused Elfego's shortcomings by explaining that he was always hampered "by his lack of fluency in English, but his record as a criminal lawyer has been of the highest, and he is credited with securing the acquittal of nineteen individuals charged with murder."[98]

Author Agnes Morley Cleaveland described an encounter with Elfego Baca and her friend, "Corky," who was charged with murder. She visited Corky in his Socorro County jail cell, and there met Elfego, his defense attorney. "This gentleman was a Mexican who spoke halting English." He bragged to her, she wrote, "'I was the first man in thees jail.'"

The rest of his conversation was pointed at convincing her to perjure herself in Corky's defense. It was all delivered in an accented English not spoken in the capital of the State of Kansas. Elfego promised a script of testimony for her to learn. She quoted him: "'I'll tell you what to say on the weetness stand,' he told me. 'You learn it good and come to my office and I cross-examine you like the deestrict attorney do, so they can't treep you up.'" The rest of Elfego's conversation, according to Cleaveland's account, was similarly accented, while the author dithered over whether those on the jury who were not Mexican-Americans should be called "white," "English," or "Anglo." Her hemming and hawing was for nothing. She didn't make it to the witness stand, with or without a script.[99]

Elfego himself later contributed to the confusion about his language abilities when he testified in Spanish in the trial of legislator Jose P. Lucero for solicitation of bribery. The trial was held in 1914. While in the witness box, Elfego said that he "came pretty near forgetting the English language" after he returned to Socorro from Topeka. He testified that even so, he was comfortable in either language.

It's probable that when he made the comment before an overwhelmingly Hispanic jury with the desire on Elfego's part to see to the conviction of Lucero, he was again trying to identify himself with the Mexican ethnics he had fought for at Frisco. At Lucero's trial, the group he reached out to was the jurors sitting in the jury box. But it also appears that Elfego commonly went out of his way to align himself with Hispanics and against Anglos; that while he sometimes reached out to the Anglos, his reason then was to play the role of bridge from them to the Hispanics, especially in the twenties, when his Spanish-language newspaper was such a backer of Anglo politician Bronson Cutting. Elfego's fluency in both languages and his status as a lawyer made his double role possible.[100]

For the rest of his professional legal career, Elfego kept an office either in Socorro or in Albuquerque. He also kept a branch office in El Paso for a short time. In 1910, he moved his office from Socorro to Albuquerque, though he was later to serve as Socorro County sheriff. Not always was his office limited to offering only legal services.

Keleher told of counseling Baca about the line between his obligations as a member of the legal profession and the standards governing private detectives. The advice came when Baca consulted Keleher, as a person he held in high regard and not for legal counseling, to seek advice on an ethical matter. When the respected lawyer told Elfego that what he proposed to do was out of bounds for an ethical lawyer, Baca had anticipated him. He admitted to Keleher that he was practicing two professions at the same time, and maybe what was forbidden to one would be okay for the second. He whipped out his business card. One side said, "Elfego Baca, Attorney-at-Law, Licensed to Practice in all courts from Justice of the Peace in New Mexico to the United States Supreme Court." The other side bore the words, "Elfego Baca, Private Detective: Discreet Shadowing Done: Civil and Criminal Investigations; Divorce Investigations our Specialty."

Keleher vetoed the suggestion that Baca might be able to act as trial attorney in the case and then testify, not as a lawyer but as a private investigator. "A man cannot ring the bell in the church steeple and walk in the procession on the ground at the same time," Keleher told him. Elfego took the advice with good grace. He backed off, giving his valued counselor's guidance the respect it deserved.

But Baca continued to beat the Albuquerque bushes for clients to serve in either of his double roles. He was a walking advertisement, though it's not clear for what. He haunted the downtown streets dressed in a flowing cape and followed by a bodyguard, passing out his dual-purpose business cards to all who would take them.[101]

The cape costume was not featured in the men's clothing offerings of the local papers of the times, and there is no indication of why Elfego chose it or when be began the display. Whatever the reason and whenever he was first caped, he hadn't been wearing the garment when the cattlemen asked him to speak at their convention in Magdalena.

18

◈   STILL QUICK ON THE DRAW

In a vindication of sorts, Elfego, the former nemesis of the Texas ranchers, was asked to speak at a convention of cattlemen held in Magdalena, a few miles west of Socorro. Although Crichton's account does not disclose the reason for the choice of Baca to make the address, perhaps the invitation came in 1906, while Elfego was attorney for the Sierra County Cattlemen's Protective Association. The group had turned to him to clean up cattle rustling in the area and then decided to use him as the association's lawyer. The appearance provided an unplanned opportunity for a revealing look into what made Elfego tick. The episode involved one Bill Saunders, a well-known gunman. Crichton wrote the story, which is retold here because of the insights it offers. It all happened after Elfego was no longer a brash kid.

Baca was present at a ball held at the Magdalena hotel that was convention headquarters, though he stood "on the outskirts," as Crichton described his lack of participation. While Elfego tried to be inconspicuous, a drunk Texas cowboy swaggered up to him, stuck his face in Elfego's and told him he wasn't going to run the dance. Elfego denied he had any intent of running anything. That wasn't good enough for the cowboy. While he jerked at his pistol, Elfego dropped him with a left hook to the jaw. Then Bill Saunders appeared.

Saunders had notches in his gun that showed three dead men to his credit. Elfego knew him and knew of his claim to fame. Elfego, curious as to what had moved the cowboy he had just decked to take him on, asked Saunders why the Texan had made his move. Saunders took offense, reached for his revolvers, found, too late, that Elfego had beaten him to the draw. There was a pistol pressed into his ribs, and Elfego Baca's finger was on the trigger.

One at a time, Elfego reached for Saunders' guns, pulled them out and threw them well out of reach. He spun the gunman around and booted him out the door. The dance hall crowd o-oh-ed and a-ah-ed and pressed forward to see who had handled bad-man Saunders so cavalierly.

But the action didn't stop there.

When the owner of the hotel scurried up to warn Elfego that he had just made a big-time mistake, that Saunders and his gang would be waiting for him outside when he left, Baca sprinted upstairs and ran back down, buckling on the rest of his armament. That done, he dashed down the street to the saloon where Bill and his henchmen hung out and where Elfego figured an ambush was being plotted. Pushing through the swinging door, Elfego strode in. Bill spotted him, made another grab for his guns while he tried to duck behind the bar. Once more, Elfego was quicker. In an instant his two revolvers materialized in his hands. It was then that the story takes on a significance that tells something more about the forty-one-year-old Elfego than how quick he was on the draw.

With Bill and the rest of the saloon crowd under control, Elfego, still pointing his six-guns at anyone who moved, ordered everyone to belly up to the bar. Crichton provided the monologue: "'Drink up!' He [Elfego] yelled. 'I'm a Texas cowboy. . . . I'm bad. . . . None of these damn Mexicans for me . . . . Texas . . . That's me. . . . drink!'"

And so it went until everyone had downed a round or two while Elfego bragged at the top of his voice that he was a Texas cowboy, mean as hell, and they'd better drink up. But it still wasn't over.

The proprietor, Mr. Allen, was wringing his hands, wiping them on his apron, calculating the tab with a secret smile, listening as Elfego ranted on, listening while Elfego thanked him for his hospitality. Listening but not understanding. Then Elfego spelled it out.

"'You surely don't expect me to pay? Not a Texas cowboy? Now, if I was one of those damned Mexicans. . . . But a Texas cowboy?'" Or words to that effect.

With a pair of pistols under his nose, Allen gave the expected answer. "'Yessir, Mr. Baca. Yessir. The drinks are on me.'"

Elfego's hostility toward the men from Texas had boiled over once again. It was twenty-two years after Frisco.[102]

In 1908, Elfego was back in Albuquerque, where he'd become the principal owner of a Spanish language weekly newspaper called *La Opinion Publica.* In May of that year, Baca, as the publisher, was asked by the owner of the building that housed the paper's printing plant at Third and Central to vacate the premises. Elfego didn't take kindly to having his newspaper's offices put out on the street, though he knew his only option was to move. *The Socorro Chieftain* told the story as another favorite son tale, quoting liberally from the prior day's edition of *The Albuquerque Citizen.*[103]

The owner of the building was a rancher named C. E. Geckler. The story doesn't say whether he ranched in Texas before becoming an Albuquerque property owner. Baca and Geckler had differing versions of a part of the occurrences that followed the notice to quit. Both agreed that they'd met while driving their buggies in opposite directions down Central Avenue in downtown Albuquerque. They stopped for conversation in the middle of the street, leaving others to guide their teams around them. After a few minutes of bickering and an exchange of words over why Geckler had taken possession of the newspaper's space before the term of the lease had expired, Geckler demanded the keys. Elfego told him he'd left them at Geckler's office, then asked the landlord to follow him to his law office, where he had a second set he would turn over to Geckler. But there was something in Geckler's behavior that set Elfego's nerves, well-honed by his experiences at Frisco, to twitching. The man kept his hand in his overcoat pocket, and he appeared to be angry.

Outside Elfego's office, Baca tied up his horse. Geckler did the same with his team, and the two went inside and up the stairs to Baca's second floor suite. Geckler declined an invitation to sit, saying his horses were waiting. But his hand stayed in his pocket.

Elfego located the keys in a drawer. Then, according to the *Chieftain*, Baca told the paper's reporter,

> "[I] pretended to hand them to him. As I did so, I let them fall to the floor. Mr. Geckler stooped to pick them up. I grasped him by the wrist, jerked his hand from his overcoat pocket and wrenched a pistol from his grasp. He had been holding it concealed in his overcoat pocket. Mr. Geckler turned and dashed out of the office and down the stairs. . . . He was in such a hurry he even left his hat behind. . . . I do not care to prosecute."

Geckler said his former tenant had it all wrong. He'd kept his hands in his coat pocket because they were cold. He was not the owner of the pistol that Baca was claiming he'd seized. "'I have never owned a gun during the eleven years I have lived in New Mexico and any of my friends, I think, will bear out my statement to that effect,'" he told the paper. Geckler talked to the district attorney. They decided not to prosecute. He was sure, Geckler said, that "'Mr. Baca would repent of his hasty actions. . . .'" He was wrong.

That is where it was left. The *Chieftain* closed its story with a rhetorical question: If the pistol did not belong to Baca, and if it was not Geckler's, then, "Who owns the gun?"

The riddle was never solved. But, as the *Chieftain* also said of the former mayor, once again Elfego had proved, "If anyone expects to get the start of Attorney Elfego Baca in a gun play he will find it necessary to get up early in the morning."[104]

Elfego was surely satisfied. He'd made the front pages of a couple of newspapers, one in Socorro, the other in Albuquerque. They both called him "Attorney" and spelled his name right.

There was another struggle, this one in the political arena, that drew Elfego into a bitter fight that damaged his political career. The issue was the so-called "blue ballot", so named because of the color of the paper on which it was printed when submitted to the voters. The controversy came up when statehood was just around the corner and a new state constitution was being put in place. An amendment to the constitution was proposed in order to make future amendments to the state constitution easier. It was printed on blue-tinted paper. David H. Stratton wrote of the devastating effect the vote had on the Republican party in New Mexico in his book, *Tempest Over Teapot Dome*.

A. B. Fall, and others, in 1911 urged Republicans, including Elfego Baca, that the blue ballot amendment to the constitution should be supported. Without the amendment the constitution would remain rigidly supportive of special interests in the new state, including railroads and ranching, Fall argued. Elfego, loudly and publicly, fought for the status quo, a constitution that could be amended only with great difficulty. Democrats, embracing the amendment in the name of standing up for the rights of the people against big business, swept the state offices. The Republican organization was left in shambles. The perception of many voters, especially Hispanic voters who had for years looked to Elfego Baca as their champion, was that the Republicans, including Elfego, had sold out. It was a stain that Elfego wore for years, shading his reputation as defender of Hispanic rights and raising suspicions that he put personal gain above principles.[105]

Elfego's escapades should be evaluated in the context of the times in which he lived. While it is true that Elfego was his own worst enemy when visions of the Texans of the past, visible only in the inner reaches of the hero's mind, caused him to interpret innocent circumstances as threats, there was more to his behavior than that. Elfego was an Hispanic in a political culture dominated by Anglos. He had to fight for every inch of advantage he gained, and he was to reach levels rarely attained by his Mexican-American peers, though he was ultimately to fail in reaching his loftiest political ambitions. The type of blood spilled in those political battles may not have run red, but it was nevertheless real, and the bravery Elfego showed in the political arena was as stirring as the heroism he demonstrated in the fight for his people against the cowboys in Frisco.

19

❖ THE GUN LAWS

There came a time, in 1906, when District Attorney Elfego found a way to justify confrontations with many of the young men of Socorro County. Best of all was that his belligerence was based on the law and executed initially with the cheers of District Judge Frank W. Parker of Socorro. The law was a statute against carrying concealed weapons.

While Elfego was D. A. for Socorro and Sierra Counties, he and Judge Parker went on a crusade against carrying arms stuck away in pockets or in boots so that they couldn't be seen. Occasionally, they took offense with firearms carried in plain view. During the December, 1907, term of court, just after Elfego left office and moved to Albuquerque, Judge Parker took public the enthusiasm for the anti-gun law that infected him. He instructed the grand jury that there were four laws in particular that needed to be enforced. On the top of the list was the law against carrying concealed weapons. But he had kicked off his crusade while Baca held down the district attorney's job, and it was during Elfego's term in that office that the ex-gunman got himself into trouble once again.[106]

For Elfego, the judge's anti-gun cause became his own. It didn't take long until his zeal for the law got the best of him. In 1906 he ordered a county under-sheriff to arrest a federal officer. The agent was Charles V. Mallet, a "Chinese inspector," meaning that Mallet had the power to enforce immigration laws against Chinese aliens. Mallet was charged with carrying a six-shooter in church and resisting arrest. When the arresting officer tried to take the inspector into custody, he'd jumped behind a tree and flourished his pistol. Elfego was there. He told the sheriff to shoot the man if he didn't surrender. Mallet came out with his hands up.[107]

Baca had public support for his actions further up the Rio Grande in Albuquerque. The *Albuquerque Evening Citizen*, in reporting the episode, said, "The action of District Attorney Baca in getting after pistol 'toters' meets the approval of all law abiding citizens." The approval was not as firmly unanimous as the newspaper suggested.[108]

Cynics among Baca's foes claimed that the real reason for the arrest was that Mallet, not Baca, had been picked to introduce the territorial governor at a reception held in Socorro by Baca's old foe, the livestock growers. Then, when Baca wanted to address the meeting, Mallet had said no, the podium belonged to him, and Elfego had not been invited to step up on it. Elfego, his detractors chortled, had been snubbed, and even though he was a county official with growing political influence, he hadn't even been recognized with a complimentary ticket to the affair.

The glee rankled Elfego. He picked up his pen and whipped out a righteous letter to the editor of the *Albuquerque Evening Citizen*. After excoriating the rival *Albuquerque Journal* for running an article that made a "feeble effort" to bring the culprit under the wing of the governor, he appealed to the church-goers of the community. He wrote:

> I fail to see anything anywhere in the laws which makes a Chinese inspector immune. The self same culprit has been carrying a pistol during the entire period of time he has been in San Marcial. He has been seen with it on his person while singing in the church choir during holy services (no Chinese present to inspect). If the law should, in any way, and I claim it does not, allow Chinese inspectors to carry arms while on duty, there certainly is no excuse for carrying one in church.

Baca wrote more. He asserted that Mallet had worn his pistol to a dance attended by the governor, "no Chinese present—consequently he was not on duty, unless he was trying to make it appear that some of the San Marcial people are Chinese. . . . " Elfego attested to personal knowledge that the residents of that community were not from Asia. Not only that, but the fellow who had signed Mallet's bond, C. E. Mead, and who had been on the reception committee for the governor's welcome in Socorro sponsored by the cattle growers, had been charged with selling liquor without a license in San Marcial, though Elfego made no claim that Mead had sold his whiskey from the choir loft. Elfego said Mead ran a drug store in San Marcial, had already been convicted once of selling booze without a license, and was known to sell "more liquor without a license than the other saloons together with a license."[109]

Elfego left the district attorney's office before the Mallet case came to trial. But not before he had primed his successor to run with the Chinese inspector's prosecution.

A Socorro County jury convicted Mallet, to the consternation of federal officials, including Assistant U. S. Attorney Medler, who had defended him. Rather than follow the conventional appeal processes to the state supreme court, Medler wrote State Mounted Policeman Fred Fornoff. He blamed his failure as a defense lawyer on prejudicial conduct by an all-Hispanic jury. Assistant Federal D. A. Medler's letter to Fornoff pleaded for intervention with the governor and accused Baca of prostituting the cause of justice. He described Elfego Baca as Fornoff's "friend," in quotation marks, while calling Mallet "a young, unsophisticated, serious-minded man. . . ." Somehow, Territorial Central Committee chair Holm O. Bursum got into the act. So did other politicos.

A Socorro lawyer, James G. Fitch, perhaps trying to reduce the legal competition in Socorro by running Baca out of town, wrote the governor, complaining that Elfego Baca was "totally unfit" to hold the office of district attorney. Then both Medler and Fitch did something they would not have gotten away with in front of a judge. Without having been present at any of the events, they gave slanted hearsay accounts in great factual detail describing the arrest of Mallet and Elfego's part in it.

Fitch rambled on. He pleaded for Mallet to be pardoned, arguing that as a federal officer Mallet could carry a pistol wherever the line of duty took him, though he skipped the issue of no Chinese in church. Then, he said, when arrested Mallet had been taken to a justice of the peace in Socorro who was the "tool" of Elfego Baca, instead of to a neutral J. P. in San Marcial; that just wasn't fair, and it was all the fault of the district attorney. Then he turned ugly. He told the governor that Baca had pleaded guilty in the W. E. Martin assault-with-intent-to-kill case, and the nature of the charges made it a felony. Statutes, he said, prevent convicted felons from practicing law, and unless Baca had been pardoned, the supreme court or the district court could disbar him. There were also a few other hearsay tidbits about Elfego Baca he laid on the table, such as receiving "bribes for not prosecuting parties, etc.," though Fitch admitted he couldn't prove it for the reason that everyone knows that persons who have been paid "hush-money are very reluctant to testify about it."

Governor Hagerman caved in to the pressure. He asked Judge Parker to get Elfego's resignation as district attorney. The judge did just that, and came away with a promise of Elfego's good-bye to the office. Publicly, Elfego blamed his resignation and departure for Albuquerque on earthquakes that were being felt in Socorro, claiming he wanted to get his family away from danger.

After Elfego telegraphed his resignation, everybody agreed publicly that Baca had not been asked to resign. The word on the street was that if the resignation had not been sent so quickly by Western Union, the governor would have gone public. Once again, Elfego had beaten the opposition to the draw.[110]

But Elfego wasn't finished with the Socorro County politicos. While he'd resigned from his position, he wouldn't move out of the courthouse. In July, 1906, the *Albuquerque Evening Citizen* reported that he'd refused to leave two rooms he had squatted in after his resignation. The county commission gave him three days to vacate, claiming they needed the space and he'd better move or the sheriff would throw him out. Baca played his trump. The judge of the district and the district attorney had left him in charge while they were gone, he said, and he wouldn't budge until they told him to. The *Citizen* figured it was "politics as usual" in Socorro County.[111]

Judge Parker eventually dismissed the case against Mallet in December, 1907. It came at about the same time he issued his strong statement to the grand jury about the evils of carrying weapons contrary to law.

20

◈   FAMILY TROUBLE

Bu ut though the Mallet case was behind Elfego by the end of 1907, some eleven years later he was back in office in Socorro County, this time as sheriff. He'd lost an election for that office in Bernalillo County in 1916, and apparently concluded that if he could not be sheriff in Albuquerque, maybe he could persuade the Socorro voters to pin a badge on his chest. They elected him in 1918.

Over the years that had elapsed since he'd been district attorney in Socorro and had run into trouble over the Chinese inspector, Elfego's enthusiasm for enforcing the anti-weapons laws hadn't slackened. Once again, as the sheriff of Socorro County during the early 1920s, in the same laws he found an opportunity for aggression under color of the law. His sheriff's badge pinned to his chest, Elfego strode through the town, grabbing revolvers like he planned to open a used pistol store. Until he ran into his sister-in-law.

One of the six-guns he seized belonged to Tomás Baca, who had served in the Great War and brought his bride back to Socorro from Baltimore in 1920. Tomás had grown so proud of the pistol he carried back with him that he wore it everywhere. Elfego spotted the weapon, seized it, locked up the war veteran, and hid the key.

When Tomás ran out of names to call the sheriff, Elfego let him use the phone. Tomás used his one call to reach his mom. Mom was Virginia Montoya de Baca, married to Abdenago Baca, Elfego's big brother, which made Tomás Elfego's nephew. That gave Virginia the right to barge right into the sheriff's office and grab the sawed-off little runt by the ear and twist it when she felt like it. And within ten minutes after the phone call came, that's what she did. Not only that, but she dragged with her the United States senator from Socorro, Holm Bursum, the same Holm Bursum who had had a run-in with Elfego when he was district attorney over the self-same anti-weapons law as it applied to the Chinese inspector. Bursum backed up Virginia every inch of the way. When she said that Elfego had no right to pick on her Tomasíto, Bursum agreed.

Virginia wouldn't back down, not even when Elfego pleaded that he treated family just like he treated everybody else: If relatives were breaking the law, too bad. Virginia gave a final, convincing twist of the ear, and Elfego found the keys, unlocked the cell door, let out Tomás. Mama left with her son, his revolver, and an attitude. Once again, Elfego lost his enthusiasm for enforcing his favorite law.

Virginia did not rest. She knew Socorro County politics inside out, and she knew how to get results. At every political meeting she attended, and she didn't miss a one, she jumped on the podium and broadcast her brother-in-law's shortcomings at the top of her voice. She wouldn't let go of Senator Bursum, either, until their soap-box speeches had carried the message to every voter in Socorro County and a few outside the county. Shortly after, Elfego lost his bid for re-election.

This time, instead of moving off to Albuquerque, he skipped over the U.S.-Mexican border. He got a job as bouncer at the Tivoli Gambling Hall, in Ciudad Juarez, Mexico, beyond the reach of Virginia's long arm. He would never have let it be known that his sister-in-law had anything to do with his leaving town.[112]

Family get-togethers were never the same again. Though there were no earthquakes on which he could lay the blame for shaking the dust of Socorro from his boots this time, as he had done following the adventure of the Chinese inspector, he may well have felt the earth tremble from the solid footsteps of the indomitable Virginia as she stalked him from meeting to meeting.

Virginia Montoya de Baca, Elfego Baca's sister-in-law and mother of Tomás Baca. Photograph courtesy of Gilbert Eugene Baca, Rio Rancho, New Mexico.

Tomás Montoya Baca, nephew of Elfego Baca and son of Virginia Montoya de Baca at age 19. Photograph courtesy of Gilbert Eugene Baca, son of Tomás Baca.

But with the conflict with Virginia behind him, Elfego faced yet another source of family discord.

21

◈ BATTLES AT HOME; BATTLES WITH CREDITORS

When Elfego sought peace and refuge from the courtroom battles, the political warfare and the enemies he believed were lying in wait to gun him down, as often as not he found little comfort at home. His relationships with his dear Francisquita rarely ran smoothly, at least until he'd aged into a state of indifference.

It's speculation to consider that his lack of success as a husband might have resulted, even in part, from irritability rooted in the dreams that haunted his nights and left him flailing his arms and moaning in sleep that brought no rest. But it seems likely. Surely, lying in the marital bed in the dark, his eyelids quivered and his body shuddered at a parade of nightmares rooted in an earlier time. During snatches of sleep he would have re-lived those days when the darkness was lessened by each shot fired by a Texan as the bullet punctured the mud wall of the *jacal*, letting in a bright point of sunshine to splash a tiny spotlight onto the dirt floor. He would have remembered how each point, each spot of light, increased the illumination—until the night came.

Surely, those dreams echoed with the whine of the bullets that sought him as they ricocheted off the face of the iron stove in the Armijo *jacal*; surely, too, as he thrashed about, wrestling with the bedclothes, he saw visions of the door bending under the kicks of the armed Texans as they screamed, "Kill him!" And he remembered there was no place to run if the hinges failed. He must have sometimes awakened, too, sweating, striking out at more shadowy figures that hunted him as they sought a clear shot that would earn the bounty offered by Pancho Villa after he'd made an enemy of the Mexican renegade.

Elfego Baca approaching middle age.
Photograph courtesy of Museum of New Mexico, Negative No. 128955.

Did he stumble out of bed, night after night, to pad through the combination residence, office and printing plant, until he woke enough to chase off the ghosts? Did Francisquita join him? Did she fire up the stove and heat milk for her troubled husband; did she rub his shoulders? Or did she wrap herself up in the blankets, grumbling that she'd been wakened once again and she was sick and tired of it? But Elfego never wrote or talked about such things. There could be no sign of weakness from the Hero of Frisco, the Savior of the Hispanics.

Whatever the reason for the marital discord that grew, the attraction between Elfego and the girl he was to marry started with a romantic tale of love found in an encounter along a dusty lane in Old Albuquerque.

Elfego rarely told the story of how he met his bride, the sixteen-year-old Francisquita Pohmer. He was strolling down an Albuquerque street on break from his trial for the murder of William Hearne. He spotted the striking Francisquita walking toward him, probably on a path by the side of the street so as to avoid the buggy and wagon traffic that Elfego would have challenged by sauntering along the middle of the road. She was on her way to her classes at Sister Blandina's Convent School. The school was located on the plaza in what is now called the Old Town section of Albuquerque. The courthouse was not far away.

Francisquita was probably wearing a school uniform with high, black shoes, a practical, long, dark skirt and equally dark jumper, perhaps with a starched white collar. The dashing young murder trial defendant was most likely spruced up with a cravat showing between his jacket lapels, worn at the instructions of his legal team so as to impress the jury with his personal habits of good grooming and gentility.

Elfego made it a point to catch the maiden's eye as they passed. It was love at first sight, at least on his part.

Surely the girls at Sister Blandina's had heard of the young hero's trial. Perhaps they had followed the episodes reported in the local papers. Their heads may have turned from their studies at the school while they sneaked quick peeks out a classroom window, hoping to catch a glimpse of the young gunman without earning a sharp scolding from the sisters. The fact that the outcome of the trial could set this Elfego Baca to swinging by his neck at the end of a rope surely added spice to their interest, leading them to compete for the first sighting of the celebrity. In any event, when Elfego came face to face with the girl, the quick gaze that lifted from the ground to return his own, though lasting only an instant before lowering again to the path, was enough to lead Elfego to do his best to arrange future chance encounters.

After only a few such meetings, young Baca mustered the nerve to ask the girl to be his wife. Her answer was conditional. There would be no prison visits with a convicted murderer-husband. She would not even think about marriage unless he were to be acquitted of the murder charges. Then, the answer would be yes.

Papa Pohmer was not pleased. The German immigrant, owner and operator of an Old Town bakery, protested his daughter's impetuousness.

The principal source of the story of the romance of Elfego and Francisquita, William A. Keleher, didn't describe the reasons for Joseph Pohmer's antagonism. They are not hard to imagine. Baca was being tried for murder; if he wiggled out from under the charge, he faced the possibility of a second murder trial; he was unemployed; he seemed to have an inclination toward law enforcement as a calling, and by dodging a few thousand bullets he was the current front-page example of just how dangerous that career choice was. There was the additional fact that he came from Socorro, in rough and tough Socorro County, and might very well spirit Francisquita back to that dusty venue. It was not a match made in heaven in the eyes of a father.[113]

The two were married in Albuquerque on August 13, 1885, some three months after the Albuquerque jury acquitted Baca. The honeymoon surely ended when a grand jury at the fall term of court in Socorro indicted the bridegroom for the killing of Young Parham.

Never asked was the question of whether for Elfego it had really been love when he met Francisquita, or whether he'd subconsciously been looking for some kind of stability to anchor him against the pressures of a murder trial to come and his fear that the Texans were still gunning for him. Whether it was love or something else, the couple set out to build a family. They were to have seven children, though one of them, Alberto, died in July, 1896, at the age of six months.[114]

After the Socorro jury acquitted Elfego for the killing of Parham, the newlyweds lived in Albuquerque for a time while Elfego worked as a deputy sheriff. When possibilities for employment opened up in Socorro, they moved there. Nothing is recorded about their life together while their children were growing up, but the continuing pressures from the political and legal heat that had become Elfego's way of life surely didn't contribute to the domestic tranquility. It's known that while the family lived in Socorro, Mrs. Baca made frequent trips to Albuquerque to visit her father, and that one of her stays stretched out when she became "indisposed." In the fall of 1894, Elfego came up to Albuquerque "with his little son" to enter him into the public school in Old Town because diptheria was so bad among the children in Socorro.[115] Son George was attending college in Las Cruces when Elfego became involved with the Mexican revolution, but little has come to light about the family as a unit.

In about 1911, Elfego's fortunes had reached the point at which he was able, with the help of a loan, to build a building on the edge of downtown Albuquerque, at the corner of Sixth Street and Gold Avenue. The *Socorro Chieftain* gave substantial coverage to the news of the construction, taking pride in the success that the project indicated its native son had earned in New Mexico's largest city. On August 26, 1911, it reported that work on the cement block building was to start that morning, and that the cost of the first story would be $5,000. It would be built, the account said, with sufficient strength so that two more stories could be added, in which event the total cost would be $25,000. It would house Baca's law office, his publishing company, La Opinion Publica, and a five room residence.[116]

At the time the building was planned, to contemplate putting himself and Mrs. Baca under one roof for most of every day of the week, Elfego must have judged that he and Francisquita were getting along. It turned out not to be a happy arrangement.

It was so unhappy that Elfego took his complaints to his lawyer and counselor, William A. Keleher. Baca sought to have Francisquita restrained by a court order from barging into his office while he was talking to clients. He told Keleher that her habit was particularly embarrassing when he was counseling with ladies, and that the "Private" sign painted on his office door did not slow down Francisquita in the slightest.

Lawyer Keleher was able to look further ahead than was his client. He explained that it would be a public issue if Elfego were to take his lady to court, since applications for restraining orders are spread out in files open for all to see, including inquiring news reporters with little else to do except nose through new filings in the district court records. Keleher, as a former newspaper reporter himself, knew that from experience. As a lawyer, Baca would have known it too. Keleher counseled that even though the court might enjoin Francisquita from entering while he was talking with clients, maybe Elfego should think twice. "All the world knows that you are a gunman, a fighter, that you have killed several men, and many people will be unable to understand how it comes that you are unable to handle Mrs. Baca," Keleher told Elfego.

His client got the point. Though Elfego left Keleher's office with the comment, "You just don't know Mrs. Baca," no application for a restraining order was filed.[117]

Francisquita's lack of respect for her husband's legal business, as witnessed by her refusal to recognize that "Private" written on his office door was intended to exclude her, may have been rooted in Elfego's inability to make his practice profitable enough to pay the bills. There came a time when the income of Francisquita's husband would no longer support the family in the style she'd enjoyed while growing up in her father's home in Old Albuquerque. On the 15th day of March, 1924, Elfego was adjudged a bankrupt in the Federal Court in Santa Fe, after admitting insolvency.

Running a detective agency to supplement his legal fees had not been enough. Or perhaps if Elfego had not been required to live with the legacy of Frisco—those dreams of the darkness inside Geronomo Armijo's *jacal*, of the bullets whizzing inches from his head as he lay flattened on the cold, dirt floor, and of the fear of shots fired in the night—he could have hired a business manager to protect his assets rather than a bodyguard to watch his back.

It was in 1923 that Elfego's finances began their irreversible dive. In 1924, when he filed his Debtor's Petition in the federal bankruptcy court, he signed the petition himself, not disclosing whether he was represented by an attorney, though his signature was notarized by John W. Wilson, a local lawyer. Wilson was later to assert that he had $200 coming as a result of having represented the bankrupt in filing the papers, so apparently he acted as Baca's lawyer in at least some of the proceedings.

Every bankruptcy petition tells a story, and Elfego's was no exception. The theme of chapter one of the sad Baca financial story appeared in the schedule of unsecured debts. It's obvious from the list that in a city that had not long before passed the 10,000 milestone in population, lawyer Baca couldn't have walked an Albuquerque downtown street without having to duck a creditor.

Francisquita Pohmer de Baca, wife of Elfego Baca. Photograph *courtesy of Juanita Hartsell, granddaughter of Mr. and Mrs. Elfego Baca. San Diego, California.*

He owed his plumber $1.75, perhaps for unplugging his sink; he'd bought a pair of shoes for $3.85 and had left behind a tab for their price; his car had broken down in Socorro, Albuquerque and Magdalena, and he owed repair shops in all those cities; his personal physician, Dr. Lovelace, was holding an unpaid bill for $500, and Elfego had stepped up to assume the fees for an operation for his granddaughter, Frances Cadina, but had left Dr. Rice with an account receivable of $191 and the hospital with a promissory note he'd given them for $200 for the girl's care. He owed his butcher, his baker, his saddle-maker. Left holding the bag were his grocer, his druggist and a sizable part of the business community. Elfego must have been more than embarrassed to face them. Perhaps he shed his flowing cloak for more modest attire that allowed him to blend in with the pedestrians as he tried to go about his business without being stopped by a creditor walking toward him to beg for a payment on account.

Chapter two of the depressing tale buried in the bankruptcy file is written in the list of secured creditors, those who held mortgages or some other security. The triple-purpose building Elfego had boasted to the *Socorro Chieftain* about putting up at the corner of Sixth Street and Gold Avenue in Albuquerque at a construction cost of $5,000, was worth that amount, but including also the value of the land. The second and third stories dreamed of had never been built. There was $4,000 due on the mortgage. The building was to be sold by the bankruptcy trustee to Bronson Cutting for $7,000, in a transaction that was to produce more litigation in later years.

Even Socorro County had let him down, failing to pay him $2,750 for fees owed him as sheriff, though maybe Elfego had gotten his money's worth in the joy of tracking down the bad guys. The debt was listed as secured, but it was not clear what the security was.

But it could have been worse. Baca's debts totaled $16,390.21, while assets were valued at $26,515.55. He listed as exempt from the claims of creditors his $1,000 equity in the Sixth and Gold building by asserting, "Petitioner is a married man living with his family at homestead above described." He also protected his office furniture and household goods from seizure and sale by creditors by listing them under a claim of homestead exemption.

But the most poignant chapters in the story filed with the court were those that related to Elfego's relationships with Mrs. Baca. Even with the bankruptcy of the head of the household, the two couldn't agree.

John F. Simms, Esq. appeared as attorney for Francisquita P. de Baca. His first step as her lawyer was to put the bankruptcy referee on notice that his client claimed a half interest in Elfego's property, and that her share wasn't subject to all those listed debts. The same letter, dated April 2, 1924, advised that Mrs. Baca had recently been sued for divorce on the ground "of cruel treatment which he [Elfego] alleged that she administered to him." The lawyer's letter disputed Elfego's claim that he lived in the residence. It claimed that Mrs. Baca was the one who was living there, and that Mr. Baca was not. "Her condition is most pitiful," Simms wrote.

Three months later Simms wrote again, saying that because of the way Mrs. Baca had been treated, he didn't want her to lose her home, and that he would try to find help for her by way of a new mortgage to raise money to buy out the bankrupt estate's interest in the building. Five months passed, and Francisquita fired Simms. Her letter of discharge said that though he'd done nothing for her, she would pay him for his time as soon as possible.[118]

Despite attorney Simms' letter dated April 2, 1924, saying that Mrs. Baca had just been sued for divorce, court records in Bernalillo County reflect that Elfego Baca didn't file a divorce complaint against Francisquita Pohmer de Baca until a year later, on April 8, 1925. It's possible that the divorce action to which Simms referred was filed in a different county but then dismissed. Occasionally, at that time in New Mexico history, parties would agree to file in counties other than the one in which they resided. It was done in order to reduce publicity in the hometown. Or Simms may have written based on a threat Elfego made that he was about to file, and Elfego did not follow through until later.

Elfego's 1925 divorce complaint told that the couple's six children were all married and in their own homes. Until the past six years, Elfego's pleading said, the couple had been happy, but then Francisquita had "deported herself in a cruel and unbecoming manner. . . ." She had begun to address him "in a disrespectful manner and by calling him bye-names [sic] and epithets, names of such vulgarity as are unmentionable in polite society." She had caused their daughters to distrust him, too, Elfego claimed. Worse yet, in January, 1924, Francisquita had called the cops "in order to further humiliate plaintiff in the eyes of his fellowman." All this, he said, had happened even though the long-suffering Elfego had given her plenty of money every week to buy "necessary things for her support as far as plaintiff's ability extends."

He asked for a divorce on the grounds of cruel and inhuman treatment, for a division of their property, and offered to pay her house rent and provide support.

Francisquita counterclaimed. Her version was that she'd lived a very unhappy life for the past "good many years." It was due to the "ill-treatment and lack of consideration to which she has been subjected at the hands of said cross defendant. . . ." Elfego, she said, had caused her "untold hardships and humiliations . . . notwithstanding the fact that . . . [she] has nursed and cared for him during his illness, and endured many hardships, in order to make things as comfortable as possible for him."

Judge Milton Helmick granted Francisquita a divorce on May

25, 1925. Elfego was ordered to pay fifty dollars each month as permanent alimony.

Five months later Elfego was back at the courthouse to plead poverty. The fifty per month was way too much, he argued. He filed a petition with the court claiming the most he could squeeze out of his paltry income as alimony was thirty-five. His pleading wailed that he'd been in a severe accident, had a lot of doctor bills, and that his legal practice was in tatters. He barely had enough, he claimed, to pay the premium on a life insurance policy he carried on his life for the benefit of Francisquita. His plea was that she didn't need alimony anyway, because she'd moved to California and was living with a daughter, and she was getting along just fine.

Francisquita hired Robert Hoath LaFollette and M. Ralph Brown, two young Albuquerque lawyers who had gotten together that year to form a partnership. LaFollette wrote about their representation in his little book about Elfego titled *Eight Notches*, though his account varies in several ways from what is recorded in the court files.

According to LaFollette, the partners picked the fight by setting out to get an order to show cause to require Elfego to appear before Judge Milton J. Helmick. Once in the judge's courtroom, Francisquita's lawyers said, they would ask Elfego to explain why the judge shouldn't hold him in contempt for ignoring the court's order that he pay Mrs. Baca her fifty dollar monthly alimony. The court file, though, shows that it was Elfego who took the initiative. He was the one who got to the courthouse first. He carried with him his sad story of yet another financial crisis that he wanted to share with Francisquita by paring his alimony down to a level he could handle.

The pleading filed by LaFollette and Brown in response to Elfego's plea for mercy called Baca's law practice "lucrative." It charged that Elfego had unilaterally decided to reduce his payments to Francisquita to thirty five dollars a month, even though he was well able to pay the fifty his honor had told him to pay. And Francisquita, though she was living in California with one daughter and being helped by another, was "not anxious to live off the charity of said daughters. . . ."

It was not until the two new partners had filed their papers and had them served, LaFollette wrote, that they learned that the fellow they were trying to pry more money out of was one of the "bad-men" of the times. With that knowledge, their introduction to Baca at the steps to the courthouse wasn't reassuring.

Though Brown and LaFollette expected trouble when they reached the courtroom, the intimidation they ran into in the sunshine outside was unexpected. As they walked up to the courthouse steps, a large limousine pulled up and a "ferocious-looking" man stepped out. A bodyguard trailed behind. Beneath his coat, each man displayed the outline of a pistol on his hip.

When the party reached the courtroom, Elfego demanded to know if the young upstarts who had reported they were representing Mrs. Baca were licensed to practice law in the state of New Mexico. Judge Helmick deflected the question. He'd had the partners in his courtroom on other occasions. Baca then demanded to see a power of attorney—anything to verify that Brown and LaFollette had Mrs. Baca's authority to appear for her. They waved their client's letter, and his honor found it acceptable. Elfego had exhausted his defenses, and he pleaded for the mercy of the court.

Elfego claimed he'd been sick. He was so pale and wan, his voice so weak, that the judge told him to try harder and do his best to pay the arrears. If he agreed, the court would take the matter under advisement and would do nothing but hold the threat of contempt of court over Baca's head until he showed he was really trying by coming up with money.

LaFollette's book doesn't report the outcome. Court records show his client lost. On February 16, 1926, Judge Helmick signed an order reducing Elfego's monthly alimony payments to thirty five dollars.[119] Presumably, Elfego left the courthouse feeling better already.

There's no record of how, or if, Elfego was paying his bodyguard or making payments on the limousine that delivered him to the courthouse to argue that he was too poor to pay for his ex-wife's upkeep. The court file doesn't show whether Mrs. Baca's two lawyers questioned him about his expenses.

Despite the divorce action and the alimony arguments, in 1932 Elfego wrote Francisquita to tell her he'd left his will in a safety deposit box in the First National Bank. He enclosed a key. He instructed her to see W. A. Keleher, "very honorable and very Catholic." The letter was signed, "Your spouse Elfego Baca."[120] At some point, probably after the date of the letter, which was mailed to Francisquita in California, the couple apparently reconciled, since they were living together in Albuquerque at the time of Elfego's death in 1945.

22

❖   BUILDING A LEGACY

With the bankruptcy and his divorce behind him, it was time for Elfego to set the record straight. What better way than to ask his trusted advisor, William A. Keleher, to write a book about his life. Surely, coming from the pen of that respected lawyer and former journalist, no one would doubt that the Baca version of the events at Frisco had really happened, that there had indeed been at least eighty Texas cowboys that he had stood off, that the count of the bullets fired at him did in fact add up to 4,000. How could the Baca bashers who raised their eyebrows and rolled their eyes when the tale of cowboy cruelty was told ever question the facts again with the weight of the Keleher reputation on the side of Elfego Baca?

But it was not to be. Keleher had a law practice and business interests to tend to, and he wasn't able to undertake the work. As an alternative, he recommended Kyle Crichton, an Albuquerque new-comer. When Elfego sought out Crichton, he accepted the job.

Crichton was a transplanted coal-town Pennsylvanian who had moved to New Mexico in the 1920s because of ill health. He was a big, good-natured man, but then, after having had the ham-like fists of saloon-keeper Milligan shaken under his nose, Elfego wasn't intimidated by size any more than he was by looking down a gun-barrel.

Apparently Crichton's writing career had begun before he came to New Mexico, but *Law and Order, Ltd.* was to be his first book. It was the springboard to further writing. Once he left New Mexico behind with credit for the Baca biography under his belt, he headed for

New York and the literary scene. He was to hone his writing teeth on pseudonymous treatises for left-wing publications, such as the *Daily Worker* and the *New Masses,* as a member of the Communist Party. His books that were published under his own name often seemed to be written more for fun than for profit. They included a biography of the Marx brothers and a story of Anthony Joseph Dexter Biddle, which, when dramatized, had some success on Broadway. He also authored a novel about a Spanish family in New Mexico titled *Proud People.* He had apparently learned some of Elfego Baca's lessons about native New Mexican culture.[121]

But if Elfego wasn't intimidated by Crichton, the same couldn't always be said about how Crichton felt about Baca. Keleher told of a confidential meeting he'd had with Elfego's second choice as biographer when Crichton was well into his work. "This man Elfego Baca scares the hell out of me," Crichton told him while trying to figure out some way to walk away from his writing job. "Here we are only about half way through the story of his life and he has already told me about killing seven men. I am afraid he will go on a rampage some fine day and murder me if I make him out in the book as a bad character. . . . "[122]

Some of Crichton's frustration also showed in his Foreword to *Law and Order, Ltd.* He wrote that friends had told him that laymen, particularly Easterners, would have trouble understanding the psychology of a man like Mr. Baca. Maybe he was describing his own reactions. He responded to the issue with what he said was "the only possible answer." He explained that, "[O]ne who knows the romantic character of the Old Southwest and better still the romantic and *insouciant* attitude of those who stem from the Spanish will not only find such things believable but also quite logical."[123] He didn't claim that he himself had reached that level of understanding.

No records have survived to disclose whether Elfego profited from Crichton's work, or whether its bottom line on the Baca's finances was reflected only in the loss of the lawyer's billable time from hours spent jawboning with his biographer.

Neither Elfego's disappointments nor his financial entanglements ended with the bankruptcy and the appearance of his biography in bookstores. They surfaced again with the death of Bronson Cutting, who had bought Baca's downtown building from the bankruptcy trustee. For many years, Elfego had been a supporter and political ally of Cutting. While serving as a United States Senator from New Mexico, Cutting died in a plane crash near Atlanta, Missouri, on May 6, 1935. He was forty-seven.

When he died, Cutting was one of the young, shining lights of the national Republican party. He was born on Long Island, New York, attended Groton School and was graduated from Harvard. He moved to New Mexico in 1910 to regain his health. He never moved back to New York.

Two years after his move he became a newspaper publisher when he took over the *Santa Fe New Mexican*. In 1927 he was appointed to the U. S. Senate as a Republican to fill a vacancy left by death. He served a year, until election of a successor. When the successor's term ended in a few months, he ran for and was elected to the Senate by the New Mexico voters in 1928. He was reelected in 1934.[124]

During much of the period of Cutting's residence in New Mexico, the Republican party was the party of Hispanic power. At about the time that Cutting's Santa Fe newspaper was occasionally touting Elfego Baca as a possible candidate for governor, the publisher was creating his own base among the Hispanics by organizing American Legion posts in predominately Hispanic counties. At the same time, Elfego was organizing "independent progressive Republican clubs," and showing Cutting how to do it. By this time, Baca was an experienced and effective organizer and skilled at shaping public opinion through his Spanish language newspaper and personal contacts. He was also a dedicated candidate, and while not always successful, his successes and failures had taught him what worked and what didn't.

Though Baca and Cutting toiled together in the Republican cause, they were not intimate friends. The Easterner and the son of the West never entirely trusted each other. Perhaps Crichton's insight about Easterners not understanding the psychology of Elfego Baca was proven right in Cutting. Some have claimed that Bronson befriended Elfego for what he could get out of the relationship, and that he would have been dismayed if his Hispanic protégé had been elected to any of the offices for which he provided token support. The two were never close, and the untamed Baca was always on the outside looking in when Cutting entertained at his Santa Fe home, playing Beethoven sonatas on his grand piano, according to William A. Keleher.[125]

What Keleher did not explain, however, was whose choice it was for Baca to skip the musical ordeals. Perhaps it was not that he received no invitation from the Easterner, but that invitations were declined because Baca never felt at home dealing with the crystal goblet and bone China society set that had been transplanted to Santa Fe. Neither Cutting or Elfego told that part of the story.

Cutting died a wealthy man. That fact caused hope to spring in the hearts of many of the politicians of the time who had borrowed money from the Senator. Cutting didn't let them down. He'd kept detailed records of his loans, and from each borrower had extracted a promissory note. His will gave each an amount equal to the sum he owed. Cutting's east coast estate representatives produced four typewritten pages of beneficiaries of his estate for the use of his New Mexico executor. Gifts ranged from $1,000 to $150,000. The list is overwhelmingly Hispanic. It's at least arguable that it discloses Cutting's prime political supporters in that ethnic group, and that the reason

Cutting had been so intimate with them as to tie them to him by means of loans was due to the influence of Elfego Baca and his newspaper. But Elfego, though he too had borrowed from Cutting, was not on the list.[126]

Some months after Cutting's fatal accident, one of the attorneys for Cutting's estate wrote Baca demanding he turn over to the executors his interest in the building at Sixth and Gold, Albuquerque. Elfego wrote back. He explained that though the building was in the name of Bronson Cutting, in fact he, Elfego Baca, was the sole owner. He invited the attorney to commence proceedings for eviction in the proper court. After a spate of letter writing, the Cutting Estate filed an ejectment suit seeking to have Elfego tossed out.

Elfego had not mellowed. He reached for his pistol for an old-fashioned shoot-out. But after a time, he thought better of his plan for a duel and decided maybe he'd better fight the fight in court. Once again he turned to William A. Keleher, who assigned the matter to lawyers A. H. McLeod and Robert Nordhaus in his office.

The Keleher firm raised two defenses. One was the claim that the deed to Cutting had been intended as a mortgage. The other was by way of an offset, by which Baca claimed that he'd provided detective services to Cutting at the publisher's request, and that he was owed $44,000.

The story Elfego told his lawyers was that the deed to Cutting came out of the financial predicament that led to his bankruptcy. Cutting, to help his sometime political ally and probably to solidify his still valuable political support, had agreed to buy the building from the bankrupt Baca estate, free and clear of its mortgage. He would then hold title for Elfego until he cleared himself of his troubles with Mrs. Baca. In that way, Elfego wouldn't have to argue about its value with Francisquita in the divorce proceeding. The claim, expressed in legalese, was that Cutting held the title in trust for Baca, and that the executors were obliged to let Baca pay off the debt owed to Cutting and then take back the title. Cutting estate attorney Reed Holloman was unimpressed with the defense. He changed his mind, though, when he saw the records that Baca had kept.

For once, Elfego had retained meticulous accounts of his time for detective work for Cutting. He had also kept years of correspondence to and from Cutting and from the lawyers for the estate, who had represented Cutting during his lifetime. Some of that correspondence proved embarrassing to attorney Holloman when he began shuffling through the pile produced by Elfego's lawyers. There was one letter which he especially wished he had never written. In it, he'd spoken derogatorily of his client's political organization. With that, and with the intervention of Bronson's mother and her big New York law firm, who urged that Baca be treated fairly, the case quickly settled.[127]

Keleher's lawyers brought perspective to the Baca-Cutting transaction. They pointed out that in the thirteen years intervening from the date of the deed to Cutting signed by the bankruptcy trustee until the settlement of the ejectment suit, Elfego had enjoyed all the benefits of ownership of the building. His newspaper was published there; it housed the Baca law offices; he paid no rent.

But Cutting profited from the deal, too. Elfego's paper, *La Opinion Publica*, had published articles in Spanish praising Cutting to its Hispanic readers. Elfego had built political support in a segment of the population that was valuable to the politician, and had kept his ally informed about how the political winds were blowing with that ethnic group. In return, Cutting had paid the taxes and insurance. The settlement ended with Baca taking title to the property.

Eventually, Elfego sold his building to the federal government for the construction of a new federal building. The sale didn't close until after he had run a handful of agents from Washington off the property with his twin six-guns.[128]

After the government began construction of its new office facility, a reminder of Elfego's tenancy at the location surfaced. Earth-moving equipment dug up the barrel and cylinder of a Colt 45 bearing the initials "E. B." It was found at the north end of the excavation, between Fifth and Sixth Streets near Gold Avenue. Historians at the time speculated that it was part of a large collection kept by Baca in his building at that corner, and that he had dropped it and lost it in the sand.[129]

It can be inferred that Elfego's preoccupation with his Spanish-language newspaper and his occasional denial of knowledge of the English language are evidence of his continued drive to feel a part of the Hispanic community. There was another series of episodes that seems to illustrate the same need. They were his experiences with the army men from south of the border. His adventures with the revolutionaries were always spiced with their latent aggression. It was a dangerous association; the men from Mexico were always on the edge of violence. But they counted on Elfego when they needed legal help in the United States.

23

◈   PANCHO WHO?

Exposure to the Mexican Revolution nearly vanquished the gun-fighter-turned-lawyer. It drew him into disputes with the federal government that resulted in his call to testify before a Congressional committee, and it produced a federal indictment on conspiracy charges, a price on his head by his one-time-friend, Pancho Villa, and a duel to the death with a phony doctor named Celestino Otero. The fees Elfego earned from his embroilment with the Mexican Generals probably did not make it all worthwhile, but the vicarious satisfaction he drew from association with a revolution intended to help impoverished Mexican peasants may have been enough compensation.

The first revolutionary Elfego met was probably Pancho Villa. The encounter happened before Villa became a military man. Crichton told the story of Elfego's first exposure to the cast from south of the border. It came in 1906, before the Mexican Revolution began.

In that year Elfego, then a forty-one year old lawyer with a reputation for an ability to evaluate mining claims, visited the Mexican town of Parral, southeast of El Paso, for the ostensible reason of checking out mining properties. The real reason was that he was tracking an American cattle thief named Gillette, for whose capture he believed a $50,000 reward had been offered in Kansas City.

Elfego had a man on the ground in Parral keeping an eye open for Gillette, who was rumored to be heading in that direction. Baca's lookout was Charley Hunt, an ex-Bernalillo County Sheriff who had left office with a smudge on his reputation. Sure enough, Charley spotted Gillette and got word back to Elfego, who hot-footed it south across the border. After he'd scouted out Parral for a couple of days, Elfego got together with Charley to plot strategy. The two devised a plan, but not before Elfego had flushed out a scheme that Charley had cooked up all on his own. Crichton did not report how Elfego reacted when he learned that Charley and Gillette had plotted that Gillette would pay Hunt $50,000, Hunt would travel to Kansas City and report that Gillette was dead, collect the reward, then return and split the money with Gillette. The scheme would have left Elfego out in the cold. However he reacted, Elfego didn't pull his revolvers. Maybe he thanked his old friend for having kept Gillette around town until he could ride in, since he moved on with his own plan with never a word about scolding Hunt for his duplicity.

Elfego told Hunt he'd made a deal with a mule merchant who was hanging out in the town—Pancho Jaime, the fellow called himself. Pancho Jaime was Pancho Villa, who'd ridden into Parral under an alias, hoping to sell the American lawyer a clutch of stolen mules. It wasn't Villa's first venture into peddling pilfered livestock. By the time of his Parral visit, Villa had a price on his head for horse theft. His skill at making off with the stock of ranchers made him just the man Elfego needed. Elfego figured that a fellow who could make a living stealing horses and mules just might be available to kidnap a human being. If he'd read his man right, Pancho Jaime could be hired to grab Gillette and spirit him to the border, where Elfego would arrest him and take him in for the reward.

It was not until March 16, 1916, ten years after meeting Elfego, that Pancho Villa would make his raid across the border into Columbus, New Mexico, and be elevated into something of a folk hero among the Mexicans who lived on both sides of the border.

But Elfego left Pancho holding the bag in Parral without learning the horse-thief's real name. The plan Elfego hatched to kidnap Gillette fell through when Elfego, with his lawyer's caution, checked with Kansas City to be sure that the reward was still offered before he set the scheme in motion. He found it had been withdrawn, and Elfego returned to Albuquerque. Pancho Jaime still had his mules to sell, and Elfego Baca was left with only memories.

Five years would pass before Elfego and Pancho Villa would meet again. At the first meeting, it had been the Mexican mule-seller who had sought the contact. The second time, the New Mexico lawyer was the one who took the initiative.

The second meeting took place in 1911. At the time, the Mexican Federalists forces held the town of Juàrez. They were surrounded by the forces of Revolutionary General Pascual Orozco. Newspapers over the Southwest were carrying the stories of the fighting just south of the Texas-Mexico border. Elfego read tales of a certain flamboyant leader of part of Orozco's forces whose name was Pancho Villa. Baca suspected he might be the former mule merchant who had called himself Pancho Jaime. Though news reports suggested that a battle for Juàrez was imminent, Elfego's curiosity wouldn't let him depend on the newspapers for information. He had to go see for himself.

Elfego crossed the border and penetrated into the camp of Orozco, where he asked if he could meet Villa. Orozco agreed and set up a meeting. He would use the occasion to present Villa with a commission confirming that he was a colonel in the revolutionary army. The reunion took place as planned. Elfego verified that Pancho Villa was indeed the former Pancho Jaime, Villa got his commission, though he couldn't read it, and Elfego went back home a happy man.[130]

It's speculation to imagine how Elfego Baca, a lawyer from Albuquerque and sometimes El Paso by way of Socorro, could have slipped over the border and through the Mexican revolutionary army lines without getting shot. His twin Colts would have been little protection against the rag-tag troops who had been whetting their appetites for killing on the battlefields for the past several months.

It might have come about because back when the Mexican revolution broke out, lawyer Elfego Baca had picked for verbal support the side of revolutionists Francisco Madero and Pascual Orozco, which ultimately became the side of Victoriano Huerta. Huerta had stepped into the Mexican presidency for a time, fled from advancing troops, and wanted to be president again. Baca was thought by Huerta to be a potential ally in the state that, with Texas, was close to the action going on just south of the border. After all, the Mexican-American lawyer was influential in the Hispanic communities of the soon-to-be state, and for years had had interests in El Paso, including a branch law office there. It was important for the revolutionaries to have a point of reference in the United States for their own security, since many of their arms and supplies were coming to them across the border, contrary to American law. So Elfego was in a position to pick up legal work if and when the revolutionaries generated entanglements with the law on the north side of the Rio Grande. One of the Mexican generals, José Ynez Salazar, who stashed his family in El Paso while he was out fighting, was to generate a good amount of it.

There were many turns in the road to revolution that would follow Elfego's second meeting with Pancho Villa. A sketch of these convolutions, extracted from scholarly accounts written by Ralph H. Vigil and Allen Gerlach, will be helpful in putting Elfego's activities in dabbles in foreign affairs into historical context.

24

❖ THE MEXICAN REVOLUTIONARIES

The Mexican revolution broke out in 1910, a result of tumult among one aspirant to the presidency after another when President Porfirio Diaz was brought down by the supporters of Francisco I. Madero. Three years following Diaz's fall, Madero's tenuous rule was ended by the forces of Victoriano Huerta, prompting more violence. The new president, Huerta, fled from Mexico to Spain shortly after, when opposing armies advanced on the capital in Mexico City. When Huerta cut and ran, the victors met in 1914 to try to unify the government. But they couldn't stop quarreling among themselves, and the result was a split. The division turned violent. The fighting between the two factions gave Huerta an opening to return and claim the presidency. Somewhere along Huerta's way home he made Elfego Baca his agent in west Texas.

Reports of Huerta's return from Spain bearing cash provided by Germany for buying weapons were verified when American intelligence officials along the Mexican-American border learned that federal neutrality laws were being flaunted by arms shipments flooding south out of Texas. The aim of the Germans was to keep Yankee troops so busy along the Mexican border that they would stay out of Europe. When Huerta popped up in El Paso to kick off his revolution in northern Mexico, the United States government tracked him down. On June 27, 1915, he and General Orozco were arrested in Newman, New Mexico, where they waited to cross the Rio Grande. Uncle Sam had finally lost his tolerance for the use of the United States as a base of operations and an ammunition dump for Mexican revolutionaries.

A month after the arrest, General José Inéz Salazar was cornered and taken in Columbus, New Mexico.[131] Salazar was at the center of Elfego Baca's exposure to the Mexican revolutionaries over the next few years.

Salazar was a prime example of the tangles that grew south of the border as the revolution waxed and waned. Between 1911 and 1916, he fought for three different sides in the Mexican revolution. For a time, he and Villa were side by side. But then Salazar switched, and was ordered to take Juárez from his former ally, Pancho Villa. Salazar failed; he was forced to flee with the troops of commanding general Mercado, leading to Salazar's arrest.[132] However, by September, 1916, Villa was at the head of a force that set out to rescue Salazar, a mission that was successful. After freeing Salazar, Villa made his former enemy his chief of staff.[133] Shortly after, General Salazar was to gain notoriety in the United States, carrying all the way to arguments on the floor of the Senate, for executing an American citizen by firing squad.[134]

It was while Salazar was supporting Huerta that Elfego Baca got his chance to step up and collect a retainer for representing the general. But before Elfego embarked on his representation, he was to meet Pancho Villa once again.

Though the time of the meeting is not entirely clear, Elfego's third encounter with Pancho Villa apparently was shortly after the conclusion of the battle of Juárez. It happened during a meeting that brought the winning generals together in Juarez. Crichton described the occasion.[135]

Madero, who had claimed the Mexican presidency after the battle, met with two of his generals, Orozco and Carranza, at Madero's house in Juárez. Villa was also to be present, but he arrived late. For some reason left unexplained, Elfego Baca was also at the table when the powers of Mexico, however temporary their rule and how tenu-ous their friendship, came together on Madero's front porch. Crich-ton's report of the gathering conveys a surrealistic quality that leaves one who pictures it from the written page some eighty-five years after the fact wondering if he has strayed into *Elfego in Wonderland.*

The victorious generals, the president, and their American lawyer, sat on Madero's verandah, sweating in their heavy uniforms in the Juarez heat, though Orozco seems to have been dressed in bat-tlefield rags. Crichton described him, based on Elfego's depiction of the meeting, as having a huge tear in the leg of his pants. He pulled and tugged at the edges to bring them together over his bare knee, trying to conceal the hole from his more spectacularly dressed com-panions, but it was too obvious to hide.

Milling around in the yard and the street in front of the ve-randah was a crowd of more than a thousand people. The horde had followed the heroes to the Madero hacienda hoping to be drawn into a part of Mexican history, though many of them were Americans.

The discussions grew as heated as the weather, and Elfego watched the action as Villa strode onto the porch and with barely a pause grabbed President Madero by the neck. Villa's aim was appar-ently to throttle the life out of him, probably because of a dispute that he'd had with Madero over whether to attack Juárez. Madero's dal-lying over launching the battle had caused Villa and Orozco to be pictured by the public as gutless incompetents, and neither had been pleased by the label.

Whatever the reason for his excess energy, Villa dragged El Presidente over the porch with his hands digging into Madero's throat, cussing him out and towing him from one end of the verandah to the other. The crowd leaned this way and that as the action moved back and forth, and the gang on the porch edged forward to watch the fun. When the President's eyes began to pop, Orozco strolled to the rescue, summoning a band of underlings to loosen Villa's grip while

Elfego wrestled with his loyalties: should he help Villa, or should he support Orozco's rescue? In the end, he sat in his chair. Villa was hustled off. Soon a report came back to the meeting that Pancho had been stood against a wall and shot. Madero, rubbing his neck, and Orozco, cracking his knuckles, shook hands, smiled falsely, the crowd cheered, friendship ruled. The new presidency was off to a roaring start, and — Elfego was there.

But that evening, after Elfego had returned to his hotel in El Paso, there came a knock at his door from the knuckles of a messenger claiming to be from Villa. After convincing Elfego that Pancho was indeed alive, the messenger escorted Baca to a dark alley, where lurked an unscathed Pancho Villa, no bullet holes in his chest. The resurrected revolutionary made the lawyer a proposition. There would be a considerable amount in it for Baca if he would only cross the border the next day and meet Villa, who would give him certain valuables to hold for him for safekeeping on the American side of the international line. Elfego agreed.

The date was never kept, Elfego reported. American troops sealed the border, and Elfego Baca was stuck in El Paso. But Villa was not one to take being stood up lightly, just as he was not one to smile and remain friends with one who had sat on his hands while he was arrested and carried off to a firing squad, imaginary though the riflemen and their ammunition might have been. Baca was later to suggest that the incident had something to do with the fact that Villa offered $30,000 for the delivery of Elfego Baca.[136]

Whether that connection was a factor or not, there was another reason for the reward.

At some point Elfego engineered the theft of one of Villa's prized Mauser rifles, one of four that had been hand tooled especially for Pancho Villa. Villa knew of Baca's part in the thievery, and he not only wanted the rifle back but would have been only too pleased had it been returned in the cold, still hand of a dead Elfego Baca.

All this to Elfego was an opportunity. There was a $30,000 reward for the delivery of his own person to Pancho Villa. The cash was just waiting to be lifted, and nothing would do except for Elfego to cook up a plot to grab the money and run.

Baca's imagination was up to the task. He would be seized and taken to Villa; his "captors" would collect the $30,000; at a pre-arranged signal, sharp-shooters just outside would riddle Villa with bullets; Elfego would escape; the whole party would return to the United States to celebrate the windfall while Villa either lay dead or sat wringing his hands over what went wrong. But it never happened.

Everything was in place except for one thing. There was too much action underway in Mexico for Villa to set out to scrape up the $30,000.[137]

As a result of all these escapades, Elfego earned a reputation as his country's expert on the principals in the Mexican Revolution. He was called to Washington to testify before a committee of Congress. The subject was Pancho Villa, and Elfego Baca was eloquent in describing him as a cattle and horse thief with an uncanny ability for furnishing his own hacienda with the spoils of war.[138]

The events that transpired after Elfego was to have crossed the border to pick up Villa's valuables for safekeeping in the U. S. at Villa's request raise unanswerable questions. Baca told Crichton that the border had been closed and he couldn't keep the date with Villa. But if that's what happened, how and when did Elfego steal Pancho's Mauser? How, when and where did Elfego learn that that the Villa hacienda was furnished so lavishly with the spoils of war if he'd been prevented from visiting it by the border closing?

How else, unless Elfego did in fact make the trip over the border, did visit Villa's place, and did carry off property to the U. S. to stash for the Mexican general? And did Elfego then keep the general's hoard, or part of it, as compensation for the risks he'd taken? If that's what happened, Elfego had the opportunity to liberate from Villa's possession that prized custom-made Mauser rifle. Otherwise, Elfego's opportunity to make away with the weapon is unexplained.

25

◆ ADVENTURES WITH GENERAL SALAZAR

While all these diversions were claiming Elfego's attention, Salazar's military career continued. In 1914, Salazar, and other Huertista generals, were forced to flee to the United States, where Salazar was arrested at Sanderson, Texas.

Salazar was indicted for violation of neutrality laws. He was tried in the federal court in Santa Fe, New Mexico, and acquitted. Salazar himself said that his attorney was Elfego Baca,[139] though Ralph H. Vigil's account of Salazar's various adventures identifies E. W. Dobson and H. C. Miller, Jr. as his counsel. For at least a short time, however, Elfego was attorney of record. The court file for Salazar's trial reflects that on May 16, 1914, Elfego Baca signed a pleading directed at the charges against Salazar, claiming that they had been so vaguely worded that he and Salazar could not decipher what it was that Salazar was charged with. The motion was dismissed and the case went to trial. Based on the jury result, Salazar should have been a free man.

But despite Salazar's acquittal, Uncle Sam hung onto him. As soon as the jury came in with its verdict, the general was re-arrested by the military and carried off to Fort Wingate, east of Gallup, New Mexico. It took the government a while to figure out its justification for failing to set the general loose, though some time during his stay charges were filed.[140]

It was in the Fort Wingate stockade that Salazar again met Elfego Baca, Esq., Huerta's representative in the United States. Baca had been lured to Fort Wingate and the side of General Salazar by Huerta's payment of a fee of $30,000 and expense money of $3,500.

Huerta forked over the funds through his Washington agent because he sorely needed his general in Mexico, and he thought that Elfego Baca was just the man to spring him out of the stockade. Huerta's plan was that with Salazar free, he'd make Salazar commander of a military district in Chihuahua, with headquarters in Juárez.[141]

At last, Elfego Baca had a return on the investment of his time spent cultivating the Mexican revolutionaries, and it would be earned by the exercise of his legal skills.

Baca rolled up his sleeves and went to work, his dapper secretary and son-in-law, J. B. McGuinnes, alongside. Their aim was to get General Salazar released by quite conventional legal means. Elfego's first step was to seek a writ of habeas corpus, asserting that the prisoner should be released because he was illegally held. Elfego's reasoning was that since the Mexican national was not incarcerated under any treaty between the two countries, Mexico and the U. S., and since he wasn't being held as a prisoner of war, the government had no justification for failing to free his client.

Elfego had a point. It appears that with the general under arrest, the U. S. attorney may have been facing something of a dilemma. Salazar had been acquitted in May, 1914, for violation of neutrality laws, and to try him again on those charges would have placed him in double jeopardy, forbidden by the constitution. Yet the military authorities did not want to turn the renegade military man loose. He had used the United States as a base for much of his operations, and somewhere on the U. S. side of the border he seemed to have a stash of armaments that he dipped into periodically for arms to carry south to Mexico. Uncle Sam did not want the acts to go unpunished. And Salazar had offended the U. S. in other ways. He admitted in his testimony in the habeas corpus hearing that he'd previously skipped bond while he was being held on federal charges in El Paso, but that did not seem to be the basis on which he was penned up in Fort Wingate.[142]

The court file shows that Elfego's petition for a writ of habeas corpus was denied by U. S. District Judge William H. Pope on September 3, 1914. Elfego told the story differently. He said that the writ was granted, and that he and his client ran afoul of hard times along the border; due to wartime pressures the Judge was overridden by Washington, leaving Salazar inside the stockade looking out through the wire.[143]

Whether the writ was denied or granted, Salazar was returned to Fort Wingate under guard. The democratic administration of Woodrow Wilson wasn't through with the general yet, nor had it even started its attack on Republican Elfego Baca.

When Salazar left Santa Fe for Fort Wingate after the habeas corpus hearing, he left behind a transcript of his testimony taken by the court reporter, Earl C. Iden. The record has been preserved in the archives of the U. S. district court for the District of New Mexico.

Salazar's testimony under questioning by his attorney, "Elfego Baca, Esquire," contained the seeds of Baca's subsequent indictment for conspiracy. It gave the U. S. attorney, after he had time to study the transcription and cook up another charge against Salazar, a reason for holding the Mexican general in jail, and if Salazar hadn't been jailed, Elfego wouldn't have been charged with the crime of conspiring to break him out.

The habeas corpus transcript reports Elfego's questioning of the general. Baca, in a skillful and pointed direct examination that moved too quickly to permit any listener to lose interest and move on to day-dreaming, brought out that Salazar had lived in the United States for half of his thirty-six years. He'd been a mining contractor for mine owners in Mogollon, Santa Rita and Lordsburg, New Mexico. At the time at issue, December, 1913, his wife and three children lived in El Paso, though during his incarceration they were to move to Fort Wingate.

Salazar's deposition testimony provides an unusual first-person eyewitness account into battlefield occurrences during the

Mexican Revolution. Salazar had risen through the ranks to become a general of division, his last promotion coming while he was behind barbed wire in Fort Bliss.[144] Salazar also explained that he had gone to the revolution in Mexico with no intention of "seeking for myself general-ship." One reason he had joined the revolutionists, he said, was that he had "seen that all the poor people in Mexico were running bare-footed because on account of the government of Don Porfirio Diaz . . . paid the laboring man a wage of 18 cents a day, and the men had to work twenty hours." It was just the kind of thing that had led Elfego a few years before to champion the poor Mexican sheepherders who were locked in his jail for failure to repay their loans to the rich sheep-owners. Perhaps that shared compassion accounted for Baca's affinity with Salazar.

The meat of Salazar's testimony, insofar as the charges of perjury that Elfego defended him against, came while he was telling about the battle for Ojinaga in Chihuahua in late December, 1913. Salazar was then a brigadier general of Huerta's forces with 1,500 troops under his command. Under attack, his army retreated illegally into the United States, but Salazar said he wasn't with them, meaning he hadn't broken any U. S. laws against entry.

Salazar's version was that while the battle was being fought, he'd received disturbing news that took him away from any engagements that followed. The court reporter's record quotes him: "At this time, I received a telegram from my house in El Paso that one of my children had been stolen or kidnapped, and, as I saw that the enemy had withdrawn, I secured permission from the Commander in Chief for a leave of absence to come to El Paso and see what had happened to my son."

At this point in Salazar's testimony, Elfego led the general to testify about how he and his commanding officer responded after he got word of the kidnapping. In the General's answers the District Attorney later found the seeds for a perjury charge:

Q [by Elfego Baca] State whether or not you were discharged on that day? [sic]

A [by General Salazar] General Mercado told me it was not necessary for me to report further, that from that time he considered me as discharged.

Q State whether or not you went away from Ojinaga at that time?

A That night I left Ojinaga.

Q State whether or not you went to El Paso to see your wife and children?

A Yes, sir.

Q Who did you find when you got there — of your family, I mean?

A I found my wife, and the child who had been lost also.[145]

The upshot of this testimony was to establish, under oath, that Salazar could not have participated in the evacuation of Ojinaga nor straggled across the river into Texas at the head or the rear of an army in retreat. Before the evacuation began he was gone — off to El Paso on emergency family leave to find out what had happened to his six-year-old son. Fortunately for the general and his little boy, it turned out that two days after the kidnapping the boy had been released by the two men who'd seized him. They turned him loose without collecting any of the $5,000 ransom they'd demanded for his return.[146]

Suspicion prompted the U. S. attorney for the district of New Mexico to investigate whether Salazar was telling the truth. He weighed the general's testimony and found it wanting, presented a transcript of the habeas corpus questions and answers to a grand jury, and got an indictment charging that Salazar had lied under Elfego's questioning. Though the general had sworn that he left the Mexican Army while under the immediate command of General Mercado on

January 5, 1914, and crossed over the border into the U. S. to see to his kidnapped son two days later, Salazar didn't believe it was true when he said it, the D. A. claimed. The charge was bolstered by two exhibits offered into evidence at the trial. One was a clipping from the *El Paso Morning Times* reporting the kidnapping of the Salazar six-year-old on December 20, 1913, the other a clipping from the *El Paso Herald* of December 22, telling of the return of the boy. General Salazar had gotten the dates wrong.

Salazar was charged with perjury. This was despite affidavits disputing the allegations, presumably obtained by Elfego Baca, from General Mercado himself and a handful of his colonels and majors. Later, though, according to Ralph Vigil's account of the occurrences, General Mercado was to write that Salazar had indeed taken part in the battle for Ojinaga, and Pancho Villa confirmed that version.[147]

Whichever was true, the result of round one of Salazar's legal battles with Elfego Baca as his counsel was that the Mexican general was buried even deeper into the morass of federal charges, though there was no suggestion made that his alleged perjury was suborned by his attorney. The matter was in the hands of the U. S. attorney's office.

Salazar was scheduled to be taken from Fort Wingate to El Paso to be held pending trial, but federal authorities got wind of a possible plot to effect the escape of the imprisoned general so that he could assume leadership of guerrilla forces south of the border. The scenario was believable because Salazar had a such large array of supporters and so many men ready to fall in behind him if he were to return to Ciudad Juárez, Mexico.[148] The U. S. attorney decided to move his prisoner.

As a result, Salazar's stay in Fort Bliss was short. He was soon taken from there to the Bernalillo County, New Mexico, jail in Albuquerque's Old Town to await trial on the perjury charge. It was there that another plot unfolded, a successful scheme that has often been attributed to Elfego Baca, though without direct verification and with vigorous denials from the alleged principals in the jailbreak that freed Salazar.

Salazar arrived at the Bernalillo County jail from El Paso on November 16, 1914. He stayed around for only four days. His departure is shrouded in intrigue which has yet to be untangled, though the essential facts are known. The cast for the jailbreak that set him free was alleged to have included Bernalillo County District Attorney Manuel Armijo, state game warden Trinidad C. De Baca, Monico Aranda, Deputy Sheriff Carlos Armijo, Porfirio Saavadra and Celestino Otero, alias Pedro Abeyta, and others, as well as the suspected ringleader, Elfego Baca. All of these men were to be indicted for allegedly conspiring to rescue Salazar from the custody of United States Marshal A. H. Hudspeth.

The events that played out, though more than one version has been told, went something like this, largely drawn from the indictment filed against Elfego Baca and the others for conspiracy to liberate the prisoner, and from Robert Hoath LaFollette's book, *Eight Notches*.

Acting sheriff Charles Armijo is on duty at the Bernalillo County jail on the night of November 20. There is also a jailer on the premises. At precisely 9:30 p.m. on that night the jail phone rings. Armijo's deputy picks up the receiver, lifts it to his ear. A voice says there's been a stabbing at the White Star Saloon on Indian School Road, and an officer better get there, quick. The deputy raises his chin to the mouthpiece of the wall-mounted instrument, says that somebody'll be right there. The jailer hangs up and trots out the door.

Enter two masked men. They jump Sheriff Armijo. They wrestle the lawman's handcuffs away from him, drag him outside, cuff him to a fence post. Armijo doesn't yell for help.

The two men dash back into the jail. They leap up the stairs to the second floor. Salazar is waiting, his suitcase packed. The two masked men unlock the door to Salazar's cell in a moment, using the key they've taken from the sheriff. No words are spoken. The threesome clatter down the stairs and out the back door. An automobile is waiting, and the two masked men jump in. Salazar follows. The car speeds off and is never seen again.

Meanwhile, downtown at the Graham saloon Elfego has just bought a round of drinks for himself, Chief Deputy U. S. Marshal Galusha and respected local citizen George Craig. Elfego pulls out his watch and studies it, puzzled. "What time is it, Marshal?" Elfego asks.

Galusha consults his railroad watch, says, "Nine-thirty, Elfego."

Elfego shakes his watch, holds it to his ear, looks at it again, turns to Craig with a question in his eyes. Craig pulls out his pocket watch, studies it, and nods agreement with Galusha.

"Nine-thirty, eh?" Elfego says. He holds up his watch, pulls out the stem and sets it. He pounds his watch against his palm. "Thanks, fellas."

While all this is going on, all but one of the other indicted alleged co-conspirators are busy forging iron-clad alibis for the time of the kidnapping. Bernalillo County District Attorney Manuel Vigil is in Gallup. Trinidad C. de Baca is with eight witnesses, nowhere near the scene. Everybody else has a verifiable excuse except for Celestino Otero, and he won't live to testify. He's shot and killed by Elfego Baca in El Paso on January 31, 1915, prior to the indictments and the conspiracy trial.[149]

The grand jury had its own version of the events, and they closely follow the account given above though the indictment names names and spells out how the escape job was pulled off. The trial is described in a later chapter.

But what of the shooting of indicted co-conspirator Celestino Otero, who didn't live to testify at the trial of Elfego Baca and the others? What of that duel to the death?

Though Otero took two fatal bullets from Elfego's gun several months after the Salazar escape was history, Elfego Baca was charged in the Texas state court in El Paso with Otero's murder prior to the time that the U. S. Attorney in Albuquerque got around to indicting Elfego and the others for conspiring to pull off the Salazar jailbreak. Nevertheless, the escape conspiracy matter got to trial first. For that reason, the conspiracy trial arising out of the jailbreak and its background will be addressed first, and the Otero killing will be described separately.

26

◈ FEDERAL COURT BATTLES

Elfego Baca's first court appearance with General Salazar came in the federal court in Albuquerque as a result of a true bill filed by the grand jury on October 10, 1912. Salazar and four others were charged with procuring "in the United States of America arms and munitions of war and to ship and export [them] from the United States of America to the United States of Mexico . . . " They had allegedly stashed some 50,000 rounds of ammunition in New Mexico while they waited for an opportune time to sneak it out of the country and carry it south to troops fighting for the revolutionists. Elfego Baca got Salazar off. He was acquitted.[150]

Elfego Baca's next federal court appearance also grew out of his ensnarement in the affairs of General Salazar. This time, he would not be seated in the chair of lawyer for a defendant but in the hot-seat of one who was himself charged with a crime.

During the April, 1915, term of court, federal grand jurors in Albuquerque returned an indictment charging that:

> Elfego Baca, Manuel U. Vigil, Trinidad C. de Baca, Monico Arranda, Carlos Armijo, Porfirio Savedra, alias Perfelio Savedra, and Celestino Otero alias Pedro Abeyta, (the last now deceased), and other persons to the grand jury unknown did willfully, knowingly and unlawfully and feloniously, conspire, combine, confederate and agree together to . . . rescue from the custody of an officer, to-wit: the United States Marshal for the District of New Mexico, a certain person, to-wit:

one Jose Inez Salazar [sic], arrested upon a warrant issued under the provisions of a law of the United States. . . .

The indictment spelled out the United States Attorney's version of the jailbreak that had freed General Salazar to return to Mexico for yet more battles. The document, signed by U. S. Attorney Summer Burkhart, laid out a scenario for the jailbreak that reads like an outline of a rejected script for yet another remake of *Mission Impossible*. The task of each of the players is summarized, and the objective of the whole scheme, to "liberate" Jose Ynez Salazar, is repeated like a kind of mantra to inspire the players to get their roles right.

Defendant Carlos Armijo was the jailer. The indictment says he "permitted the cell of the said jail, in which the said Jose Inez Salazar was confined, to be opened, and the said Jose Inez Salazar taken thence and liberated. . . ."

Celestino Otero, who by the time of the issuance of the indictment had died at Elfego's hand alongside the Santa Fe tracks in El Paso, and Monico Arranda "went to the said jail and caused" Salazar to be liberated. Presumably, they were the masked men who overpowered the (allegedly willing) jailer.

Trinidad C. de Baca was charged as the driver of the escape car.

That left tasks unassigned to indicted co-conspirators Elfego Baca, Manuel U. Vigil, and Porfirio Savedra, alias Perfelio Savedra. The implication was that they were the masterminds who put the plan together, cast the other players, and wrote the script for the participants.

The defendants did not sit idly by after they read the U. S. attorney's handiwork. They didn't care much about what the government's case was because they had their alibis, and they would prove they were true if only Uncle Sam would pay for the subpoenas to get their witnesses to the courthouse.

The court file is replete with affidavits signed by various of the defendants. They plead poverty and beg the court to provide them with free process so that they can subpoena the witnesses needed to establish that they were most everywhere except the county jail when Salazar walked out its open door. In each instance, the affidavits outline the expected testimony of the witnesses the defendants wanted to have subpoenaed. In reading the documents, the handwriting on the wall spelling doom for the government's case takes form. They develop an overwhelming brief that would surely lead to acquittals if only half of what the affidavits recited were to be believed by the trial jurors. U. S. attorney Summer Burkhart, as he read the pleas for free subpoenas, must have sensed his case melting away.[151]

But the alleged leaders of the plot didn't ask the court to pay for their subpoenaes, so there's no record of what the witnesses for Elfego Baca and the others Burkhart thought were in charge were expected to swear to. And once the preliminaries were out of the way, it was time for the court and the jury to get down to the business of hearing the evidence.

The prosecution's opening statement was delivered by District Attorney Summer Burkhart himself. An account was carried by *The El Paso Times*. After Burkhart had gone through a prosecutor's usual attempts to ingratiate himself with the jury, he launched into accusing Elfego Baca of masterminding the entire scheme. Then he overstepped. He accused Elfego of "murdering" one of the participants in the jailbreak, Celestino Otero.

Elfego's lawyer, Octaviano Larrazolo, leaped to his feet to object.

It was early in the trial and His Honor was not inclined to let matters get out of hand. He banged his gavel, sustained the objection, and admonished the D. A. not to say or suggest again that Elfego Baca had murdered Celestino Otero. He could say he was killed, but not that he was murdered. That issue would be decided by the jury, His Honor said.

The eleventh witness called by the prosecution was Mrs. Ofelia Ortega de Otero, wife of the victim. She was to be recalled later to testify for the prosecution a second time.

Mrs. Otero was not a happy witness, though she seemed overjoyed to have the chance to fire verbal shots at the killer who'd gunned down her husband. She didn't care that the judge had told the prosecution to steer away from accusing Elfego Baca of murdering her Celestino. The term that described what Elfego had done to her spouse was "murdered;" she'd call a spade a spade no matter what, and the devil take the judge.

Her tale was that her husband had known Elfego Baca well. So well that Baca had agreed to slip him $1,000 for playing a role in Salazar's escape. The reason Otero had been in El Paso, she testified, had to do with the escape plot. Baca had enticed him to go to that city, where he had then murdered him because her husband wanted his promised pay for a job well done. She had to admit that the only thing she knew about the alleged escape scheme and the $1,000 pay-off was what her dead husband had told her, which made her testimony hearsay.

One of the fireworks displays thrown off during the trial was Mrs. Otero's cross examination. Defense counsel tried a ploy that many times backfires in front of a jury. He set out to discredit her testimony by attacking her reputation. Counsel asked her if it were not true that she had been a prostitute before and after her marriage to Otero. She didn't take the suggestion lying down. "It's none of your business!" she spit. The judge apparently agreed, since there's no indication that the question was pursued any further.[152]

Both Elfego Baca and George Craig were sworn in. Though surviving records are silent about their testimony, they surely told about the amazing coincidence of how they and Chief Deputy U. S. Marshal Galusha were all bending their elbows together and checking their watches at 9:30 p.m., when the jailbreak happened. Galusha wasn't called.

In total, the defense team marched thirty-eight citizens to the witness box, according to the court file, which named the witnesses who were put under oath. The thirty-five produced for the prosecution were no match for them, and on the 18th of December, 1915, the jury returned a string of verdicts of acquittal signed by foreman Jose Varela, one for each and every one of the six defendants.

Six acquittals giving a walk to each of six defendants surely throw a reasonable doubt on the accuracy of the charges in the indictment. But wherever stories of Elfego Baca are told, even today, it's suggested that he engineered the Salazar escape.

So how did the escape happen? Who pulled it off? What was Elfego Baca's role, if anything?

As with so many tales of Elfego Baca, what's left is to turn to the hero himself for an explanation. Since U. S. Attorney S. Burkhart's fanciful story was reduced by the jury to the status of one of the tales of the Brothers Grimm, what better place to look than into the memory of Elfego Baca?

In denying any part in the jailhouse events of the evening of the breakout, Elfego told his biographer, Kyle Crichton, a version far different from others that had been told or speculated about. His story centered on a young woman whose multiple talents might have been learned at the feet of the famous World War I spy, Mata Hari.

The seductive female Elfego told about, known only as the beautiful Señorita Margherita, was the caller who lured the jailer away from his post. Crichton produced her picture. She stood looking into the camera, posing in a wide-brimmed hat framing a face that smiled enigmatically. Her hands hung at her sides, she was dressed in a baggy blouson dress and heeled shoes with bows tied over her insteps.[153]

The way Elfego told the story, the 9:30 telephone call made by the lady wasn't from the White Star Saloon at all, but from the ten hundred block on North Twelfth Street. It reported that the home of a certain Mrs. Chavez was being burglarized, and she needed help pronto.

The information proved to be a hoax. The deputy who investigated the report searched high and low for a Mrs. Chavez at the given address. He found nobody there by that name, no person in distress, and no suggestion of a burglary. This according to the way Elfego told it to Crichton in explaining the skills of the admirable Señorita Margherita.

In Elfego's version, the mysterious señorita was a secret service operative for General Huerta. The general not only had the lovely lady on his payroll, but also was the one who'd paid Elfego for Salazar's defense, presumably giving Elfego inside knowledge of how the escape plot was hatched, despite his innocence. Elfego said that Margherita was one of two undercover agents sent to Albuquerque to scout the lay of the land at the jailhouse and plot out an escape route. The woman was not only beautiful, Elfego claimed, but had a way with "rough men," and a skill at operating in the camps of the enemy, whoever the enemy might be.

In addition to the tasks assigned to the señorita, the escape script disclosed by Baca also included roles played by General Orozco and eight other Mexican generals plus a lone colonel. This battalion of the top military echelon of the Mexican Federalists traveled by train from El Paso to Colorado, then back to Albuquerque. The brass of the army had put aside their magnificent uniforms to dress in the dungarees of migrant farm workers with the aim of grubby, inconspicuous anonymity. If stopped by American authorities, they were prepared to explain that they'd been toiling in the Colorado beet fields, and they had the stubs from their train tickets to prove they'd come from that direction.

The task of this collection of army men was said by Elfego to be to lounge on various Albuquerque street corners ready to interfere with pursuit of Salazar once he'd been sprung, if any chase developed. Nothing in the report of Crichton, as told to him by Baca, divulged who was minding the battlefields in Mexico while eight generals and the lone colonel sought to free yet another general from custody, though the account admits that if they'd been caught Huerta's revolution would have come to a quick end. Nothing, either, told how this contingent of military brass was put together so quickly and hustled onto a train for Colorado. The story is silent, also, about how the timing so exquisitely fell into place, allowing the band to reverse directions and chug back into Albuquerque while the exquisite señorita blew into town with her accomplice and eyed the terrain, all during the four days Salazar unexpectedly spent in the Bernalillo County hoosegow.

By Crichton's account, acting Sheriff Armijo wasn't cuffed to a fence post at all, but was tied to a chair and gagged, then slugged in the jaw. The masked men who rescued him, and the General himself, all jumped into the same car and drove down Central Avenue eastward, past the Graham Bar. Elfego said he learned later about a rumor that Salazar had leaned out the window as the vehicle passed the bar and waved in the direction of his lawyer and bid him farewell. The trio caught the 10:05 train to El Paso, and the jailer returned to the jail at 10:20 to find his famous prisoner long gone.

While posses combed Albuquerque for days, searching for Salazar, rousting citizens from their beds and shadowing Elfego Baca as he went about his daily activities, Salazar and the clutch of generals, trailed by the single colonel, made it all the way to Mexico, where they once again took up their banners.[154]

As for Elfego Baca, he could take consolation in the fact that his fee for defending General Salazar had been paid in advance. But alas for Elfego's finances, he learned after his retainer was handed over that he'd misjudged how much to ask for when he requested $30,000. The general's Washington representative was authorized to write him a check for up to $100,000.[155]

But where does all this leave the advocate for Elfego Baca in deciding which version of the jail break is the true tale? How did it really happen? What was Elfego's part, if any, in the general's escape?

District Attorney Burkhart's take on the occurrences was thoroughly discredited when the jury handed him six acquittal verdicts telling him he was dead wrong. So Elfego's story line, the shadowy, improbable Señorita Margherita and all, is all that was left standing at the end of the day. It remains as the most credible surviving report of the jailbreak, though on the face of it it's incredible indeed. But it has never been voted down by a jury of twelve good and true peers of the Hero of Frisco.

So Elfego's energetic detractors have been left to resurrect the indictment story that the jury of twelve rejected after having heard it from the mouths of witnesses called with all the majesty the United States government could muster. And Baca critics have been able to assemble no new evidence to show that the jurors were wrong.

But Elfego was not yet out of the legal woods. He still had to face that murder charge for killing Celestino Otero. And he'd be standing before a judge and jury in El Paso rather than in one of the familiar courtrooms in Socorro or Albuquerque.

27

◈ SET-UP FOR MURDER

Albuquerque residents who stepped through their front doors and into the cold to pick up their copies of *The Albuquerque Morning Journal* on February 1, 1915, found their papers folded to the headline: "ELFEGO BACA SHOOTS AND KILLS CELESTINO OTERO ON STREETS OF EL PASO; THEN GIVES HIMSELF UP."

As they stood there, shivering in their bathrobes, their eyes would have dropped to the subheading: "Turbulent Mexican Politics Believed to be at Bottom of Tragedy Enacted Last Night."[156] Surely, their cold feet would have been forgotten, replaced in their minds by a string of questions prompted by the message carried in the thirty point type.

How had Elfego dug himself into such a hole? Had he buried himself this time? Would a conviction for murder followed by the hangman finally lead him to the grave he had escaped so often? Or would he pull himself out of the latest mess without so much as a speck of dust on his black woolen suit?

Everyone in Albuquerque over the age of twelve knew that Baca and a cadre of suspected co-conspirators, including Otero, were the subjects of publicized snooping by federal detectives into how they had planned, aided and abetted the escape of General José Inéz Salazar from the Bernalillo County jail. To the Baca bashers, it was all so obvious. All one had to have done was read the papers that reported General Salazar's jailbreak a few months earlier. In the days that had followed the general's flight, the speculations of the feds had been spread as fact over the front pages. *The Albuquerque Morning*

Journal had named the names of the suspects, featured their faces in two column pictures, and published maps and drawings of how the escape was pulled off. It was as though the reporter had been there taking notes. It was just a matter of time until the settling dust would bury Elfego and his friends.

One of the names of suspects that had been listed was Celestino Otero. Maybe he needed to be silenced; maybe Baca had blown away Otero because he was about to sell out Elfego and his henchmen by cooperating with the United States attorney. But would even the Hero of Frisco have taken such a huge risk at a time that the U. S. marshals and prosecutors were half a step behind and getting closer? So what had really happened?

The preliminary facts weren't disputed, though versions of why and how the shooting came about began to proliferate with the first issues of the newspapers to carry the story. Even in the early accounts the bulk of the shadow cast by Elfego Baca over all the facts began to shape the telling. He wasted no time in releasing a preemptive statement for those who wrote the news.

It's sometimes said by lawyers that "any publicity is good publicity as long as they spell your name right." If that's true, beginning with the first issues of the newspapers to follow the shooting, Elfego Baca reaped a harvest by killing Otero. The El Paso and Albuquerque papers had a field day with the events of January 31, 1915, and the aftermath down through the reports of the murder trial.

Elfego's picture was spread across the *Albuquerque Morning Journal* of February 1. No mug shot with height scale behind and a number across the chest for Elfego. Beneath the black-suited portrait of the somber but confident lawyer, reflecting the avoirdupois and the gravitas of middle age, was the caption: "ELFEGO BACA. Noted politician and lawyer of Albuquerque, who killed Celestino Otero, also of Albuquerque, in El Paso, Sunday afternoon." Elfego sat there, looking into the center of the camera's eye, a full head of black hair that hadn't receded at all, heavy black eyebrows and mustache, black bow tie, black suit. He held both hands over his chest, the right grasping a lapel, the left resting over his heart as though swearing to tell the truth. It wasn't difficult to see why some of his cronies had awarded him the nickname "Nap," short for Napoleon. With two hands on his chest he'd gone the classic hand-in-the-coat pose of the French Emperor one better.

The write-up under the photo wasn't limited to the facts of the shooting. The reporter might have been accused of acting as a paid publicist for Elfego Baca. He wrote:

> In a country where, in the past, picturesque characters have been the rule rather than the exception, it is doubtful if a more picturesque character than Elfego Baca ever lived. A man of undoubted courage, he has lived through some of the most stirring events in the history of New Mexico, and there have been many occasions when his nerve was put to the supreme test. . . . [I]t is generally believed that there are several notches on the Elfego Baca gun, for he was at one time deputy sheriff of Socorro County during a period when a peace officer needed to be extremely handy with firearms, and it is a well known fact that he is the deadest of dead shots.

The reporter then summarized the story of the standoff at Frisco, concluding the tale of Baca's heroism by saying, "This was in the year 1884, when Mr. Baca was little more than a boy . . . ."

A collection of more articles about Elfego, Pancho Villa and the jailbreak appeared on the day following the killing, and each and every one of the stories spelled Elfego Baca's name correctly. Gone were the days when reporters called him "Elfigo."

While the newsmen were gathering their facts, Elfego made it easy for them. There was that statement he issued setting out his version of how he had happened to kill Celestino Otero. Added to Elfego's hand-out, three separate court hearings in two days spit out more information than the average reporter could digest in a year. Through it all, a handful of facts emerged.

Elfego Baca shot and killed Celestino Otero in El Paso on Sunday afternoon, January 31, 1915. Elfego was in town to look for his son, George, who had disappeared from the New Mexico State Agricultural College campus in Mesilla Park, on the edge of the southern New Mexico city of Las Cruces. George had spent the Christmas holiday visiting with his sister, Mrs. Garcia, who lived in El Paso. Elfego thought he might find the young man still hanging out in the Texas city, which is only a few miles south of Las Cruces.

In El Paso, Elfego asserted in the statement released to the press just in time for the Albuquerque readers of the editions of February 2, he had met his old friend, Dr. F. B. Romero. The distraught father was ready for a break in the search for young George. What better distraction than to visit the training camp of world heavyweight champion boxer Jess Willard. The Champ had set up a training camp in Ysleta, just east of El Paso, to prepare for his next bout, which was to be held in the border city. Dr. Romero and Elfego met at the Paso del Norte Hotel, where Elfego had a room. From there, they had planned to drive to the Willard camp.

Dr. Romero parked his car on the street, entered, and asked the desk clerk to ring Baca's room. The pair was ready to retrieve Dr. Romero's car for the drive when Celestino Otero walked into the lobby. The day was overcast and cold, and Otero wore an overcoat.

According to Elfego's own account, he knew Otero "only slightly." When Otero sidled up, Elfego greeted him and introduced him to Dr. Romero. Baca noticed that Otero kept his hand in his overcoat pocket and was reluctant to shake hands, though he finally did. Otero said he wanted to talk business with Elfego, but he said he didn't want to visit in a corner of the hotel lobby. He begged off by explaining that the subject for discussion was too private for such a public area. He turned down an invitation to talk in Elfego's room, instead suggesting that they go to the saloon owned by an M. Andujo (Marsial Andujos), who had been a client of Baca's and who also wanted to see the lawyer. Elfego agreed, believing that Andujo probably wanted to talk. It was a logical conclusion. The man owed him some money as a result of legal services provided to him in obtaining his release from charges of neutrality law violations as a co-defendant with General José Inéz Salazar and others.[157]

Dr. Romero and Elfego headed toward the doctor's car to drive to Andujo's bar after Otero turned down their offer of a lift. Otero asked them to let him have a head start since they would be driving and he'd be walking. They noted that as Otero left, he was joined by a man Elfego believed he recognized as a former officer in General Salazar's army, Sylvestre Quevedo, though he wasn't sure. The *Journal* account identified Quevedo as "a noted bandit whose case he [Baca] refused to take when Quevedo was held at Fort Bliss."

Baca's press release explained his tenuous connection with Quevedo. While he was defending General Salazar, it said, he'd ignored a letter from Quevedo seeking to hire him to defend against the same kind of charges that were pending against Salazar. That was the extent of the contact.

All in all, the presence of Quevedo wasn't reassuring to Elfego. Combine the attendance of a Mexican revolutionary warrior disgruntled because of rejection by the lawyer he wanted to hire with the other coincidences of Otero's behavior, and there was enough suspicion to titillate Elfego's nerve endings into working overtime.

En route to the saloon, Romero drove "a roundabout way" so that Otero would have time to reach Andujo's place. When Dr. Romero pulled up to the saloon, it was obvious that it wasn't open since it was a Sunday, though there were a number of Mexicans standing around outside. Dr. Romero and Elfego couldn't see Andujo among the men. Baca told Dr. Romero to drive on—he was uncomfortable stopping near a crowd in that part of town.

Dr. Romero slowly rolled his car past the standing men. As the two in the auto reached the Santa Fe Railroad tracks not far from the saloon, the car had to stop for a switch engine. The delay allowed Otero and his companion to come up behind them on foot. Otero hailed them from the sidewalk when the locomotive had passed. Dr. Romero made a U-turn and stopped. Elfego opened his door and got out to find out what Otero had to say.[158]

Elfego told of the occurrences at the railroad crossing in detail during the habeas corpus hearing. In the process, he made it clear that though he was forty-five, his reflexes were those of a far younger man. His testimony was quoted in *The Albuquerque Morning Journal* of February 3.

> I got out of the automobile and walked several feet towards Otero. He told me to go on down to the saloon and I refused, saying that he could say anything to me he wished right there. I noticed that he held his hand in his coat pocket, and asked him his reason for such action.
>
> "I'll show you, you — — — — —-," he replied and jerked his gun from his pocket, firing at me as he drew it. Before he had his arm straightened out in front of him I whirled to one side and the bullet passed through the front of my coat. As I whirled I drew my own automatic and fired. He staggered back, attempting at the same time to fire his revolver, which seemed to be jammed. I fired a second shot and he fell to the ground, his pistol falling from his hand at the same time. He raised himself up on one hand and felt about him on the ground as if looking for his gun and cried to me, "Don't shoot again."

Otero was taken to an emergency hospital, where he lived for about fifteen minutes. As for Elfego, he was facing yet another murder rap, this one in Texas, But he had once faced Texas six-gun justice and come out on top, so surely he could handle an appearance before Texans in the civilized atmosphere of an oak-paneled courtroom.

28

◆ WHAT HAPPENED?

After the killing, Elfego held a press conference. He announced to newsmen that he had been suspicious about Otero, prompted by the man's furtive behavior. Those suspicions explained why he was so alert when Otero drew his pistol. "I confidently believe that Otero intended to kill me in the hotel. His hesitancy to shake hands and the fact that he kept his hands in his overcoat led me to believe that he was only deterred from shooting me by the cordiality with which he was received."[159]

The *Albuquerque Journal* repeated the story that Otero's automatic pistol had jammed after Otero had fired the shot that ripped through Baca's coat, and that Baca then fired while Otero was trying to shoot again. As Otero fell to the sidewalk, Quevedo, or whoever the man with Otero had been, raced off toward Mexico.[160]

The *El Paso Morning Times* reported that an Inspector Briggs of the Custom House was the first "American" to reach the scene. He had heard the firing from about a block away and looked up. When he saw what was going on, he sprinted toward the action. As Briggs was running, he watched Dr. Romero and Elfego drive off. He came upon Otero lying on the ground, groaning, his .32 Savage automatic near his outstretched hand. Clutched in the hand was a small knife, unopened, he said.[161] When Briggs picked up Otero's pistol, it discharged in his hand. Eight cartridges, two of them fired, were found in the magazine when the weapon was turned over to the police.[162]

Meanwhile, after the shooting Dr. Romero drove his friend away from the scene to the house of George Armijo, who lived in

Palms Court on West Missouri Street. There, Baca called the police and turned himself in, handing over the Colt .32 revolver he had used to kill Otero. He admitted the killing. The police took him into custody and hustled him off to the city lockup. At the jail, Elfego showed police the bullet hole in the front of his coat just below the second button. There was no scorching and no powder burns, as the lawmen would have expected had the shots been fired from very close range.[163]

Before sunset on the day of the shooting, Baca had hired attorney Harris Walthal of El Paso. Exactly twenty-four hours after Otero died, Elfego was indicted for murder by the El Paso grand jury. The speed came about because Elfego waived a preliminary hearing and asked for the grand jury indictment. It was a shocking move. A "Special Dispatch to Morning Journal" of February 2 said, "The indictment was made at his own request, which so far as is known is the first time that a man accused of murder has ever requested to be indicted by a Texas grand jury."

The police held Baca overnight since a bond hearing couldn't be scheduled until the next day. When morning came, after the examining hearing on the criminal complaint filed before a magistrate, there was a habeas corpus hearing. The result was that Elfego was freed on $7,500 bail. No reason was given in the papers for the unprecedented request for an immediate grand jury indictment.

The next morning, after news reporters had scribbled their notes at the examining trial and at the habeas corpus hearing on the issuance of bond, and after rumors had leaked out about testimony at the secret grand jury proceedings, at least three versions of what had prompted the shooting were floated out, and soon there was to be a fourth. The first was the reason Elfego gave: self-defense. He'd been fired at, and he had to fire back or die. But that explanation was too easy for Baca's enemies.

The second, and the story that excited the Baca detractors the most, was the claim that the killing was a set-up and an ambush. The plot was orchestrated, they said, and pulled off by Elfego Baca himself, because Otero was about to blow the whistle on Baca and other alleged co-conspirators who were believed to have sprung José Ynéz Salazar from the Bernalillo County jail. Baca had planted the gun on the ground near his victim, the story went, and Baca hadn't acted in self-defense at all.

The ambush version came from El Paso District Attorney Bridgers himself. His theory about motive, one that his office released to the press in Albuquerque and El Paso, had Elfego Baca and Celestino Otero hand in glove in the scheme to liberate José Ynéz Salazar, and had Elfego killing Otero to keep him from testifying. The possibility that Elfego had shot a guy who might be a witness against him was plenty enough for motive, Bridgers believed.

The prosecutor's theory that Elfego had killed Otero in a cold-blooded ambush and then covered it up didn't go far. It was born at the bond hearing and expired at the same place. Bridgers claimed that Baca had planted the gun found with Otero near the dying man's hand. Elfego had bought the gun at an El Paso pawnshop shortly before the killing, Bridgers said, though the Albuquerque paper that reported his tale told of no proof to back up the D. A.'s brainstorm.

So Bridgers struck out. Nobody showed up at the hearing to back up his concoction. Nobody who watched or listened in the courtroom bought it. With no facts, and with no way to challenge eyewitnesses who said Otero had shot first, the claim that the gun was planted seems to have shriveled and died. It wasn't reported, either, that the prosecutor had any response to earlier comments Baca had made about fear for his life. It was those declarations that formed the foundation of yet another version of the motive for the killing, though this version tied into the ambush theory.

That motive was reported in the *Albuquerque Journal*, in its February 1, 1915, coverage of the shooting and its aftermath. The story told was that when Baca was in El Paso a month or so earlier, he had been interviewed about how he was affected by the revolution started by his client, José Ynéz Salazar. Baca's response to the reporter's questions was unexpected: "[T]he Albuquerque lawyer admitted to newspaper men that he was being shadowed by [Pancho] Villa's secret agents in El Paso and feared he would be shot in the back from ambush. . . ." The would-be assassin was identified as "Gachupin," a name commonly applied, the paper said, "to all Spaniards."

The same issue of the paper reported that Elfego had been told by one who had seen General Villa's "proscription list" that Baca's name was "at the top of the roll."[164] All that tied into motive, the D. A. figured, when he speculated that Elfego thought Otero was Villa's agent who was out to execute him, and that Elfego had shot him preemptively to save himself.

So had the Hero of Frisco grown paranoid? Was Elfego ducking shadows? Were his worries farfetched?

To one who'd known from past experiences how Salazar's enemy, General Villa, was bound to have his vengeance for betrayal, it would have been only reasonable if Elfego harbored some degree of suspicion. Elfego was mindful of the fact that at one time Pancho Villa had put a $30,000 reward on his head over something as trifling as a stolen rifle worth a fraction of that amount. And the worries would not have been trivialized by one who knew that Pancho Villa, when crossed, had had no better judgment than to dare the armies of the United States to take him on when he led a handful of raiders across the border into Columbus, in southern New Mexico. Now, Elfego Baca had re-declared himself an enemy of Villa by aligning himself as the attorney for Villa's perennial nemesis, General Salazar. And Villa was known to have his tentacles firmly extended into Texas along the border.

But who was Celestino Otero and why was he gunning for Elfego Baca? How did he fit into the jailbreak of General Salazar? Was he on Pancho Villa's payroll?

Otero had had some troubles of his own with the law. He'd been indicted by a grand jury the year before his death, and he'd once been
charged with attempting to stab a man during a quarrel in an alley
behind an Albuquerque bar.

Otero had also been prosecuted in New Mexico for practicing medicine without a license when he branched out from his patent
medicine sales business and started prescribing treatments and medi-
cines for his customers. Otero had then left Albuquerque for Texas,
and it was known on the streets of the New Mexico city that he had
been in other trouble with Albuquerque authorities. In El Paso he was
known as Dr. Pedro Abeyta, so he may have been carrying on his un-
licensed medical practice in that city.[165]

The part of Otero's life that fueled the fires under the prosecutors in both Albuquerque and El Paso was the connection to Celestino
Otero as one of the other indicted alleged conspirators in the federal
court jailbreak case. Though the charges that named Otero wouldn't
be filed in court until after Otero's death, he was named as a defendant and one of the conspirators. Another named defendant would be
Bernalillo County District Attorney Manuel U. Vigil.

When Otero's widow appeared before the El Paso grand jury,
she admitted that she and her husband had been tenants on a ranch
owned by Vigil within sight of the church in Alameda, just north of
Albuquerque. It was the place where Salazar was believed to have
holed up just after he walked out of the Bernalillo County jail, as had
been reported by Albuquerque newspapers at length. This connection led to speculation as to the involvement of Otero and Vigil, right
along with guesswork about Elfego Baca's role. Similar speculation
had been splashed over the pages of the Albuquerque morning paper
the days following the break, leading to conjecture in El Paso that Elf-

ego might have wanted to close Otero's mouth.

The United States attorney's version of Otero's role had it that Celestino Otero, alias Pedro Abeyta, and Monico Arranda liberated the imprisoned José Ynéz Salazar from jail once the cell door had been opened by jailer Carlos Armijo. Presumably, the Otero-Arranda pair were the masked men described by some who worked up tales of the escape. Eye-witnesses had reported that one of the masked men was short, one was tall. Otero was "Andalusion" and short, as the *Albuquerque Morning Journal* described him. Arranda was tall. For some, the match in height was enough to convict. The district attorney was certain that Salazar had been taken to the Vigil ranch by the two men to wait out the initial searches following his liberation. Whatever his part, if any, Otero had not stuck around Albuquerque to celebrate the General's freedom.

If anything definitive were to be learned about exactly what had happened, it would have to come out at Elfego's trial.

29

◈ TRIED AGAIN FOR MURDER

The timing of Elfego Baca's trial for the murder of Celestino Otero could scarcely have been worse for Elfego. General Salazar was tried for perjury in Santa Fe the week of December 6, 1915, with the jury returning its verdict on December 9. Though the indictment against Salazar had arisen out of statements made by the general under the questioning of attorney Elfego Baca, Elfego saw no barrier to his representation of the general, so he had planned to represent Salazar at his trial for perjury. But there was too much at stake for Elfego personally in all the charges pending against him to let him ignore his own defense while he fought for General Salazar. Though Elfego retained an interest in the outcome and probably attended the trial, he passed the defense on to another attorney. As a result, Elfego lost his fee from Salazar, and he would have needed the cash to pay his own lawyers in El Paso.

Less than a week after Salazar's acquittal, the conspiracy trial against Elfego and his alleged crew in the escape of General Salazar was called in the same courtroom. The harvest of acquittals in that prosecution came in on December 18. Elfego then had a month and six days for celebrating Christmas and getting himself down to El Paso for the defense of the case against him for murder. The Otero trial was to start on January 24, 1916.

The Baca family celebration of Christmas was surely abbreviated by necessity and made less than spiritual by anxiety. No sooner had the ink dried on the acquittal verdicts in the jailbreak prosecution than Elfego had to hustle south by train to El Paso to meet with his defense counsel and track down witnesses for the Otero murder trial.

In the three weeks between Christmas and the commencement of the El Paso trial, Elfego dug up an eyewitness the newspapers and the prosecution had missed.

Perhaps it was that last-minute dogged preparation and the unearthing of someone who had seen the whole episode but had kept his mouth shut about it until Baca nosed around that led to the story that even today is often told in New Mexico with a grin when the subject of Elfego Baca comes up. The tale goes like this: Elfego, sitting in his Albuquerque office, is sent a retainer by telegraph to bind his representation of a man in Texas who is charged with a murder in that state. Elfego fires a telegram right back: "Leaving on next train. Bringing eyewitness."[166]

The eyewitness Elfego discovered in the days just before the Otero trial was Jeff Bransford, who worked for the Reclamation Service in El Paso as a patrolman on a canal near the place of the shooting. The *El Paso Morning Times* called Bransford the "star witness for the defense." Bransford surfaced when a friend of Elfego's, Louie Hill, and Bransford got into an argument about the Otero shooting. Hill was defending the accuracy of a version he'd read in a local newspaper account. Bransford trumped him by bragging that he was there and had seen it all.

Baca learned of Bransford by accident when he dropped into Hill's office to talk to his friend. Hill told him he'd run into a man who knew something about the case. Elfego wanted to know all about it, and when Hill told him, he reacted. He had Bransford standing by to testify when the defense opened its case. The trial was called in the El Paso County courthouse. Presiding was Judge W. D. Howe.

Throughout jury selection and the entire trial, Elfego dressed in the suit he'd worn when he killed Otero. Though not marked as an exhibit, the suit would, in fact, parade before the jury as Exhibit A for the defense. Elfego had done nothing to mend the bullet hole through the front of the jacket.

It takes no stretch of the imagination to visualize the picture: the rotund figure straining to sit up telegraph-pole straight behind the table reserved for the defendant and his lawyers, making sure that the hole wouldn't be hidden from the jurors below the table top; Elfego worrying the hole with pokes of his finger through it while his lawyer points at him, asking each jury panel member examined if he knew the man who killed Celestino Otero. Self defense was being acted out from the moment the defense team set up at their assigned places.

Elfego took a "lively interest' in the selection of the jury, according to the *Albuquerque Morning Journal* of January 25. During the jury voir dire, opening statements and the prosecution's case, he sat at the defense table surrounded by his three lawyers, Harris Walthal, T. A. Falvey and E. R. Elfers, fiddling with that hole in his suit coat and probably scribbling notes and passing them to his defense team.

When the jury was seated and after opening statements, the prosecution began its case before a full courtroom. It called four witnesses on the first day. The lead-off star was the widow Ophelia Otero.

Mrs. Otero told the jury that she and Celestino had been living on a ranch owned by Bernalillo County, New Mexico, District Attorney Manuel U. Vigil. The couple had come to El Paso about a month before the shooting, she said, so her husband could collect some money from Elfego Baca. She didn't explain why the money was owed. She had known Baca about eight years. Otero knew him, too. She knew this for a fact because Elfego had given her husband a ride in his automobile one day while they left her behind on the curb, waiting.

After laying this background, District Attorney W. W. Bridgers coaxed his witness into discussing the Salazar jailbreak under the guise of pinning down when Baca had given her husband a ride.

Asked if she knew Salazar, she said, "He was hiding at the ranch."

Defense counsel Walthal leaped to his feet, shouted an objection, and moved to strike the comment. Judge Howe pounded his gavel, leaned forward, admonished the witness to answer the questions put to her, to listen to them carefully and not to anticipate what the next question might be, and to stop the ad libbing. Turning to the jury, he said, "The last answer by Mrs. Otero is stricken. You are instructed not to consider her answer."

But Bridgers didn't hold back. The questioning that followed was reported by the *El Paso Morning Times*. Bridgers, over defense objections, pushed for information on when it was that Elfego gave her husband a ride with respect to the time General Salazar was at her house. The D. A. was probably disappointed when she answered that it was several days before the General came. It was also true, she said, that Manuel Vigil gave her money to come to El Paso.[167]

Again the defense attorney was on his feet, too late to interrupt the answer. Again he shouted an objection. Again Judge Howe sustained and instructed the jury to ignore Mrs. Otero's response.

To close out the account of the first day of the trial reported in the *Albuquerque Morning Journal*, the reporter didn't hesitate to speculate about what Mrs. Otero might say on the second day of the trial, or to mix rumor with testimony. He wrote:

> The principal witness for the prosecution this afternoon was Mrs. Otero. . . . Her testimony, so far as introduced this afternoon, was to the effect that Baca deliberately killed her husband. . . .
>
> [T]he story is generally well known to those who followed the trial of the conspiracy case at Santa Fe a few weeks ago. It was to the effect that General Salazar had been secreted at Otero's home at Albuquerque, and that Manuel Vigil and Baca were to pay him for his services in the escape of the Mexican

officer. The money was slow in coming, she said, and he had made demands on these parties. He was told to go to El Paso and the matter would be taken care of. This he did, and on the day of the killing he was deliberately inveigled to the place of the shooting and put out of the way. . . .

Just how far the present witness will be allowed to testify is not certain. The defense is fighting every statement made.

Jim Briggs, the customs inspector, walked up to the stand at the call of the prosecution the second day. He'd picked up the gun that was either Otero's or had been planted by Elfego, he said, put it in his pocket, then found a phone and called the police. Later, he took out the weapon and it discharged in his hand. There were six other cartridges in the magazine.

Santa Fe Railroad employees who had been on the switch engine when Dr. Romero stopped his automobile to let it pass were also called. R. A. McCoy, a switchman, gave his version of what he saw. Though he heard some shots and turned his head to look, he couldn't say who fired the shots. When he first saw Otero, the man was staggering. Though McCoy saw Otero's hands, he saw no pistol in them, though there was a weapon lying ten or twelve feet away.

Though when considered singly, the testimony produced by the District Attorney's witnesses was ambiguous at best, the prosecution was able to put on enough of a case to withstand the motions of the defense for a directed verdict of acquittal. It was the turn of the defense team.

The jury listened, leaning forward, hands cupped to their ears while Trinidad Zamora, a porter in Andugo's saloon, where Elfego had gone to meet Otero at the latter's request, told his tale in tortured English. He said he lived in Juarez, but was in El Paso during the month of January.

Zamora had seen Otero and Baca at the saloon on various occasions, he said, though the reporter's account of the cross-examination didn't say whether they'd been there at the same time. Baca had been there the day before the shooting. When the shooting took place, Zamora was outside the saloon, doubtless one of the crowd of men hanging around the front door that caused Elfego to tell Dr. Romero to drive on.[168]

Zamora had known Baca six days before the killing, and had known Otero for twenty days. The *El Paso Morning Times* quoted a part of Zamora's examination that was omitted by the Albuquerque paper, and it was more direct than anything the prosecution had come up with:

> I saw Mr. Baca before the killing. That was about 3 o'clock. About fifteen minutes later the killing happened. Baca was in an automobile. The deceased raised his hand and the automobile stopped. The deceased raised his hand up and fired a shot at Mr. Baca. Mr. Baca then fired two shots at him. The deceased fell.
> What did you do then?
> I left.
> Where did you go?
> I went to a picture show.[169]

Standing by to testify for Elfego were several prominent citizens from Albuquerque. District Attorney Manuel U. Vigil was a witness for the defense. Judges F. W. Parker and W. H. H. Llewellyn were there as character witnesses for lawyer Elfego Baca. So was E. L. Medler, who as an assistant U. S. prosecutor had written a letter to the state mounted police castigating Elfego Baca for his handling of the Chinese inspector and suggesting that the Department of Justice look into the matter.

Dr. Romero took the stand. His added little to other testimony, though he had his own perspective from having been closer to the action. His testimony, too, was recorded by the El Paso reporter. Defense counsel took him through events at the scene of Otero's shooting:

> [Q] What was [Otero] doing at the time Baca got out of the machine?
> [A] He had his hand in his right pocket. He told Baca to get out of the machine.
> [Q] What was the first thing these two men said to each other?
> [A] "Well," Otero said, "why didn't you go to the place you said you would meet me?" Baca said, "what have you got in your pocket?" Otero pulled out his gun, cursed Baca and his mother and then shot. He was walking back. His teeth were grinding. Baca drew his gun from his right hand hip pocket. He did not shoot until Otero had shot at him. Baca shot twice.

As for Jeff Bransford, the last minute witness Elfego had unearthed when he went to El Paso to prepare for the trial saw the shooting from about 300 to 350 feet away and didn't equivocate about who had fired first. The dead man had fired the first shot, and Bransford knew because he had seen it all.

The district attorney wasn't happy about the happenstance that Bransford had been found only days before the trial began. Though he tried to discredit the witness, the only result was that the story was repeated again and again for the jurors.

Elfego took the oath and testified in his own behalf. He told about his meeting with Dr. Romero and their decision to visit the Willard training camp. After the two had made their plans in the hotel lobby, Baca explained that he "went up and got my pistol because there had been so much talk about this Salazar business." He explained to the jury that he had been deputy sheriff, United States marshal, county superintendent, district attorney and city mayor. Currently, he said, he was publisher of *La Opinion Publica*, and "a story to the effect that Otero had assaulted a woman had appeared in the paper." He left it to the jury to connect Otero's anger at the reporting of the assault to his motive for taking a shot at him.

Elfego also denied any part in Salazar's escape. He denied that he had ever ridden in any automobile with Otero, as Otero's wife had testified. Authenticating his own testimony, he solemnly raised his hand, saying, "If any reputable citizen of Albuquerque will testify that they saw me riding with that man, I will enter a plea of guilty to this charge."[170]

Closing arguments were an anti-climax. Despite his pre-trial huffing and puffing accusing Baca of having planted the gun found near Otero, District Attorney Bridgers seemed to have had the air let out of him.

The El Paso paper's front page when the jury came in was headlined, "ELFEGO BACA FOUND GUILTLESS OF MURDER OF CELESTINO OTERO." The story that followed summarized Bridgers' closing argument, making it sound as though Bridgers knew he had a loser on his hands:

> Only brief arguments were made when the case was submitted to the jury. District Attorney W. W. Bridgers made a short statement to the effect that if it was believed that Otero fired first at Baca, he should be acquitted. [Defense counsel] Palvey stated to the jury that witness [sic] for the defense had testified that this was a fact, which state's witness [sic] had not denied it and would not say Baca had not been fired on when he returned the fire.

The jury took twelve minutes to elect a foreman, vote, and return with its verdict of not guilty.[171]

Though the murder charges were history, among those who currently tell tales of the Hero of Frisco the telling of the Otero incident does something to Baca's reputation that the jury refused to do after it heard all the testimony. Today, the skewed facts that have survived to be told have convicted Baca of a crime he wasn't charged with, and one that didn't happen. As presently told, with the "everybody knows this" preface, the story is that the rascally Elfego once planned a jailbreak that freed a Mexican revolutionary called General Salazar, and when a sleazy character who had aided in the escape was about to run to the federal district attorney and blow the whistle, Elfego Baca hired an assassin in El Paso and had him gunned down.[172]

With the Otero incident behind him, once again Elfego Baca was a free man with no criminal charges hanging over his head. Now all he had to do was reclaim his legal practice and rebuild his reputation as a law-abiding citizen.[173] But the soot that had fallen on him from the charges arising out of the Salazar escape and the Otero killing were not all that had soiled his reputation. There was another affair that left a residue of innuendo that he had to clean off before he could once again stand proud as the hero of the Mexican-Americans. That was the matter of the state legislators Baca accused of having their hands out.

30

◈ TANGLING WITH THE LEGISLATURE

When Elfego stuck his neck out to try to stamp out what he perceived as corruption on the part of a handful of state legislators, he became mired deeper in political mud than he'd thought
possible. His adventure centered on a quartet of state legislators who
were allegedly willing to sell their votes for cash during the election
of New Mexico's first United States senators when New Mexico first
became a state.

Elfego's troubles played out over several years, leaving a residue of embarrassment and injury to his reputation that he never completely overcame. The last chapter in the episode was the appeal of
a conviction for solicitation of bribery by one of the state legislators,
and Elfego was the one who had forked over the money. Though he
didn't appear as attorney for any of the litigants nor as a party to
the lawsuit, Elfego had a stake in the outcome that outweighed the
importance to him of any other case in which he had ever had a role.
Baca's name was sprinkled all over the opinion written by the state
supreme court.

State vs Lucero[174] was decided in January, 1915. Elfego Baca,
a member of the bar and a vigorous seeker of public office, was im-
plicitly accused of having paid money under the table in exchange
for a state legislator's vote for Baca's political crony, though a careful
reading of the documents submitted to the supreme court shows that
allegation was never made. It was a high profile case, since before it
hit the courts it had already been tried in the state legislature and in
the front pages of newspapers over the state.

Jose P. Lucero was a member of the first state legislature seated after President Taft announced that New Mexico had been made the forty seventh state, in January, 1912. The legislature had the job of electing the first senators and first member of congress for the new state. Before that first-ever session, Elfego worked to get himself elected to the U. S. House of Representatives. He had been nominated at the Republican convention in 1911, "eloquently," by A. B. Fall, later to become Secretary of the Interior and to be felled by the Teapot Dome oil reserves scandal. Though Elfego ran a good race at the convention, he fell behind and lost.

Equally hard-fought contests for the nomination of the first senators followed, and in all of them Elfego was a hard-working lobbyist for his favorites. His ferocious activity was an ideal breeding ground for the notion that he might be open to paying a bribe. For such a fighter, there was always the perception that he played his version of the political game with a wad of cash.[175] The game that led to criminal charges against Lucero played out in a hotel in Santa Fe just before the first a session of the legislature.

According to the court's opinion, prior to that first session of the legislature Elfego Baca and four legislators, including Jose P. Lucero, got their heads together to talk about events surrounding the election, including who was supporting whom. As a result of that meeting and the events that followed it, the grand jury in Santa Fe County issued an indictment reading, in part, as follows:

> That Jose P. Lucero . . . on the eighteenth day of March (1912) then and there being a . . . member of the First State Legislature . . . feloniously and corruptly did solicit, take and receive of and from one Elfego Baca five hundred dollars . . . for the vote and influence of him, the said Jose P. Lucero as a member of the First State Legislature, and . . . agreed to and with the said Elfego Baca to vote and use the influence of him, the said Jose

P. Lucero, as a member of the said First State Legislature in the matter of the election of two Senators of the United States.

The *Santa Fe New Mexican* provided a comprehensive account of the action. Its story was picked up in full by the *Socorro Chieftain*. The papers reported details not deemed important by the supreme court, notably that the under-the-table payment that Elfego handed over was the spring on a trap.

The *New Mexican,* as recorded by the *Socorro Chieftain*, said:

"It was a dramatic prelude that was enacted last evening at 10:30 o'clock, at the Palace Hotel [in Santa Fe] when four members of the house, Jose P. Lucero and Julian C. Trujillo of Rio Arriba county, and Manuel Cordova and Luis R. Montoya of Taos county, were caught in a trap set by the republican state central committee, but which the legislators this forenoon assert was a trap they had set to get hold of the 'higher-ups.' Much credit also belongs to . . . Attorney Elfego Baca . . . [and the state republican chair, the Supreme Court Clerk, and a Mounted Policeman] who staged the affair. . . .

"Last Saturday, so the accusers of the four legislators relate, word was sent to Judge [A. B.] Fall that the four statesmen desired to see him. They made arrangements through Attorney Elfego Baca for an interview at which Judge Fall assured the four that he would be pleased to have their support [for the United States Senate] and that if the Spanish-Americans nominated some man with a clean record and possessing ability, that no doubt a number of Fall supporters, would vote for such a man for the second senatorship. Fall then left the room and the four men gradually unfolded to Attorney Baca that they would cast their ballots twice for Fall for senator for $500 and would stay with him to the last ballot for $1250 a piece [sic]. Attorney Baca called attention to the nefariousness of their offer, the severe penalty provided by law, but apparently left them unmoved, their retort being that the fellows at Washington would make $50,000 at one fell swoop in perhaps a sugar [tariff vote scam] or some other deal."

No sooner was the deal made than Elfego ran to the state chairman of the republican central committee and helped make the arrangements for a trap. It was to be sprung in room 44 of the Palace Hotel. In place in an adjoining bathroom that connected also to room 46 were state chairman Vencestao Jaramillo, supreme court clerk Jose D. Sena, and mounted policeman Apolonio A. Sena. The plan went off without a hitch, though there was a near miss. One of the legislators, already on edge, panicked at a noise from one of the three lurking in the connecting bathroom, but Elfego explained it was the occupant of the next room using the toilet. The newspaper story recorded that when the legislators had been calmed, at a clap from Elfego's hands the trio burst out of the bathroom. The Chieftain continued to quote from the *New Mexican's* telling of the tale:

> "Attorney Elfego Baca had just completed counting out the money to the four, when the men hidden in the bathroom stepped out. One of the legislators still had the money in his hands, another had stuffed it into his pockets. One man had a $20 gold piece in his vest pocket and the rest of the money in the pockets of his trousers. One shoved it under the table and the fourth under a bed sheet. They were immediately placed under arrest."

The state chairman was well prepared. He left for a moment and quickly returned to whip from his pocket four blank forms of resignation from the legislature for the signatures of the captives. They signed, while one of the four wept real tears. But after a night in jail, the foursome regrouped, having had time to stitch together a claim that they themselves were victims of a trap they'd intended to spring on the very guys who'd snared them.

The *Chieftain* account promised more to come: "Sensational developments may occur at almost any hour and the investigation may take a turn that will have a startling denouement."[176]

A full transcript of the hearing conducted by the first state legislature to be seated, including the verbatim testimony of Elfego Baca, is preserved in the *Proceedings of the Investigating Committee of the House of Representatives.*[177] In that record, Lucero appears to have been the principal spokesman for the four legislators when they negotiated with Elfego, which may explain why he was apparently the only one charged and convicted of a crime. The legislative investigation and the criminal prosecution, both based on the same facts, would turn out so differently that they might have involved different people and a different transaction.

But away from the halls of the legislature, the district attorney and the state attorney general went to work with the law books, pouring over the statutes and constitution to determine the legal effect of bribery by entrapment as contrasted to "real" bribery. They found that in order to justify booting out a member, the legislature's rules required a three-step proof, requiring first, the solicitation of the bribe; second, receipt of the bribe money; third, completion of the underhanded deal by the act of voting. The D. A. and his back-up from the attorney general's office then determined that the criminal statutes were less stringent. They made the bare solicitation of a bribe a crime; there was no need for proof that the bribe had actually been received or that the bought vote had been cast. The legal issues were shaping up, and it appeared to the prosecutors that Mr. Lucero had committed a crime, even though he may not have broken the legislature's rules.

The prosecutors took Lucero to trial. Lucero was actually convicted of *solicitation* of bribery, though not of accepting a bribe. It was a distinction that would have been important for Elfego's reputation, since the legislature had already smeared his name by finding he had conspired to set up the four lawmakers.

Lucero took an appeal. The language of the indictment was at the core of Lucero's hope that he might be able to upset his conviction. It charged that Jose Lucero had sought money from Elfego Baca, and that Baca had paid him. In exchange, Lucero would vote the way Baca told him to for the election of the first two senators to be sent to Washington to represent the brand-new state. Lucero would influence other legislators to do the same when the vote was called.[178]

Despite the apparent clarity of the language of the charges, to Lucero and his attorney the indictment wasn't clear at all. They claimed that it was too fuzzy to understand, and that because they couldn't understand it, the whole case should have been thrown out before it started. The supreme court didn't buy the argument, and Lucero's conviction stood.

Elfego testified at some length at Lucero's trial in the Santa Fe district court. A copy of the transcript of all the trial testimony has survived. The trial record shines light not only on the bribery case, but gives a rare insight into a phase of Elfego's state of mind and a view of his command of English and Spanish thirty-two years after his return from Topeka.

When called as a witness, Elfego requested permission to testify in Spanish. Defense counsel Edward P. Davies demanded to hear everything in English. The court told Davies it was up to Elfego. Elfego chose Spanish, so the questioning went on in that language. But when it was Davies' turn to cross-examine, the defense lawyer had his chance to ask Baca about his ability to testify in English, trying to embarrass the witness by showing he was only playing up to the Hispanic jurors.

After he'd established how long Elfego had lived in New Mexico and in Albuquerque after leaving Kansas, the transcript records that counsel Davies asked these questions and got these answers:

Q. [by Mr. Davies] Born in Kansas, were you?
A. [by Mr. Baca] I was born in Socorro, New Mexico and my father and mother went to Topeka, Kansas, about the time I became one year old.
Q. And you moved back to New Mexico about when did you say?
A. I came back to New Mexico I think when I was about fifteen years old after my mother died in Topeka.
Q. Then up to the time, - from the time you were about one year old up until you were fifteen you lived in Kansas?
A. Yes, sir.
Q. In Topeka?
A. More or less.
Q. There were not many Spanish Speaking people in Topeka, Kansas, were there?
A. No, it was only my father and mother and the family by the name of Sanchez that I remember.
Q. And I presume you attended a school where English was spoken and taught almost exclusively, did you not?
A. Yes, I think I did.
Q. Then up to the time you were about fifteen years old you spoke a great deal more English than you did Spanish, did you not?
A. Yes. When I came to New Mexico I couldn't talk Spanish at all and there were no Americans here and I came pretty near forgetting the English language.

Davies was apparently satisfied, though it is unclear just what the exchange had won for him. When lawyer Davies finally reached the meat of his cross-examination, Elfego used his time as witness to play to the jury of eleven Hispanics and one Anglo. Asked to admit that he "formed a trap to catch these men," he denied it. But he gave his reasons for his participation in the matter. Once again he cast himself in the role of champion of the Spanish-American population. He acted, he told the jury, because he was concerned about the integrity of Hispanics, he said, and the four legislators who had offered to sell their votes were a disgrace to all New Mexicans of that ethnicity. Elfego testified:

> One of them [on the executive committee of the republican party] suggested that I should make an affidavit, particularly I think it was Venceslao Jaramillo, he was in doubt as to the conduct of these men I spoke about, and I told them I wouldn't like to make an affidavit but I was a republican and I thought it was for the interest of the republican party, and especially for our Spanish speaking people. . . .It was decided there also that this move was to be made by our own people. There was not a single of the so-called Americans that had anything to do with it and who was at the lead of it was Solomon Luna, Venceslao Jaramillo, Jose Sena, etc. . . . It was shameful to have the kind of people that these [vote-sellers] were in the State Legislature and under those circumstances we couldn't claim nothing. That was when we were seeking to have a Spanish American as one of the United States Senators.

When asked if he were astounded when the legislators "mentioned money for their influence or vote," he answered, "Yes. Especially when I saw it from my people."

A few pages later in his testimony Elfego again came down hard on the four for betraying the Mexican-American people:

When I continued to talk to them, Mr. Davies, I did it for the purpose to see if I had sufficient words to convince them that they were not only a distrace [sic] to themselves but to the whole race in this state. . . .

The supreme court affirmed Lucero's trial court conviction. By refusing to speak English, and by his skillful disparagement of the conspirators for disgracing the whole race he had tried for so long to elevate, first at the gun battle, later through his newspaper and in other ways, Elfego had denied alliance with the English-speaking population to stand once more with the Hispanic population of New Mexico.[179]

Had that been all there was to it, Elfego Baca would have walked away covered with honor for his role in exposing a gang of legislators-for-sale who were trying to sell their influence in the new State of New Mexico. But the legislature, before the criminal matter involving Lucero had reached the state's highest court, rescued the reputations of the four members of its club by smearing Elfego Baca with political mud. The politicians showed to Elfego Baca, who was not a member of the body, none of the care and concern granted by the members of the supreme court to Elfego as one of its own, a member of the State Bar.

In the legislative committee hearings, Elfego was expertly examined by the legislators' attorney, Colonel Pritchard. The Colonel phrased question after question to suggest that Baca had pulled a series of dirty tricks in encouraging the four legislators to do something they never would have done if Baca hadn't led them by the nose. Based on the recommendation of the legislative committee assigned to conduct the hearing, Baca and his team were found by the legislature to have entrapped the four legislators, and that the quartet was nothing more than four dupes of a clever plot to keep them from voting because Elfego and friends couldn't control them. The committee report adopted by the legislature, in restoring the four to their seats, read, in part:

> This committee is of the belief that the accused have been made the victims of a conspiracy against them, that they were inveigled to room 44 of the Palace hotel on the night of the 18th of March by the witness Baca in furtherance of that conspiracy. . . . The secrecy with which the business was carried on makes it apparent to this committee that the action taken by those in the scheme was inspired by a desire to get these members out of the legislature, for the reason that they could not be controlled by those who wanted to control them in the matter of voting for United States Senators.

One of the participants in the "scheme," an employee of the legislature who came out of the bathroom to nab the four, was censured. Elfego's reputation was for years to carry the dirt from claims that he had set up the plot to his own political advantage.[180] He'd been tarred by the legislature, and though the courts had found Jose P. Lucero guilty and Elfego Baca clean as a whistle, it was the legislature's actions that earned the front page coverage. Elfego's giant step forward in condemning those who soiled the cause of the Mexican-Americans had resulted in two steps backwards.

The *Lucero* trial and supreme court case rated no mention in Crichton's biography of Elfego Baca. The entire incident of Elfego's bribery by four state legislators is given only a single paragraph, and the few lines written there claim that Elfego was sometimes credited with electing Fall to the United States Senate and with trapping four legislators "in such a way as to preclude the possibility of denial that they had accepted a bribe to vote against Fall." The account steers clear of any hint of the actions of the state legislature in reinstating their fallen brothers or of the smears that were painted on Elfego Baca by lawmakers looking to protect their own by rules inadequate to provide for punishment for soliciting a bribe.[181]

As for Elfego, he could take comfort in having started out as a citizen of the new State of New Mexico by championing the Hispanics, vindicated in the eyes of those who knew him by the verdict of the Lucero case jury.

There were many other cases, however, in which Elfego had an interest in the outcome as an attorney for one of the parties or as a litigant, and some of those reached the state supreme court through the appellate route. For those cases, written court opinions were issued, giving the student of the life of Elfego Baca a glimpse into the man's abilities as an attorney and into his personal financial affairs.

31

❖ NEW MEXICO SUPREME COURT BATTLES

Four times Elfego Baca appeared in the Supreme Court of New Mexico as a counsel of record for a party, always with co-counsel. alongside. From the fact that he never made a solo appearance it may be inferred that he lacked confidence in his brief-writing skills and so brought in reinforcements. It would have been to his credit that he recognized that his training for the bar lacked lessons in legal writing and research. In six other cases he was one of the parties to the appealed lawsuit. Another opinion, in the *Lucero* bribery case, reported his name as an essential witness. All ten of the lawsuits are mentioned in this chapter as indicators of the activity of the hero and the causes he devoted himself to.

Elfego's first appearance was more memorable for his association with co-counsel than for the law of the case. H. B. Fergusson and Elfego Baca appeared side-by-side as attorneys for the appellants, H. C. Crary, and others, in a case entitled *Dye vs McCrary*.[182] The matter reached the Territory's highest court in 1906. The fact that the pair was together on the same side may lead to an inference that hard feelings resulting from the fight at Frisco and the murder trials that followed had been smoothed over, at least among fellow lawyers.

Harvey B. Fergusson, as district attorney of the Second District of the Territory of New Mexico, signed the grand jury indictment charging Elfego with the killing of Young Parham twenty years before. Fergusson prosecuted the case amid accusations by Baca and the rest of the Frisco Nine that his actions were financed by the cattlemen's association. In another six years after *Dye vs McCrary*, he and Elfego would be fighting again, this time going toe to toe for election to the first Congressional seat for the new State of New Mexico. Fergusson was a Democrat, Baca a Republican. Fergusson would win.

Since Fergusson not only was a party to the *Dye* lawsuit but also sat in the seat of counsel for McCrary and the other plaintiffs in the case, he must have had a voice in the selection of his co-counsel. What led to the pick of Elfego Baca is unknown. What's left is speculation about the conversation between the two lawyers when Fergusson and his co-plaintiffs called on Elfego Baca to hire him to help Fergusson handle the case and to represent him at the same time. But Elfego was a pragmatist. To the always cash-strapped lawyer, the promise of a fee would certainly have overcome any lingering resentment he had against the former D. A.

There would seem to have been only one reason why a well-educated, former teacher of Greek, and skilled lawyer like Fergusson would have hired Elfego, whose "scanty preparation" for the bar was well known among the handful of lawyers in the Territory: he needed a fighter at his side. No one at the bar better fit that job description than Elfego Baca.[183]

As it turned out, the team of Fergusson and Baca was unsuccessful in obtaining title to the gold-mining claims involved in the suit for Fergusson and his co-adventurers. The only result of *Dye vs McCrary* was to provide a published opinion that studied the law of estoppel in the Territory while fostering curiosity about the association of former prosecutor Fergusson with his one-time prey, Elfego Baca.

In 1915, the New Mexico State Supreme Court issued its opinion in a case in which Elfego had a personal stake: he was the plaintiff.

Baca vs City of Albuquerque[184] started with Elfego driving his buggy down a street in downtown Albuquerque, minding his own business. He was run into by a city fire wagon and pitched into the dirt and horse manure covering the street. He suffered injuries "that should by all rights have finished him." Elfego seems to have suggested to his biographer, Crichton, that the collision was deliberate. Crichton reported that "it failed of its purpose."[185]

Elfego didn't keep quiet about his injuries or about the city's role in causing them. During visits to Socorro, and in conversations with Socorroans he encountered in Albuquerque, he let it be known that he'd been hurt and how it had happened. The *Socorro Chieftain* of November 14, 1907, reported that the native son "was recently run down by a fire wagon in Albuquerque and had two ribs broken." Over a year later, on December 12, 1908, the same paper said that Baca was in town and still hadn't fully recovered from his injuries.

Elfego sued the city, asking for $5,000 in damages, claiming that the city's agents had driven the wagon negligently. The City denied all, while pointing the finger at Baca for being contributorily negligent. Such a defense at that time, if proven, would have resulted in a denial of all damages even if some negligence on the part of the City had also contributed to the injuries.

The supreme court opinion didn't say which one of Baca's lawyers with the firm of Vigil & Jamison made the opening statement to the jury once twelve men had been seated. Whoever it was suffered the most extreme embarrassment a trial judge can inflict on a trial attorney.

When the lawyer sat down after telling what he was about to prove, the judge called for the city's lawyer to state his case. Instead, the city moved for an instructed verdict that would throw out the case. Grounds were that the opening statement made by Elfego's lawyer had shown that there were no facts to back up the Baca claim. The judge agreed. He banged his gavel. "Case dismissed," he bellowed, and stood up to leave. Elfego and his lawyers sat in shocked silence.

City lawyers had found a statute that protected city employees from suits arising out of acts performed by authority of the city, such as driving a fire wagon. The city itself had the protection of immunity granted to governmental units. The problem with Elfego's case was that Vigil and Jamison, at Elfego's request, had filed suit when the statutes said they couldn't.

The jury went home. The lawyers packed their briefcases. Elfego slunk back to his offices. But he recovered his spirits in time to prod his lawyers to appeal. They did.

A lawyer reading the Supreme Court's opinion in *Baca vs City of Albuquerque* would wonder if city attorney John C. Lewis might have had it in for Baca, or maybe for Vigil & Jamison. The motion the city's lawyer made when the opening statement concluded could have been raised earlier, based on the allegations set out in the complaint filed on Baca's behalf. Had that been done, the arguments of the lawyers would probably have been made more privately, in the judge's chambers; they would have received little or no attention from newsmen, and the judge's ruling surely would have been the same as made publicly in the courtroom in front of a full house, including reporters.

When the supreme court heard the appeal, it agreed with trial judge Raynolds, though it took nearly seven years from the date of the injury to finalize the claim. Elfego was left with no damages for his injuries, no salve for his mortification, no reminder of the case except the ache of his broken ribs, a sheaf of legal briefs, and his name memorialized in the title of a case he'd lost.

No case Elfego was involved in reached the supreme court on appeal after the 1915 *Lucero* case until 1918 brought him grief at the hands of John W. Murphy. The case reveals just what financial travails Elfego was experiencing as an aftermath of the expenses he had incurred in his multiple criminal defenses and the fees he had lost while defending himself.

In *Murphy vs Baca et al*,[186] Elfego appealed a judgment against him taken in Socorro County. Baca had been sued on a promissory note secured by a mortgage on real estate. Elfego and his co-debtors were told to pay up or have their land sold. The record doesn't show whether Elfego scraped up the money or lost the land. The case, while insignificant for legal precedent, foretold just how critical Elfego's financial condition would become. *Murphy*, and the case that follows, both lay bare the fact that Elfego seemed to be spending more time on his own financial affairs than on the paying business of clients.

Two years later Elfego was back before the supreme court in another civil suit, *Baca vs Fleming*.[187] Elfego had filed his complaint when a used car he bought threw a connecting rod and ruined the engine. He claimed the oral contract of purchase he'd made required the seller to pay for repairs. The case shed more light on his mounting financial difficulties, and may have been filed to stall off a creditor when money was tight for the hero. The *Fleming* case also demonstrated Elfego's weakness when he strayed out of the field of criminal law, in which he had proven expertise, and into the arena of contract law.

Baca's unfamiliarity with civil law is not simply a deduction drawn from his record in the supreme court. William A. Keleher, who represented him in litigation over the ownership of his combination office, printing plant and residential building at Sixth and Gold, Albuquerque, wrote, "Elfego Baca was an ideal client in many respects, admitting that he was pretty much a stranger to civil litigation, saying that most of his practice had been in criminal law."[188]

In the *Fleming* matter, Elfego was again unable to grasp the complexities of the civil law. If he had, it is not likely that he would have filed the suit. Was his lack of education the handicap he labored under? Other New Mexico lawyers who read the law in the offices of established lawyers rose to respected positions, including Federal Judge Verle Payne, who distinguished the federal bench with his wise rulings and careful attention to the law. Or was the reason, or part of it, for Elfego's inability to focus on issues long enough to pull together the multiple threads of a complicated civil case due to the shadows of Texans with blazing six-guns flitting through his subconscious? Perhaps so. Veteran's hospital psychiatrists are kept busy with long-term PTSD patients today, some of them still responding reflexively to images of World War Two and Korea, decades after peace.

As for Elfego, we are left only to make informed guesses. Whatever the reason, he lost the *Fleming* case and was never able to master the civil law.

At long last, Elfego broke his string of consistent defeats at the hands of the state supreme court. Once more he was a party to the litigation, and once more the case centered on his financial affairs. In *Baca vs Padilla*,[189] Elfego sued for money he claimed was due to him for prosecuting a criminal case on a unique contingent fee basis that only Elfego Baca could have dreamed up. His client had hired him as a private attorney to prosecute a criminal case in Valencia County, New Mexico, and to try to get a conviction. The deal he made was that if the parties Baca was to prosecute were acquitted, Padilla would pay him a "reasonable fee." If they were convicted, he was to be paid a "big fee."

The defendants were convicted. Elfego had earned his "big fee." He sent a bill for $5,000. "Too big," his client claimed, and refused to pay. Elfego sued to get it.

The trial court allowed him $500. Padilla appealed, pleading that the deal he'd made with Elfego was void because it was against public policy, and that a fee of nothing would be just right. Padilla's counsel argued Elfego's fee arrangement gave him a personal stake in the matter, and that it wasn't in the state's best interest to encourage that kind of activity by lawyers, even though Padilla had had the benefit of the bargain.

The justices found that no one had ever before argued the point that Elfego raised — the argument that it was perfectly okay for a private lawyer to prosecute a criminal case for a client for a fee whose size was based on getting a conviction. Their opinion broke new legal ground. The author of the opinion came down on the side of public policy, but not quite one hundred eighty degrees away from Elfego's position. The state provides a prosecutor, Justice Roberts wrote, pays his salary, provides him with a staff, and demands he be disinterested. But when a private attorney is hired, and when the size of his fee depends on conviction whether the defendant is guilty or innocent, that goes against the grain.

But the opinion found a way for Elfego to get a piece of the $5,000 into his pocket. The justice wrote that the public policy against contingent fees for the prosecution of criminal cases won't entirely prevent an award of a fee as long as it's not based on a contract for a "contingent fee," since such contracts are void. But, if the lawyer is paid for the value of service actually rendered, then it's okay to collect. The justices figured Elfego's services had been worth, coincidentally, the amount the trial court had awarded him: $500. Elfego got his fee, though only a tenth of the $5,000, though through the back door, and though far from the "big" fee Padilla had agreed to pay. There was no inquiry into whether Elfego's zeal resulting from the hope of a "big fee" had resulted in the conviction of an innocent man.

The next three cases that took Elfego to the Santa Fe chambers of the state's highest court again demonstrated Baca's difficulty in handling cases in sedate fields of law remote from the battlegrounds of criminal law. The matters were *Baca vs Winters, et al*,[190] and *Baca vs Buel (two*

cases).[191] They arose out of the estate of W. H. Byerts, deceased, and from Elfego's venture into the maze of probate law.

In the 1920s, when these cases came up, there was no such thing as specialization in the New Mexico Bar, or doubtless in any state's bar, and there wouldn't be for some fifty years. All lawyers were created equal, and they would find their skills evaluated only in the marketplace of those who hired lawyers.

In the Byerts estate cases, Elfego's need for fees to support his family once again led him to stray into a field he hadn't tilled while he was reading law in Judge Hamilton's offices. This time, the area was probate. Once again, he spent more time and effort in digging himself out of the trouble he'd gotten himself into by jumping into a field of law he hadn't studied than he was able to recoup in fees awarded by the court.

Elfego was to visit the state supreme court two more times. One trip was as counsel in a criminal case, *State vs Layman,*[192] the other was a probate matter, *In re Candelaria's Estate, Candelario et al. vs De Lucero.*[193] Elfego and his co-counsel obtained a reversal of Layman's second-degree murder conviction, but he lost the probate matter hands down.

In the latter case, Elfego and his co-counsel, George R. Craig and I. V. Gallegos, were opposed by a distinguished battery of Albuquerque lawyers, Mechem & Hannett and Donald B. Moses, who ultimately prevailed in a case that was more concerned with adoption law than with the probate code. Once again Elfego had stumbled when faced with civil law. Once again, the gaps in his legal education had overcome his motivation to help the underdog.

One of the lawyers in the *Candelaria* case confirmed the difficulties Elfego had with grasping many of the principles of the law. "I was in court with him many times," Donald B. Moses, Esq., said in an interview. "Members of the bar thought of him as something of a clown. By that I don't mean they thought he was a funny guy. I mean the other attorneys in town thought he wasn't much of a lawyer. Not because he didn't try. He just didn't have any education. There were times, though, when he did some funny things, especially in [U. S. District] Judge Neblett's court." Moses then told the story of the time Elfego defended a Mexican against charges of selling liquor to an Indian.

"His client was charged with selling Crab Apple Whiskey to this Indian. That was the label on the bottle. When the evidence was in and the lawyers were giving their closing arguments, Baca got up and argued that the prosecutor had not met its obligation of proving what was in the bottle. Nobody had tasted the contents or smelled it, yet his client was charged with selling whiskey. All the prosecutor had done was show the jury a sealed bottle labeled "Crab Apple Whiskey," and that wasn't enough to distinguish the contents from cold tea.

"There was a recess called about that time. When everybody came back, Elfego walked up to the jury to finish what he'd been saying. He had a sign hanging around his neck. It said, 'Jesus Christ.' Elfego pointed to it and said, 'Does this make me the Savior?' The jury laughed. And acquitted."

Moses added another episode involving whiskey. He said that when one of the lawyers for the Estate of Bronson Cutting went to Baca's home to ask if he intended to pay the debt owed to the representative of the deceased Cutting, he found Elfego drunk in bed, a whiskey bottle alongside and Mrs. Baca explaining that her husband was "sick."[194]

In the divorce action shortly after, Mrs. Baca told of nursing him through his "sickness" without disclosing its nature.[195]

Elfego's own appraisal of his law practice waxed and waned with the times or the setting. In his own divorce action, when he went back to court to try to whittle a few dollars a month off his alimony payments, his lawyer complained that he couldn't pay "on account of his failure to secure business as an attorney. . . ." But a decade and a half earlier, under cross-examination in the bribery trial of Jose P. Lucero, he testified under oath, "Well, I can say, I have just as good a practice as any attorney in New Mexico I guess."[196]

A versatile lawyer? No. Unconventional? Yes. Effective? As long as he stayed in the criminal arena.

Elfego Baca, still quick on the draw at an advanced age. Inscribed "To my dear friend George Fitzpatrick. Elfego Baca."
Photograph courtesy of Museum of New Mexico, Negative no. 128796.

32

◈   NEVER GIVE UP

When Elfego went on the payroll at the Tivoli in Juarez, Mexico, he was quick to let it be known among his Socorro and Albuquerque associates that he'd not taken a second class job. He was the head of a fourteen member "police force," and to call him the head bouncer was a slap in the face, and nobody slapped Elfego Baca in the face. The purpose of the "police force," he said, was to keep order in the only government-sanctioned gambling den in the border city. The position gave him plenty of opportunities for aggression.

It was at the Tivoli that Elfego's biographer, Kyle Crichton, first met him. Crichton had gone to El Paso to hear famous opera diva Mary Garden sing. Crichton found her trying her luck one afternoon at the Tivoli gambling palace. When she won at one of the tables, the crowd following her turned raucous, with cheers, laughter and applause so loud that the head bouncer/police chief walked over to ask the group to tone it down.

In writing of the episode, Crichton told his first impression of his client-to-be. "At the time we first saw him," Crichton wrote, "we knew of him solely by a reputation not overly favorable." It's not clear that Crichton's opinion ever changed after he began his writing task for the head bouncer's biography a few years later.

Crichton wrote of one of Elfego's Tivoli confrontations when he told the story of *Numero Ocho*. It was one more opportunity for aggression by the Hero of Frisco.

Numero Ocho, or Number Eight, headed the Juarez underworld when Elfego Baca was hired to captain the Tivoli police force. Before

Elfego came on board, *Numero Ocho* and his gang helped themselves to the receipts of the Tivoli just about any time they were short of cash. Their practice of quick raids on the tables and games with never an arrest or hot pursuit by the police, led Elfego to suspect that they had a special relationship with the local cops. Things changed when Elfego took over security.

One of the first things Elfego did was to keep the lighting system manned. The Tivoli had two master circuits. When there was an attempted raid, the habit of the robbers was to cut the lights, scoop up the money lying on the tables and run. To do it they probably had inside help. Elfego devised a simple plan. When the bad guys cut off the lights, his man would activate the second lighting system, spotlighting the thieves so that part two of his plan could go into effect. Part two was to have his fourteen man police force train their guns on the gambling tables.

While this two-part tactic eliminated raids during Elfego's entire tenure at the Tivoli, it didn't get to the cause of it all. The cause was *Numero Ocho*, and as Crichton wrote, "Elfego Baca, to this day, makes it a habit of confronting anyone with whom he has a disagreement." There was nothing left except to confront the kingpin.

Elfego's anger at the threat to his new domain drove him to track down *Ocho* in the cellar of the gang's hideout, where he was surrounded by his henchmen. When Elfego asked which was *Ocho*, a seated Mexican raised a finger. There was no offer of a handshake, but *Numero Ocho*'s head jerked back a fraction when Elfego announced his name. Elfego stepped up to *Ocho*, ignoring the six or seven other men, some seated and some standing around their leader, and demanded he get to his feet.

Ocho checked out the intruder, and bemused, raised himself to his feet, warily. Squaring off and with no warning, Elfego slapped the man on the side of his mouth, threw a left hook into his stomach, and slapped him two more times as he doubled up.

Ocho had had enough. He straightened, raised a hand from his stomach to motion to his men, turned his head toward Baca and nodded. The gang reached for their guns. Before the weapons cleared their holsters Elfego had his twin pistols out, waving them around the circle. Hands raised a respectful distance above gun handles.

Elfego re-sheathed one pistol. With his now free hand he spun *Ocho* around, then booted him toward the door. *Ocho* stumbled out of the room.

Pulling his second pistol again, Elfego motioned the thugs toward the door, not wanting any to stay behind him for a shot in the back as he left. "You fellas. I see any of you step inside the Tivoli, you're dead," he said. "If you don't know Elfego Baca means it, try me and see." Or words to that effect.

The party was over.

Elfego and the Tivoli had no more trouble with *Numero Ocho* or his gang during the rest of Elfego's tenure at the gambling palace.

Not long after this episode Elfego's reign over the Tivoli police force came to an end. Though *Numero Ocho* was top dog in the underworld, the chief of police himself was *numero uno*, number one, in Juárez, and Elfego knew it. He also knew that his career in the Mexican city was over when he discovered that a man he had arrested was the son of the police chief. Elfego held no illusions about either Mexican politics or Mexican graft. He asked for his final pay-out in cash and headed north.[197]

But before he walked away from the bouncer's job at the Tivoli, Elfego received a call from A. B. Fall, former New Mexico district court judge, and former United States Senator from New Mexico. Following the bribery scandal over the state legislators and Fall's election to the U. S. Senate, Fall owed Baca, and it was pay-back time.

Whether or not Elfego's role in the vote scandal had helped put Fall over the top in his bid for the senate, when Fall resigned his senate seat to accept appointment as President Warren G. Harding's Interior Secretary in 1921, he named Elfego as an Indian and land inspector for the Department of the Interior.

Elfego served for only a couple of years, for that was the length of the term Fall served as Interior Secretary. In 1923, Fall resigned, and not long after was sentenced to a term in prison for accepting bribes to induce him to issue leases to federal oil lands in what was known as the Teapot Dome Scandal. Elfego returned home to Albuquerque. Fall was disgraced, and his cronies in New Mexico couldn't believe how far their mentor had fallen.

The inspector's job was to be the last of any consequence that Elfego held, other than the practice of law, though not because he gave up. After returning to Albuquerque from Washington, Baca hung out his legal shingle once more, but the domestic problems with Mrs. Baca and the battles with his creditors were enough to engage his full attention. Nevertheless, in 1924 he resolved that it was time to become a district judge in Bernalillo County.

He approached the Republican Party. They didn't want him. He meditated, fretted, and decided that rejection didn't become him. He filed as an independent. His platform promised that litigants wouldn't be judged based on their politics, nationality or religion. He would stop the practice of district attorneys talking to jailed persons accused of a crime, and he would prevent deputies from eavesdropping on attorney-client conversations. And no more third degree interrogations if he were elected.[198]

His campaign lasted only a couple of weeks. He passed out handbills and made pitches for himself to any group that opened its doors to listen to candidates. When the count was tallied, he'd lost, but he had collected enough support to split the republican vote and assure victory for the democratic candidate. His popularity wasn't enhanced among the republicans. Once again, Elfego had had his revenge.[199]

It was then that he turned to William Keleher, who made the referral to Kyle Crichton, to write his biography.

The unsuccessful run for district judge in 1924 didn't end Elfego's quest for public office. In 1934 he threw his hat into the ring for governor of New Mexico. He was sixty-nine, running as an independent. He'd left the republican party sometime around 1930 to become a loyal democrat because he felt the republicans had turned their backs on the Hispanics, but once again he had no party endorsement.

The "Manifesto" Baca published and circulated in support of his candidacy listed a nineteen point platform. Many of his planks are still being raised by candidates over seventy-five years later; others have since become law.

He proposed repealing the laws against carrying concealed weapons since criminals will carry them whether there's a law or not, and his experiences had taught him that a man with a gun can take care of himself. He supported legislation requiring couples seeking a marriage license to have a health examination; every poor person charged with a crime was to be given a lawyer; each Saturday, he would pardon a convicted prisoner from the penitentiary. His number one issue, appearing under a picture of the steely-eyed candidate in his brochure, was, "I AM IN FAVOR OF REPEALING THE SALES TAX LAW."

His campaign wasn't taken seriously, and he received few votes. Licking his wounds, he retreated back to his law practice.

Elfego made another try for district judge in 1940. His campaign was much like he'd run in 1934 — low to no budget. He lost to Judge Johnson, but he claimed he'd picked up 3879 votes.[200]

Though Elfego was seventy-five when he made the run against Judge Johnson, Professor Larry D. Ball wrote that he decided before his death that he had at least one more race in him. He tried again for district judge and failed.[201] The phrase "give up" was not in Elfego's vocabulary.

Some event, or series of events, probably in the late 1920s or early 1930s, seems to have mellowed Elfego. Perhaps it was finally getting his story out through Crichton's biography. Maybe it was his financial woes and his marriage breakup. It may have been no more than aging. Whatever, the result was a more gentle Elfego.

Only in the last twenty years or so of his life was he reported as joking, and then, as his nephew, A. B. Baca, who knew him when he was aging, said in a 1981 interview, "He liked kids and old folks."[202] Perhaps it was because they posed no threat. His granddaughter, Juanita Hartson of San Diego, said in a 2002 interview that he visited his daughters in California twice a year when he was old and she was growing up, and that he was a "great guy." A family photo pictures her at fourteen and him at seventy, both smiling while she shows him her tennis racket and tap-dancing shoes. Her grandmother, she said, "ruled the roost at home." But during his California visits, Elfego stayed with daughter Josephina, not with Francisquita, who lived in San Diego while he lived in Albuquerque.[203]

Elfego Baca in his 70s with his granddaughter, Juanita E. (Mrs. Robert L.) Hartson, who is showing him her tennis racket and tap-dancing shoes on a visit by Elfego to San Diego. Photograph courtesy of Juanita E. Hartson.

George Fitzpatrick, editor of *New Mexico Magazine*, knew Baca for the last twenty years of the hero's life. During that period, he wrote, Baca had "a robust sense of humor and he loved particularly to recount the amusing incidents."[204]

Charley McCarthy, grandson of the cowhand Charley McCarthy whom Baca arrested, related during a telephone interview that he recalled his grandfather taking him into a saloon in Magdalena when he was a small boy. There, they ran into Elfego Baca. The young Charley remembered his grandfather and Elfego hoisting a few beers together and laughing and joking about the events in Frisco when both were young. Neither seemed to bear any hard feelings.[205]

But there was another, more touching and revealing episode about Baca's later years. Professor Ball's book reported an interview the author had by telephone with Elfego's former paper boy, Donald Ecklund, a history professor at the time of the conversation. Ecklund told of delivering Elfego's newspaper to him at 5:30 a. m. According to Dr. Ball, Ecklund said that sometimes when he made his delivery he would see, and presumably hear, Elfego playing the fiddle, jumping around, seeming to enjoy himself.[206] But Elfego was all alone during those sightings—jigging and fiddling by himself at 5:30 a. m. Having a good time—solo. It's the only story of Elfego's fiddling or jigging to be found. And though he's reported to have attended dances, no one has written about seeing him on the dance floor, whirling and spinning around with a partner, smiling and having a good time and enjoying the music.

Descriptions of Elfego as a fun-lover during his earlier years are non-existent, and Crichton feared the subject of his work. There also remains the speculation about the sickness Elfego had and that Francisquita referred to in cross-claiming for divorce, and her observation that her husband was passed out on his bed with a whiskey bottle alongside, "sick" when another attorney called on him. Was Elfego plagued by the sickness of alcohol abuse? It seems likely.

◈ ◈ ◈

The Hero of Frisco died on August 27, 1945. Francisquita wrote to U. S. Representative Clinton P. Anderson, whom Elfego had admired, telling him that when death came her husband was sitting by the radio waiting to hear him speak. Apparently Elfego and Francisquita had reconciled by that time, though granddaughter Juanita Hartson in a telephone conversation could not explain how or when. Pallbearers were M. J. McGuinness, sheriff J. A. Flaska, and four Albuquerque lawyers, including his sometimes advisor, W. A. Keleher.[207]

Elfego's political tract-turned-autobiography, which served him so often but so unsuccessfully over the years, ended by stating his life objective. He wrote that he was taken to Albuquerque to stand trial for the killing of William Hearne wearing two pairs of handcuffs, one welded in place by a blacksmith, and two sets of leg shackles. As the blacksmith hired by the sheriff to remove the irons was doing his work, Baca little autobiography recalled, he thought:

> From then on I made up my mind, I wanted the outlaws to hear my steps a block away from me. I always had been for law and order and I will be until I die. Since that time I wanted to be an 'A No.1 peace officer, likewise a criminal lawyer.[208]

He was both. He could have no better epitaph.

❖ AUTHOR'S CONCLUSIONS—CLOSING ARGUMENT

It's time somebody stood up to speak for the Hero of Frisco. It's time to fire back at those who take cheap shots at Elfego Baca, who offered his very life to save the Hispanic settlers.

So, this is the closing argument in the Case for Elfego Baca.

Let's start with firing back at those who challenge the count of Texans lined up against Elfego and the number of shots they fired. Those anti-Baca arguments are the ones that come up most often. Later, we'll move on to the positives about the hero of Frisco.

The typical positions of the detractors are eloquently set out in a newspaper article by writer and former rancher, the late Bill McGaw. McGaw's story was clipped, copied and pasted inside the front cover of a 1970 reprint of Kyle S. Crichton's biography of Elfego Baca titled *Law and Order Limited. The Rousing Life of Elfego Baca of New Mexico*, published by Rio Grande Press of Glorieta, New Mexico.The publisher's preface to the book records that the clipping came from the *El Paso Herald Post.* The date of the article, "Stories About Elfego Baca Standing off 80 Men Are a 'Lot of Nonsense,' N.M. Rancher Says," is not supplied.

McGaw's arguments came from a Joe Porter, nephew of Joe Armstrong, who was a trail boss for the Slaughter outfit when it came into New Mexico from Texas. Neither Porter nor Armstrong is said to have been at Frisco when the action was hot and heavy, but reliance on speculation has never slowed down those who ridicule the hero.

Here are just two of the verbal shots taken by Porter as record-ed by McGaw, and used by him to make fun of the hero who faced the real lead bullets.

He asks: Were there really 4,000 shots fired into the *jacal*?

He asks: Were there really 80 cowboys present?

McGaw says "No," to both questions, and for both relies on Porter. Let's look first at the number of shots fired.

Based on his interview of Porter, McGaw's article says that the old cowboy and rancher calculated that 4,000 rounds of .45 lead am-munition would have weighed 500 to 600 pounds, and bullets would have had to have been carted in by burro train to keep the Texans supplied. "Somebody could stake a mining claim for the quarter-ton or so of lead which must be there someplace," Porter chortled.

Porter was way off, and here's how we fire back with real facts raised earlier in this book.

James Cook himself confirmed the 4,000 shots in his eyewit-ness account. "The evidence showed that 4,000 shots had been fired into the *jacal* in which Baca had been hiding since he killed Herne." No choking at the 4,000 count can be found in the statement by the partisan Cook, who was there from beginning to end, and who fired his share of those 4,000 shots.

And the cowboys had plenty of ammunition, despite Porter's giggling.

Two years before the 1884 gunfight, a handful of Apaches broke out of a reservation in eastern Arizona, sending western New Mexico ranchers and their ranch hands into a panic. According to p. 42 of James Cook's book, "We then opened several cases of cartridges and placed them near the arms they fitted. (We always kept a good supply of arms and ammunition at the ranch.)" The mini-uprising was quelled with no shots fired from the entrenched New Mexicans. And it was *cases* of ammunition that were opened, not boxes.

If Cook, who led the shooting at Baca, broke out "several cases" of cartridges when some twenty-five Apaches were loose in western Arizona, how many would he have broken out and issued to his men to fend off the army of Mexicans "on the warpath" he had been told were taking over Frisco, right down the road? The armed cowboys did not ride into town for a Saturday night frolic when Cook sent them out to put down the revolution, but to fight a war. They came with their saddlebags full of ammunition, their guns loaded and their ammunition belts full.

And eighty cowhands, each packing six-and-a-half pounds of lead ammunition, exceed the five hundred pounds that Porter figured would have had to be carted in by burro. It calculates to be some 52 rounds each, including in the chambers of their six-guns, in their ammunition belts, and in their saddlebags. Out of reason? No.

McGaw asks another question: Did Elfego really stand off *eighty* cowboys? He says no, based again on his interview of Porter. Porter claimed that there were not that many cowhands in the whole area. He figured "8 to 10 firing at him at any one time . . . and no more than 20 or so around here altogether."

Again, he's wrong.

Here's the count. Justice of the Peace Lopez told Elfego that there were some 150 cattlemen working on a single ranch in the area. Cook said that "quite a crowd" assembled in Frisco, later estimating around eighty. French calculated that "twenty or thirty" rode into the upper plaza. But there was already a "crowd" present. Jerome Wadsworth calculated there were "forty-five or fifty" there. French's thirty plus Wadsworth's fifty add up to eighty.

But enough of rebutting those who disparage our hero.

Now, let's look at the positives for Elfego Baca.

Here are the issues:

A) Has Elfego's heroism in offering his life to save the Mexican settlers of the Frisco area from abuse earned him a lasting place of honor in the hearts and minds of not only those he saved but also of all Americans who deplore racism in whatever form it takes?

B) Or—do the troubles that weighed Elfego down—those repetitive PTSD-induced scrapes and brawls, his bankruptcy, his questionable political dealings, his divorce, his tussles with alcohol—so strip him of his heroism that Baca should be forgotten, to remain no more than a curiosity in the scrap-yard of New Mexico history as a thirty-six-hour-wonder with a six-gun?

The only conclusion that can be drawn is that the hero's legacy as the defender of the Hispanics should live on.

There are three points in Baca's favor: 1) Elfego willingly offered his life to save the Mexican-American settlers from abuse when a savior was sorely needed; 2) his accomplishments after Frisco were unparalleled for his times; and 3) he achieved them against odds that would have beaten down a lesser man.

1. Elfego Baca offered his life to save the Hispanics from abuse.

The only one who recorded the story of why Elfego Baca rode to Frisco is the man himself. Elfego's words:

> He [Deputy Sarracino] told me that before he left Frisco for Socorro about six or seven cowboys, drinking at his place got hold of a Mexican called "El Burro." They laid him on a counter, one of the boys sat on his chest and arms and the other one on his lap and right there and then the poor Burro was alterated [sic] in the presence of everybody. . . . Then they used Epitacio [Martinez, who had protested] as a target and they betted the drinks on who was the better shooter. . . . I told Sarracino the deputy sheriff that he should be ashamed of himself, having the law on his side to permit the cowboys to do what they did. He told me that if I wanted to, I could take his job. I told him that if he would take me back to Frisco with him, that I

would make myself a self-made deputy. We left . . . [209]

To counter this description, so simple and direct that it carries the ring of truth, Baca detractors claim that Elfego cooked up a bogus reason for his trip to Frisco—made it all up—after the fact in order to make himself into a hero. They say that the real reason he came to town was to campaign for the re-election of Sheriff Pedro Simpson.

It's a red herring. It's a red herring for two reasons.

First, Elfego was a hero whether the teen-ager rode out to save the Mexican-American settlers from cowboy abuse or whether he stepped up and arrested one of the riders for breaches of the peace of the settlers occurring after he got there. Either way, the result was the same: the "Mexican" kid arrested a Texas cowboy who should have been brought in; he did it when there was no one else in the entire Territory, Hispanic or "American," who had the guts to stand up to the men from Texas—not Deputy Sarracino, not Sheriff Simpson, no one. No "Mexican" had ever before had the guts to stand up to the arrogant men from Texas. And doing it put Elfego's life on the line. That's the measure of his bravery.

Second, the claim that Elfego rode into Frisco to campaign for Sheriff Simpson's reelection bid makes no sense. It makes no sense because Elfego could not understand the Spanish that the leaders of the cowboys shouted at him while trying to negotiate to end the gunfight. Would Sheriff Simpson, to whom the Spanish-speaking voters were so significant that he changed his name from Pete to Pedro, have sent a man able to speak only English and too young to cast a ballot as his representative to the voters in heavily Hispanic Western Socorro County? Not while he had the bi-lingual Pedro Sarracino working for him? To ask the question is to answer it.

So the time was right, and the right person stepped up.

For the context in which young Elfego found himself when he moved to Socorro at age fifteen called for a savior, a champion.

Texas cowmen had invaded the New Mexico Territory searching for cattle and grazing lands; bands of white-capped Mexicans raided the eastern plains burning railroad buildings, haystacks and other Anglo-owned property; Mexican-hating cowboys still angry over the Alamo shot up Mexican villages, terrorizing their inhabitants, and all-Anglo vigilante posses scoured the Socorro County countryside for Mexicans who had committed the most trivial of offenses. "Hispanophobia," with its pattern of discrimination, contempt and violence, infected the Anglo population. Mexicans feared to step outside their homes, and parents frightened their children with threats that the *Tejanos* would return and take them away. Racial tensions were at an all-time high, and there was no one to put an end to the abuse; no one to step up.

Not until Elfego Baca heard Deputy Pedro Sarracino's report of the abuses at Frisco. Not until Elfego Baca heard the call and answered it.

Elfego rode into Frisco to save his people. He ended the abuse, and he lived to tell about it.

2.   **Elfego Baca's accomplishments following Frisco were unparalleled for his times.**

To allow the sometimes irrational acts that plagued Elfego after the Frisco battle to erase the memories of the sacrificial good deed he performed and to forget his later accomplishments is to give the *Tejanos* their revenge. It's true that for every noble deed Elfego followed up with some irresponsible act that erased memories of the good in the man. Yet, to focus on the faults when evaluating his heroism misses the point that Elfego was a hero because of what he did at Frisco. If his record as a hero, lawman, political candidate and lawyer seems overshadowed by his failings, that does not diminish the valor that started him on his life course. His positive accomplishments after Frisco are simply the frosting on the cake. So what did he accomplish?

When he was not far into his twenties the boy whose education stopped when he was fifteen was sworn in as an attorney. He had read enough law to satisfy the judges and lawyers of the time, some of whom had come the Territory with classic educations. His mentor was one of the leading attorneys of the Territory, who spotted the raw talent in the young man. And while the young lawyers in the 1940s, when Baca was in his late seventies, did not think much of his skills as a civil law attorney because of his lack of formal education (or maybe because of his age), he maintained his law license, won lawsuits for his clients, and was said to have won acquittals of nineteen persons accused of murder.

Elfego earned his lawyer stripes in the criminal courts. The criminal cases whose transcripts of testimony have survived show an aggressive, effective advocate. The federal court matters he handled were complex, tried before real judges applying the law of the land, a far cry from off-the-cuff frontier justice of the peace law that prevailed in outlying communities. What Elfego may have lacked in legal knowledge he made up by the same courage he had shown in Frisco. He tried case after case against the educated and the eloquent attorneys of the Territory.

Baca's clients included the rich and powerful in the Territory: the Cattlemen's Association, whose members ran to him though he had alienated them only a few years earlier; the suave Harvey B. Fergusson (later United States Congressman), who had earned three degrees from Washington and Lee University, and his gold-mining venture investors; and the President of Mexico and his generals. He was tapped for federal government service by Secretary of the Interior Albert B. Fall before Fall was disgraced by the Teapot Dome scandal. Elfego's business and political associations were with solid citizens such as Groton and Harvard educated Bronson Cutting, the senator whose promising future was cut off by an airplane crash. But though Elfego held his own in lofty circles, his heart was always with his downtrodden Hispanic brothers and sisters. He never lost his touch with them.

He constantly championed the poor Mexican-Americans of the Territory and the State. He freed the Mexican sheepherder-debtors from the Socorro county jail and forced repeal of the law that had put them there, he fed the poor Mexicans of Kelly with the inventory from his cousin's store, he risked his reputation by enlisting others to participate with him in trapping Hispanic members of the first State legislature because their offer to sell their votes disgraced all Mexican-Americans, he started and published a Spanish-language newspaper to advocate for his people's rights, he jousted against the Anglo politicians of the time, though his bid to be elected as the new State's first representative to Congress fell short by an inch. When he saw that the republican party was moving away from being the party of the Hispanics, he switched and became a democrat.

And—he laid his life on the line to rescue the Mexican settlers in the Frisco vicinity.

3.   Elfego Baca's accomplishments were achieved against odds that would have beaten down a lesser man.

Elfego's sometimes irrational acts are explainable and excusable. With knowledge of the psychiatric disorder that plagued him, they are predictable.

If any conclusion can drawn from the repetitive belligerence and turmoil that Baca was drawn into over his life, it is that the man has earned sympathy and understanding: he rose above the disorder of PTSD to champion the cause of the Mexican-Americans of New Mexico. While he was not the first Hispanic in Territorial politics, he carried the highest profile, he could be reviled but never ignored, and he showed the way despite the burden of his psychiatric disorder.

The argument that Elfego suffered from PTSD was not grabbed out of thin air.

Two psychologists have reviewed the facts of Elfego's life. Both are thoughtful practitioners. One was at the time associated with the University of New Mexico Cancer Center, the other evaluates veterans for PTSD for the Veterans Administration. Both concluded that PTSD was a strong possibility, though neither then or later ventured to make a diagnosis a century after so many of the relevant events had occurred . But they added insight. They shed the light of their expertise on just how Elfego's painful childhood probably affected the boy and just how both his early life and the Frisco episode combined to shape the man. They also provided guidance for more research into the probable connections between these important life events and Elfego's personality.

Based on his interviews, guidance, and the research Dr. Gonçalves suggested, the conclusion is inevitable that the defining feature of Elfego's childhood, the abandonment caused by the three family deaths and the desertion by his father, all when he was seven, probably created a personality marred by feelings of inferiority. One expert writes, "[A]nxiety stems from an unconscious conflict that began in the individual's past. These conflicts arose from discomfort during infancy or childhood."[210] "Discomfort" is inadequate to describe the feelings left in Elfego by the multiple family deaths followed by the sight of his father's back as he walked out the door.

Probably Elfego came out of his tragic childhood with an impaired ability to cope with trauma — like the constant gunfire and the fear of death.[211] During those first years of his life Elfego's vulnerability was planted.

With a basis for vulnerability to stress established, the patterns of the few years after the fifteen-year-old moved back to Socorro from Topeka become more significant. The vulnerable child had grown into a vulnerable teenager, but the hero-in-the-making chose to overcome the feelings of inadequacy and inferiority, not to give in to them.

The force of suppressed anger, hostility and feelings of lack of control over the instability of that early life most likely gave energy to his drive to rescue his father from jail. In that episode there may also have been an element of the need to fit into the family he had rejoined in Socorro when he came back from Topeka that same year.

Shortly after, an adventure with a young man who called himself Billy the Kid introduced Elfego to the six-gun. By age sixteen, Baca had discovered its influence as an equalizer. From then on, Elfego was rarely without a gun. A weapon represented power and control to the young man who had grown up with neither. But there were other forces that pushed Elfego into his role as savior of the Hispanics.

As an outsider, he wanted to fit into the Hispanic community he had moved into when he returned to Socorro. Socorro was a Spanish-speaking town, but Elfego spoke only English. One way to fit in was to champion the Mexican-Americans. Nowhere did they need a champion like they did in Frisco. Without much conscious thought beyond the anger that drove him for the moment, he took out after the Texans. How better to become truly Hispanic?

But Elfego was open to effects from Frisco that might not have influenced another person as dramatically. As one expert has said, "traumatized adults with childhood histories of severe neglect have a particularly poor long term prognosis [for resisting the after-effects of trauma].[212] When he rode into Frisco, Elfego was headed into the kind of trauma that trained armies marching into war have experienced over the centuries, but the self-made deputy was untrained. And his childhood had left him vulnerable.

The trauma he underwent was severe: the death threats, four thousand shots fired by a mob of eighty out to kill the lone "Mexican," exploding dynamite and flaming logs. There was an immediate effect. When Elfego emerged from the hut, as French wrote, "He was like a wild animal, stripped to his shirt, with a revolver in each hand, looking suspiciously on every side of him, as if fearing treachery."[213]

Elfego's stress was no longer hidden by the darkness of the *jacal*.

But symptoms continued long after he was jailed in Socorro. The anxiety lingered for years, causing Baca to be vigilant and reactive to an unnatural degree. The psychologists consulted supported the deduction that the probable root from which Elfego's frequent fights, confrontations and brawls grew was Post Traumatic Stress Disorder.[214]

That likelihood is consistent with an authoritative publication of the American Psychiatric Association used as a research tool for this argument. DSTM-IV says that if a pattern of symptoms continues for more than a month after stressful events, then it can be diagnosed as Post Traumatic Stress Disorder.[215]

The diagnostic criteria begin with stress factors accompanied by a threat of death or of serious injury accompanied by extreme fear or helplessness. Recall the stress at Frisco: the death threats, shots and other attacks.

There are more symptoms needed to earn the PTSD diagnosis, and the hero meets them all. One expert says the symptoms of the disorder feature preoccupation with and an anticipation of future stressors, leading to hyper-vigilance and anxious apprehension.[216] The telltale bodyguard Baca hired tells the story.

The American Psychiatric Association spells out three additional sets of diagnostic criteria once the traumatic event and the reaction of fear or helplessness are established. They include persistent re-experiencing of the event, such as by physiological "reactivity" when faced with some kind of prompting that symbolizes the traumatic event. The pages of this book describe multiple examples of reactivity, including pulling a gun on a woman, a knife fight, and firing shots at legislator Wilson. There was the time he outdrew Bill Sanders, chased him down in a saloon, ordered drinks for the crowd then refused to pay because he was a "Texan" and not a "damned Mexican," in an outcry against the unequal treatment his people received at the hands of the Anglo frontier population.

The second diagnostic criterion is persistent avoidance of the kinds of stimuli that can be associated with the traumatic events, such as by the inability to have loving feelings or close relationships.[217] What is known of Elfego's relationship with his wife matches. There were Francisquita's repeated efforts to get her husband's attention when she marched time and again into Elfego's office. She often escaped from her husband to go to her father; the pair divorced when Catholics just didn't do that. When Elfego talked to lawyer Keleher about his difficulties with Francisquita, he expressed no love for his wife, no concern for his children.

The third diagnostic factor is persistent symptoms of increased arousal characterized by extraordinary vigilance and an over-active startle response demonstrated through irritability and anger or difficulty in concentrating. The years of overreactions that anticipated danger reveal what was going on in Elfego's head.

Finally, there are the DSTM diagnostic requirements that the symptoms identified above last for more than a month, and that they cause significant impairment in important areas of functioning, such as occupational or social. Elfego's turbulent life attests to the lasting nature of the legacy imposed on him by the cowboys.

The psychologists have agreed that the facts of Elfego's reactive behavior spanning decades seem to confirm the likelihood that Baca suffered from PTSD. Dr. Huyser evaluates veterans to confirm or deny that they have the disorder. When asked if he still sees veterans of World War II who show the symptoms of the psychiatric disorder, Dr. Huyser replied, "Yes, even over fifty years after the firing ended. And yes, the diagnostic factors published by the American Psychiatric Association in DSTM are what we use to determine the presence or absence of the disorder." In response to a question about Elfego Baca and PTSD, his response was, "Well, fifty plus years after Mr. Baca's death and with no way to interview him or those who knew him intimately, no firm diagnosis can be made. But based on the stressors in that gunfight and his subsequent behavior, a diagnosis of PTSD is consistent and cannot be ruled out."[218]

The fact that in his later years Elfego was reported as laughing and having a good time isn't inconsistent with a diagnosis of PTSD. If Elfego was anything, he was a fighter. Long-term adaptations vary substantially among those who suffer from the effects of post traumatic stress. People do tend to adjust. Most of the physical brawls Elfego engaged in took place in the few years after Frisco, though confrontations continued for another couple of decades. The pattern fits. McFarlane and Yehuda, writing in *Traumatic Stress,* found that the intensity of symptoms tends to decrease with the passage of time.[219]

But even so, recollections of the trauma tend to stay vivid for those who have PTSD,[220] as they did for Elfego for sixty long, long years.

So pause for a moment and ask: How high would Elfego Baca have risen had he not carried the burden of PTSD?

The question cannot be answered, but the hero's persistent overcoming marks real heroism. He channeled his anxieties and he channeled his latent tendency to violence into law enforcement and into battles in the courtroom. Though he could not always tether his reactive responses, it is to his everlasting credit that he tried, and that he was as successful as he was.

Elfego should not continue to bear the slurs that sprung from the psychic wounds he suffered. To keep him in obscurity is to award the ultimate victory to the cowboys he bested. To list him only among the frontier gunfighters is to give the abusive *Tejanos* the revenge they sought in order to salvage their reputations as "white knights" of the frontier given them by overenthusiastic writers of the time, a time when the Hispanics had not voice in the literature of the frontier.

In evaluating the place in history earned by Elfego Baca, judge him on the courage he showed at Frisco in ending the oppression of the Hispanic farmers. The scale of his achievements after Frisco is magnified by the fact that all the while he was fighting ghostly mental images of the Texans who had circled his flimsy hideaway, firing their six-guns relentlessly over a period of thirty-six hours. He should be recognized as a true hero, undiminished by his psychiatric disorder.

This postage-stamp-sized park on the north side of the plaza in Socorro is dedicated to the memory of Elfego Baca. The cutout inscriptions on the signs read, "Elfego Baca 1865 - 1945" and "Heritage Park." Photograph by the author.

And so, this is the Case for Elfego Baca. Hero — or goat?

He risked his life for what was right; he saved his people; he overcame incalculable odds to achieve unequalled accomplishments for the time and place in which he found himself.

He's earned a tribute — and so, ¡Viva Elfego!

1. Roberts, Susan A. and Calvin A. Roberts. *A History of New Mexico. Second Revised Edition.* Albuquerque: University of New Mexico Press. 1998. See also, Trapp, Robert. "Elfego Gets no Respect." *Rio Grande Sun.* Mar. 23, 2000. NMSRCA History Files.
2. Rosales, F. Arturo. *Chicano! The History of the Mexican American Civil Rights Movement.* Houston: Arte Público Press. 1996.
3. Interviews with Antonio Gonçalves, Ph.D., Albuquerque. Feb. 24, Mar 4, 2002; and with Bruce Huyser, Ph.D. Albuquerque. October 1, 2003.
4. Conron, John P. *Socorro: A Historic Survey.* Albuquerque: University of New Mexico Press, 1980. 13, 14.
5. Baca, Elfego. *Here Comes Elfego!* Albuquerque: Vinegar Tom Press. Undated. Originally published as *Political Record of Elfego Baca and a Brief History of His Life,* 1924?. 15, 16.
6. Interview with Gilberto Espinosa, Esq. Albuquerque. ca 1968.
7. French, William. *Recollections of a Western Ranchman.* Reprint. Silver City, NM: High-Lonesome Books, 1990. 42-52. Cook, James H. *Fifty Years on the Old Frontier.* Reprint. Norman, OK: University of Oklahoma Press, 1980. 221-227. Baca. 15-22. Crichton, Kyle S. *Law and Order. Ltd. The Rousing Life of Elfego Baca of New Mexico.* Reprint. Glorieta, NM: The Rio Grande Press, 1970. 27-48. *Albuquerque Evening Democrat.* May 8, 9, 1885.
8. French. 21.
9. *Albuquerque Evening Democrat.* May 9, 1885.
10. Cook. 221.
11. Baca. 18.
12. Crichton. 33.
13. *Albuquerque Evening Democrat.* May 9, 1885. Elfego testified that the hut had only one door and one window.
14. Ibid.
15. French. 52.
16. Cleaveland, Agnes Morley. *No Life for a Lady.* Reprint. Lincoln: University of Nebraska Press, 1977. 265.
17. *Albuquerque Evening Democrat.* May 9, 1885.

18. Cox, Mike. "J. Evetts Haley: A True Texas Legend." *Texana Book Reviews*, 1997. http://site17575.dellhost.com/lsj/cox97feb.htm

19. Haley, J. Evetts. *Jeff Milton: A Good Man with a Gun*. Norman: University of Oklahoma Press, 1948. 109-111.

20. For another writer who had difficulty with Mr. Stanley's sources, see: L'Aloge, Robert. *The Incident of Socorro's Nightriders,* Sunnyside, WA: BJS Brand Books, 1992, fn 36. 19.

21. Stanley, F. *The Reserve (New Mexico) Story*. Nazareth, TX: publisher unidentified, 1973. 8.

22. Personal interview with Henry Martinez, October 9, 2003.

23. Telephone interview with Henry Martinez. October 30, 2003.

24. Personal interview with Max L. Kiehne. March 13, 2002.

25. N. C. Laughlin file. NMSRCA.

26. *Albuquerque Evening Democrat*. May 8, 1885.

27. Crichton. 33, 34.

28. Ibid. 47.

29. N. C. Laughlin file. NMSRCA.

30. Ibid.

31. Ibid.

32. Socorro County District Court Case file No. 783. NMSRCA.

33. Curry, George. *George B. Curry, 1861-1947: an Autobiography*. H. B. Hening, Ed. Albuquerque: University of New Mexico Press, 1958. 260-262.

34. Socorro County District Court Case file No. 783. NMSRCA.

35. Ibid.

36. Ibid.

37. Ibid.

38. Cook. 223.

39. *Albuquerque Morning Journal*. February 25, 1912. "The Texas-Santa Fe Expedition. The Thrilling Story of the Fighting of the Forties in New Mexico. From 'Leading Facts of New Mexico History'—By Ralph Emerson Twitchell, Las Vegas, N.M."

40. Beck, Warren A., *New Mexico: A History of Four Centuries*. Norman: University of Oklahoma Press, 1962, 142.

41. Ibid.

42. Otero, Miguel. *My Life on the Frontier 1864-1882*. New York: Press of the Pioneers, 1935, 62, 63.

43. Ibid.

44. McWilliams, Cary. *North from Mexico: The Spanish Speaking People of the United States*. Reprint. New York: Greenwood Press Publishers, 1968. 110-121.

45. Dobie, J. Frank. *A Vaquero of the Brush Country*. New York: Gossett & Dunlap, 1929. xiv.

46. Gann, L. H. and Peter J. Dunigan. *The Hispanics in the United States*. Boulder and London: Westview Press, 1986. 25.

47. Weber, David J. *The Spanish Frontier in North America*. New Haven and London: Yale University Press, 1992. 340.

48. Ibid. 42.

49. L'Aloge. 34 – 52.

50. Potter, Chester D. "Reminiscences of the Socorro Vigilantes." *New Mexico Historical Review*. XL:1. January, 1965. pp. 24-30, 35-40. Edited by Paige W. Christiansen. Reproduced from the *Pittsburgh Dispatch*. May 25, 1913, et seq.

51. Personal interview with Gilbert Eugene Baca, great-grandson of Abdenago Baca, Elfego's brother, Rio Rancho, NM. January 20, 2002.

52. Gonzales, David and Jonathan A. Ortega, "Onofre Baca—Socorro Lynching Victim and his Brother Elfego Baca—an American Legend." *Herencia*. January issue, 1995.

53. L'Aloge. 49, 50.

54. Ibid. 50 - 52. Chester Potter (fn. 50) said that Abran was "hung" and that Onofre was acquitted.

55. Potter. 25.

56. Baca. 9.

57. Ball, Larry D. *Elfego Baca in Life and Legend*. El Paso: Texas Western Press. 1992. 2.

58. Ibid. 10.

59. Crichton. 7. For the information about Elfego's time in an orphanage, see Ball, Larry D. *Elfego Baca in Life and Legend*. El Paso: Texas Western Press, 1993. 3. Professor Ball attributes the report to Abe B. Baca, Elfego's nephew.

60. Personal interviews with Antonio Gonçalves, Ph.D., Feb. 24, Mar 4, 2002. The conclusions reached by Dr. Gonçalves are reinforced by an article on the subject by van der Kolk, Bessel A. "The Complexity of Adaptation to Trauma Self-Regulation, Stimulus Discrimination, and Characterological Development." *Traumatic Stress*. Ed. by van der Kolk, Bessel A., Alexander C. McFarlane and Lars Weisaeth, New York, London: The Guilford Press, 1996. 185.

61. Doctor, Ronald M., Ph.D. and Ada P. Khan. *The Encyclopedia of Phobias, Fears and Anxieties*. New York, Oxford: Facts on File, 1989. 52.

62. McFarlane, Alexander C. and Rachel Yehuda. "Resilience, Vulnerability, and the Course of Posttraumatic Reactions. *Traumatic Stress*. 157.

63. Baca. 10. Crichton. 11.

64. *State of New Mexico vs Jose P. Lucero*. "Transcript of Record." New Mexico Supreme Court case No. 1674. 62. Microfilm files of the Supreme Court of New Mexico.

65. Crichton. 8.

66. *Daily New Mexican*. December 31, 1880.

67. Crichton. 8-13.

68. Baca. 10.

69. Crichton. 17, 18.

70. Baca. 12.

71. Ibid. 13.

72. Interviews with Dr. Gonçalves.

73. *Territory vs Elfego Baca.* Bernalillo County District Court Journal C. 1886. NMS-RCA. *Albuquerque Journal.* August 15, 1886.

74. *Territory vs Elfego Baca.* Bernalillo County District Court criminal file 1053. 1887. NMSRCA.

75. *Albuquerque Morning Democrat.* Sep. 11, 1888.

76. *Albuquerque Daily Citizen.* July 27, 1891; April 19, 1893.

77. Ibid. October 24, 1893. Issues of the *Albuquerque Daily Citizen* reported visits to Albuquerque by Socorro county probate clerk Elfego Baca. Jan 27, Sept 8, 1894. It is probable that the jobs of county clerk and probate clerk were filled by the same person at that time.

78. *Territory vs Elfego Baca.* Socorro County District Court criminal file 1548. 1896. NMSRCA

79. Record Book B. Socorro County Criminal Cases, docket book. NMSRCA. *Rio Grande Republican.* April 24, 1896. For reference to William E. Wilson as District Court Clerk, see, The *Socorro Chieftain,* December 7, 1907. It is not clear when Wilson took office.

80. Baca. 5.

81. Ashcroft, Bruce. *The Territorial History of Socorro, New Mexico.* El Paso: Texas Western Press, 1988. pp. 6-13.

82. Keleher. *Memoirs.* 154, 155.

83. Baca. 7, 8.

84. Ibid. 7.

85. *Albuquerque Evening Citizen.* September 15, 1919.

86. Smith, Janet. "Interview with Elfego Baca. Outlaws. Joe Fowler, Henry Coleman." July 27, 1936. NMSRCA; Library of Congress, Manuscript Division, WPA Writers' Project Collection.

87. Crichton. 111-117.

88. Curry. 1958.

89. Smith, Janet. "II Interview with Elfego Baca." October 23, 1936. Library of Congress, Manuscript Division, WPA Writers' Project Collection.

90. Ibid. 85-99.

91. Crichton. 49-55.

92. Ibid. 99-101.

93. Smith, Janet. "Interview with Elfego Baca: Outlaws." July 27, 1937. Library of Congress, Manuscript Division.

94. Keleher, William A. *Memoirs: 1892-1969.* Santa Fe: The Rydal Press, 1969. 179.

95. Ibid.

96. Crichton. 198.

97. Keleher. *Memoirs.* 179.

98. Crichton. 199.

99. Cleaveland. 254, 266.

100. *State of New Mexico vs Jose P. Lucero.* "Transcript of Record." 62.

101. Keleher. *Memoirs.* 154, 155. Simmons, Marc. *Albuquerque: A Narrative History.* Albuquerque: University of New Mexico Press. 1982, 356. *Albuquerque Morning Journal.* May 15, 16.

102. Crichton. 186-192. TANM 19, frame 102, SRCA, Santa Fe, discloses a letter from Elfego Baca dated Dec. 29, 1906, with letterhead identifying him as "Attorney and Counsellor at Law" for the Sierra County Cattlemen's Protective Association.

103. *Socorro Chieftain.* May 9, 1908.

104. Ibid.

105. Stratton, David H. *Tempest over Teapot Dome.* Norman, OK: University of Oklahoma Press, 1998. 100.

106. *Socorro Chieftain.* Dec. 7, 1907.

107. Ibid. Mar. 31, 1906. See also TANM 163, Frame 110. SRCA, Santa Fe for more details on the Mallet episode and Baca's departure from the District Attorney's office.

108. *Albuquerque Evening Citizen,* March 29, 1906.

109. Ibid. April 30, 1906; letter to editor.

110. Baca. 5, 6. *Albuquerque Evening Citizen,* July 24, 1906. TANM Reel 23, March 16, 1905, May 15, 1906.

111. *Socorro Chieftain.* July 7, 1906.

112. Personal interviews with Gilbert Eugene Baca, Rio Rancho, NM, grandson of Abdenago and Virginia Baca, and son of Tomás. Jan. 20, Feb. 23, 2002. Tomás Baca carried a gun all his life.

113. *Albuquerque Evening Citizen,* January 27, 1894. William A. Keleher identified Pohmer as owner of the "best meat market in Old Albuquerque." *Memoirs.* 170.

114. *Albuquerque Daily Citizen.* July 16, 1896.

115. Ibid. May 24, 1893; September 8, 1894.

116. *Socorro Chieftain.* August 26, 1911.

117. Ibid. 180, 181.

118. *In the Matter of Elfego Baca, Bankrupt.* Federal bankruptcy file, NARA, Denver, 21 New Mexico—Bankruptcy Cases Box 88, Case No. 575.

119. LaFollette, Robert Hoath. *Eight Notches.* Albuquerque: Valliant Printing Co., 1950. 4, 5. *Elfego Baca vs Francisco Pohmer de Baca.* Case No. 15069. Bernalillo County District Court.

120. Keleher. *Memoirs.* 181.

121 "Kyle Crichton, Peale's Most Famous Son." quoted from *The Writer in Pennsylvania, 1681-1981. www.osu.edu/*

122. Keleher. *Memoirs*. 156.

123. Crichton. iii, iv.

124. *Biographical Directory of the United States Congress. http://bioguide.congress.gov/scripts/biodisplay*pl?index=C001028

125. Keleher. *Memoirs*. 182.

126. "Papers of Manuel Sanchez," Santa Fe District Court file 16084. NMSRCA.

127. Ibid. 182-190.

128. Ibid. 191.

129. Undated newspaper clipping, probably *Albuquerque Journal*. Provided by courtesy of Gilbert Eugene Baca from the family files of A. B. Baca.

130. Crichton. 114-116.

131. Gerlach, Allen. "Conditions Along the Border—1915; The Plan of San Diego. *New Mexico Historical Review XLIII: 1968*. 195-196.

132. Vigil, Ralph H. "Revolution and Confusion: the Peculiar Case of Josè Inèz Salazar." *New Mexico Historical Review 53:2*. 150, 151

133. Ibid. 157.

134. Vigil. 150.

135. Crichton. 115-117.

136. Ibid. 119-123.

137. Ibid. 128, 129. Fitzpatrick, George. "The Real Elfego Baca." *New Mexico Magazine*. Vol. 38 No. 4. April, 1960. 3, 4.

138. Ibid. 123.

139. *In the Matter of the Petition of Jose Inez Salazar for Writ of Habeas Corpus.* United States District Court for the District of New Mexico. Transcript of testimony of Salazar given September 2, 1914. 14. Unnumbered court file. NARA, Denver.

140. Vigil. 152, 156.

141. Ibid. 132, 133.

142. *Petition of Jose Inez Salazar for a Writ of Habeas Corpus.* Transcript. 12.

143. Crichton. 136, 137.

144. Petition of Jose Inez Salazar for a Writ of Habeas Corpus. Transcript. 9.

145. Ibid. Transcript 6.

146. El Paso Herald. December 22, 1913. Plaintiff's Exhibit B, Criminal case 282, In the District Court of the United States for the District of New Mexico, United States of America, Plaintiff, vs Jose Inez Salazar, Defendant. NARA, Denver.

147. Vigil. 153.

148. Ibid. 153, 154.

149. This account is culled from Vigil, Ralph H., "Revolution and Confusion." 145-165, which closely follows the indictment; Elfego's establishment of his alibi is based on Robert Hoath LaFollette's chapter "Gen. Salazar's Attorney Establishes his Alibi." *Eight Notches*. 7, 8.

150. *United States of America vs Inez Salazar*, et al, Criminal Case no. 84. In the District Court for the District Court of New Mexico. NARA, Denver. The court file discloses the conviction of defendant Tovar but is silent as to the outcome for the other defendants. Salazar, in his testimony in his habeas corpus case, said he was acquitted.

151. *United States of America vs Elfego Baca, et al.* Criminal Case no. 335. In the District Court for the District of New Mexico. 1915. NARA, Denver.

152. Bryan, Howard. *Incredible Elfego Baca. Good Man, Bad Man of the Old West.* Santa Fe: Clear Light Publishers, 1993. pp. 79-81.

153. Crichton. Facing 145.

154. Ibid. 137-145.

155. Keleher. *Memoirs.* 184.

156. *Albuquerque Morning Journal.* February 1, 1915.

157. *United States of America vs Alanis, Salazar, Gomez, Tovar and Andujos.* Criminal Case no. 84. In the District Court for the District of New Mexico. NARA. Denver.

158. *El Paso Morning Times.* February 1, 1915.

159. *Albuquerque Morning Journal.* February 2, 1915.

160. *Albuquerque Morning Journal.* February 3, 1915.

161. *El Paso Morning Times.* February 1, 1915.

162. *Albuquerque Morning Journal.* February 1, 1915.

163. *El Paso Morning Times.* February 1, 1915.

164. *Albuquerque Morning Journal.* February 1, 1915.

165. Ibid.

166. Personal interview with the Honorable Ross Sanchez, Bernalillo County District Judge. Albuquerque. December 17, 2001. Constance Connor Modrall records the story slightly differently. The telegram is from a man jailed for murder. Elfego responds: "Send me one thousand dollars and I will be there in the morning with two eyewitnesses." Modrall, Constance Connor. *Courtroom Humor.* Albuquerque: Calvin Horn Publisher, Inc., 1974. 41. Howard Bryan upped the count of eyewitnesses Elfego offered to bring to three in the Introduction to *Incredible Elfego Baca.* 3.

167. *El Paso Morning Times.* January 26, 1916.

168. *Albuquerque Morning Journal.* January 26, 1916.

169. *El Paso Morning Times.* January 26, 1916.

170. Ibid.

171. Ibid.

172. Interview with Eric Sedillo Jeffries, Esq., Albuquerque. January 22, 2002.

173. Professor Larry D. Ball, in his thoroughly-researched book *Elfego Baca in Life and Legend,* pp. 69-70, says that District Attorney Manuel U. Vigil, "perhaps the most promising Hispano political leader in New Mexico," had his hopes for higher office destroyed by the Salazar affair, while Elfego's popularity was enhanced."

174. State vs Lucero. 20 N.M. 55, 146 P. 407. 1915.

175. Curry. 257-259.

176. *Socorro Chieftain*. March 23, 1912, quoting from the Santa Fe New Mexican. For a brief account of the episode, see *The Two Alberts: Fountain and Fall*. Gordon R. Owen. Las Cruces, NM: Yucca Tree Press, 1996. 370-372. Another account of the occurrences in Room 44 appears in *Tempest Over Teapot Dome*. David H. Stratton. Norman, OK: University of Oklahoma Press, 1998. 102-107.

177. *Proceedings of the Investigating Committee of the House of Representatives*. 1912. NMSRCA.

178. Ibid. 212.

179. *State of New Mexico vs Jose P. Lucero*. "Transcript of Record." 61-62, 67, 74.

180. *Proceedings of the Investigating Committee of the House of Representatives*. 1912. Esp. 47-55 and 211-214.

181. Crichton. 179.

182. *Benjamin H. Dye, et al., Appellees, vs H. C. Crary, et al., Appellants*. 13 NM 439, 85 P. 1038. 1906.

183. Keleher, William A. *The Fabulous Frontier*. Albuquerque: University of New Mexico Press. Revised edition, 1962. 38 n.

184. *Elfego Baca, Appellant, vs City of Albuquerque, Appellee*. 19 N.M. 472, 145 P. 110. 1914

185. Crichton. 200-201.

186. *Murphy vs Baca et al*. 24 NM 657, 176 P. 816. 1918.

187. *Baca vs Fleming*. 25 NM 643, 187 P. 277. 1920.

188. Keleher. *Memoirs*. 186.

189. *Baca vs Padilla*. 26 NM 223, 190 P. 730, 1920.

190. *Baca vs Winters, et al*. 26 NM 340, 192 P. 479. 1920.

191. *Baca vs Buel (two cases)*. 28 NM 225, 210 P. 571. 1922.

192. 39 NM 127, 42 P2d 201. 1935.

193. 41 NM 211, 67 P.2d 235. 1937.

194. Telephone interview with Donald B. Moses, Esq., Albuquerque, April 12, 2002.

195. *Elfego Baca vs Francisco Pohmer de Baca*. Case No. 15069. Bernalillo County District Court. Cross-Complaint.

196. *Elfego Baca vs Francisquita Baca*. Bernalillo County case no. 15069. *State of New Mexico vs Jose P. Lucero*. New Mexico Supreme Court case no. 1674. "Transcript of Record." 62.

197. Crichton. 159-168.

198. Baca. 3-8.

199. Crichton. 210, 211.

200. Baca, Elfego. "Open Letter." *Albuquerque Tribune*. November 4, 1940. "Manifesto of Elfego Baca, Candidate for Governor." Both in CSWR, UNM. Collection MSS 249, Box SC, Folder 1.

201. Ball. 103.

202. Hamm, Ron. "A. B. Baca's Uncle Elfego."

203. Telephone interview. July 15, 2002.

204. Fitzpatrick, George. "The Real Elfego Baca." *New Mexico Magazine,* Vol. 38, No. 4. April, 1960.

205. Telephone interview. April 5, 2002.

206. Ball. 99, 100.

207. Baca, Mrs. Elfego. Letter to Mr. Clinton P. Anderson. Sept. 2, 1945. CSWR, UNM; Funeral Memoriam. CSWR, UNM.

208. Baca. 22.

209. Baca. 15, 16.

210. Doctor, Ronald M. Ph.D., and Ada P. Khan. *The Encyclopedia of Phobias, Fears and Anxieties.* New York, Oxford: Facts on File, 1989. 52.

211. McFarlane, Alexander C. and Rachel Yehuda. "Resilience, Vulnerability, and the Course of Posttraumatic Reactions. *Traumatic Stress.* Ed. by van der Kolk, Bessel A., Alexander C. McFarlane and Lars Weisaeth. New York, London: The Guilford Press, 1996. 157.

212. van der. Kolk, Bessel A. "The Complexity of Adaptation to Trauma Self-Regulation, Stimulus Discrimination, and Characterological Development." *Traumatic Stress.* 185.

213. French. 51.

214. Interviews with Antonio Gonçalves, Ph.D. Feb. 24, Mar. 4, 2002. Although the Author's Conclusions follow certain directions suggested by Dr. Gonçalves, the responsibility for the arguments advanced, the conclusions reached and for all errors that might appear is the author's.

215. DSTM IV-TR. 427.

216. Brett, Elizabeth A. "The Classification of Posttraumatic Stress Syndrome." *Traumatic Stress.* 121.

217. DSTM IV-TR. 468.

218. Personal interview with Bruce Huyser, Ph.D. Albuquerque. October 1, 2003.

219. McFarlane and Yehuda. "Resilience." *Traumatic Stress.* 159, 160.

220. van der Kolk and McFarlane, "The Black Hole of Trauma." *Traumatic Stress.* 8, 9.